Ibn 'Arabi and Modern Thought

THE HISTORY OF TAKING METAPHYSICS SERIOUSLY

Also available from Anqa Publishing

The Seven Days of the Heart: awrād al-usbūʿ, by Ibn ʿArabī
Translated by Pablo Beneito and Stephen Hirtenstein

Contemplation of the Holy Mysteries: mashāhid al-asrār, by Ibn ʿArabī
Translated by Cecilia Twinch and Pablo Beneito

Divine Sayings: mishkāt al-anwār, by Ibn ʿArabī
Translated by Stephen Hirtenstein and Martin Notcutt

The Universal Tree and the Four Birds: al-ittiḥād al-kawnī, by Ibn ʿArabī
Translated by Angela Jaffray

A Prayer for Spiritual Elevation and Protection: al-dawr al-aʿlā,
by Ibn ʿArabī
Study, translation, transliteration and Arabi text by
Suha Taji-Farouki

The Unlimited Mercifier: the Spiritual Life and Thought of Ibn ʿArabī
Stephen Hirtenstein

The Nightingale in the Garden of Love: the Poems of Üftade
Paul Ballanfat; translated from French by Angela Culme-Seymour

*Beshara and Ibn ʿArabi: A Movement of Sufi Spirituality in
the Modern World*
Suha Taji-Farouki

Ibn 'Arabi and Modern Thought

THE HISTORY OF TAKING METAPHYSICS SERIOUSLY

Peter Coates

ANQA PUBLISHING • OXFORD

Published by Anqa Publishing
PO Box 1178
Oxford OX2 8YS, UK
www.ibn-arabi.com

First published 2002
Reprinted 2008, with amendments

A CIP catalogue record for this book is available
from the British Library

ISBN 10: 0 9534513 7 2
ISBN 13: 978 09534513 7 1

Cover by Iota Design

Printed on totally chlorine-free paper.
The paper used for the text pages of this book is FSC certified.
FSC (Forest Stewardship Council) is an international network
to promote responsible management of the world's forests.

Mixed Sources
Product group from well-managed
forests and other controlled sources
www.fsc.org Cert no. SGS-COC-2482
© 1996 Forest Stewardship Council
FSC

Printed and bound in Great Britain by TJ International
Padstow, Cornwall

To Barbara, Ursula and Paul

Acknowledgements

My deepest gratitude and debt to the late Bulent Rauf for his patience and encouragement, and for providing a wonderful opportunity for me, and many others, to be introduced to the study of Ibn 'Arabi. To Barbara for her unfailing support and role as sounding-board. I also dearly thank Mrs Elizabeth Roberts and Dr Michael Cohen for their helpful and insightful suggestions, and Dr Niels Detert for his diligent and overall comments on much of the material. There are many others, students and friends, too numerous to mention, who have contributed, wittingly or unwittingly, to many of the ideas contained in this book. For introducing me, very many years ago, to the whole area of the study of religion, philosophy and modern thought, I would like to thank, in particular, the late Professor Ninian Smart and his inaugural department at Lancaster.

And last but not least, my thanks to Stephen Hirtenstein, Michael Tiernan and Judy Kearns for all their help in the production of this book.

Contents

"God never commanded His Prophet to seek increase of anything except knowledge, since all good (*khayr*) lies therein. It is the greatest charismatic gift. Idleness with knowledge is better than ignorance with good works ... By knowledge I mean only knowledge of God, of the next world, and of that, which is appropriate for this world, in relationship to that for which this world was created and established. Then man's affairs will be 'upon insight' wherever he is, and he will be ignorant of nothing in himself and his activities."

Ibn 'Arabi, *Futuhat al-Makkiyah*; trans. W. C. Chittick, *The Sufi Path of Knowledge*, p. 148.

"The possessor of consideration is delimited by the ruling power of his reflection, but reflection can only roam in its own specific playing field, which is one of many fields. Each faculty in man has a playing field in which it roams and beyond which it should not step."

Ibn 'Arabi, *Futuhat al-Makkiyah*; trans. W. C. Chittick, *The Sufi Path of Knowledge*, p. 165.

Since his retirement the author has, in the context of courses offered by the Beshara School of Intensive Esoteric Education, been involved in residential courses for students of Ibn 'Arabi, both in the UK and Australia.

1 The orientation of this study

Introduction

As the subtitle suggests, the approach of this study is to examine certain aspects of contemporary thought and theorizing in the light of the metaphysical teachings of the twelfth-century Andalusian Muhyiddin Ibn 'Arabi. With some notable exceptions, much modern thought has not felt it necessary to delve deeply into its own metaphysical foundations nor to take seriously the history of metaphysics in general. At the risk of oversimplifying it is arguable that the intellectual influence of the early twentieth-century revolution in British philosophy, the general alignment in the West of science and technology with the calculative rationality of industrial capitalism, and the equating of science and technology with human and social progress engendered an intellectual atmosphere in which there did not seem to be much room left for metaphysics. In some cases, metaphysics was regarded with outright intellectual hostility. In short, the relationship between modern thought and metaphysics has had a chequered career. In one form or another metaphysics has endured. It has endured partly because the relationship between metaphysics and knowledge has always been a key issue, from Plato's *Republic*[1] through to Ludwig Wittgenstein's *Tractatus Logico-Philosophicus*[2] and beyond, into the relativistic view of knowledge of that which is called postmodernism. The promise of industrial capitalism also suffered some severe setbacks in the twentieth century and there is a feeling that its human costs are beginning to noticeably outweigh its human benefits: it is engendering its own metaphysical crisis.[3]

The availability of English translations of the writings of Ibn 'Arabi offer an extraordinary opportunity to re-examine the depth and significance of the issue of the relationship between metaphysics and modern thought in the light of one of the most profound metaphysical teachings the world has ever known.

Without the outstanding contribution to the studies of Ibn 'Arabi of such scholars as Henry Corbin, Claude Addas, Ralph Austin, Michel Chodkiewicz, William Chittick, Toshihiko Izutsu and James Morris (to cite some of the central figures to whom the present study is indebted) such a task would simply not have been feasible.

In this respect it is perhaps useful to point out to those who want to situate the thought and ideas of Ibn 'Arabi in their historical and cultural setting, the recent study by Addas, *Quest for the Red Sulphur*, a masterpiece of scholarship, insight and exposition. Alternatively, for an emphasis on the elucidation of Ibn 'Arabi's key philosophical ideas consult the excellent study by Izutsu, *Sufism and Taoism*. Equally, for a study which situates the recurring themes of Ibn 'Arabi in their Quranic setting, consult Chittick's *The Sufi Path of Knowledge*. Because such studies as these cover the historical and exegetical ground admirably the present study does not engage in detailed historical analysis of the life and works of Ibn 'Arabi. Finally, for an excellent and accessible introduction to the teachings of Ibn 'Arabi, consult *The Unlimited Mercifier* by Stephen Hirtenstein.

I mention these recent studies to differentiate their respective orientations from that of the present study which, although also exegetical, analytical and comparative, is so in quite a different sense. There is enough material, however, in the present study for the reader who is new to the metaphysical teachings of Ibn 'Arabi to grasp the logic, power and beauty of his overall picture of reality. The basic orientation of this study is to analyse the underlying conception of knowledge that permeates the metaphysics of Ibn 'Arabi and compare it with the paradigmatic assumptions about knowledge that permeated much of twentieth-century theoretical culture.

Ibn 'Arabi's picture of reality

Without doubt, the key to understanding the entire corpus of Ibn 'Arabi lies in the central idea of *wahdat al-wujud*[4] – the Oneness of Being. For Ibn 'Arabi, *wahdat al-wujud* (also translated as the Unity or Oneness of Existence) is an inescapable ontological fact. The referent of this condensed description is Being – not a particular being – but Being in general, as it were. It has as its referent that Being which is the source and ground of all beings. In this sense, God is Being (*wujud*). This formulaic description, whilst perfectly according with Ibn 'Arabi's view, has to be treated with care in this truncated form.[5] The Arabic triliteral *wujud* also means 'to find'. For Ibn 'Arabi this implies that it is incumbent upon the human person to find out what the Oneness of Being means for them, their lives and their existence. This is not simply an intellectual or conceptual "finding" but a journey into the experiential depths of their reality posited as no other than an individuated expression of the Oneness of Being itself. In fact, it is the concept of the Oneness of Being that negates, for Ibn 'Arabi, any implication of an ontological duality. There is only One Unique Being which reveals itself in a multiplicity and infinity of its own forms, and which possesses two fundamental dimensions, transcendence and immanence. This is why Ibn 'Arabi's doctrine of *wahdat al-wujud* is misdescribed if it is described over-simplistically and disparagingly as pantheism[6] for the One Unique Being transcends the immanence of its own forms. It transcends its "theatre of manifestation" whether this be the human-social world, the world of nature, the cosmos, or any other possible mode of manifestation.

Ibn 'Arabi unfolds the extraordinary human implications of the ontological fact alluded to by the phrase *wahdat al-wujud*[7] with an optimistic, relentless and disarming logic. Above all, Ibn 'Arabi insists on the central role and privileged status of the Human Self, or at least each individual's potential status as a possible exemplar of the archetypal human, known as *insan-i-kamil*, the complete or perfect human being. In his general metaphysical scheme of things *insan-i-kamil*, or the fully developed human being, can be conceived of as a bridge or isthmus which connects the internal or interior aspects of the Single Unique Reality with its external or exterior aspects.

The status of the isthmus resides not in itself but in what it connects and summarizes: the *insan-i-kamil* combines the inward and outward aspects of Reality. Hence, the true ontological dignity of the human-kind cannot be over-rated. For Ibn 'Arabi, the essential dignity of humankind resides in the fact that God, out of His love to be known, created man in His image. For the student who is just beginning to grasp the magnitude which Ibn 'Arabi accords to human poten-tial (and its grounds), it becomes abundantly clear that Ibn 'Arabi's philosophy is one of profound hope and is in perfect concordance with the sentiments of another of his contemporaries, Jalaluddin Rumi, when Rumi writes "Come, come whoever you are ... ours is not a caravan of despair". As Addas also concludes, the "dominant quality" of the writings of Ibn 'Arabi is "the quality of a universal message of hope".[8]

The concept of *insan-i-kamil* represents the ideal to which human beings can aspire. As S. H. Nasr[9] carefully points out, such an aspira-tional philosophy places before us the grandeur of what a human being can be (or can become), and contrasts it with the pettiness of what in most cases a human being is. Ibn 'Arabi's universal philo-sophy addresses itself to the potential or the ideal. It addresses itself to the inescapable metaphysical foundations of human reality: the inseparability of all human life and potential from its source or essence. It implies no Utopian idealism for it is firmly grounded in the facts of humanly lived experience and the means of its transformation from the only too human to the more than human, or perhaps the truly human.

The question about questions: knowledge and its essential direction

For Ibn 'Arabi the foundation of all knowledge, no matter how objective or impersonal some forms of knowledge appear to be, has its grounds in self-knowledge: the kind of knowledge which cannot be ultimately divorced from the knower nor from the thing known. To put the matter in contemporary existentialist terms Ibn 'Arabi's is a participatory[10] view of knowledge which recognizes that in every act of knowing stands the knower. All knowledge for Ibn 'Arabi is necessarily a form of self-knowledge. The basic question becomes "Who is known?" rather than, simply, "What is known?". In this reorientation of epistemological emphasis it is the question "Who is known?" which becomes the question to be borne in mind in every situation and in all domains of knowledge. This fundamental question is, for Ibn 'Arabi, capable of giving the quest for knowledge its proper direction and centrality. In the metaphysics of *wahdat al-wujud* there is only One Being and only One Knower. Because of this it is necessary for the *'arif*, the knower, in the contemplation of his or her self-experience, to recognize who it is that is the true knower and the known.

This is why Ibn 'Arabi can write so evocatively: "What ails thee that thou wouldst not sense me through the tangibles? what ails thee that thou wouldst not comprehend me through the scents? what ails thee that thou wouldst not see me? what ails thee that thou wouldst not hear me? what ails thee? what ails thee? what ails thee?"[11]

Let us explore further this idea that all knowledge is a form of self-knowledge. Consider, for example, a domain of knowledge which seems remote from the personal and the intimate – that is, basic arithmetic. The basic truths of arithmetic, such as $2 + 2 = 4$, seem to be objective, impersonal and abstract truths whose validity is independent of the knowing subject and whose truths are independent of anyone knowing them to be true. Such a view accounts well for the non-arbitrary nature of the arithmetical enterprise and allows for further mathematical discovery and analysis.[12] It is such features of mathematical truth which lead some mathematicians to a Platonic understanding of the nature of mathematical knowledge itself. Such a view is encapsulated in the following statement by Bertrand Russell made early in his mathematical career: "mathematics takes ... us from what is human into the region of absolute necessity, to which not only the actual world, but every possible world, must conform ... it builds an habitation ... eternally standing ... where our ideals are fully satisfied."[13]

If we choose to describe such a view as Platonic it must be in a loose sense if for no other reason than the fact that the fundamental orientation of Plato's theory of knowledge was the realignment of the soul towards that which it already knows,[14] and it certainly seems unlikely that Russell would have had this in mind. Also, for Plato, this entailed no escape from what is human but a realization of what human reality essentially is. Plato's view of knowledge, in essence, is a form of self-knowledge of the kind exactly recommended by Ibn 'Arabi. Interestingly, one of Ibn 'Arabi's appellations was Son of Plato and Ibn 'Arabi himself referred to Plato as the Divine Plato. But this point aside, Russell's early view of the nature of mathematics underwent a profound sea-change in later life. He says, for example, that "mathematics has ceased to seem to me non-human in its subject matter. I fear that, to a mind of sufficient intellectual power, the whole of mathematics would appear as trivial, as trivial as the statement that a four-footed animal is an animal."[15]

This view suggests that the propositions of mathematics are simply human productions having no eternal standing. In this regard the mathematical universe can be considered as an aspect of the general human capacity to construct symbolic worlds. Mathematics, like many other forms of human knowledge, is rooted in the human subject's capacity to wonder, to create and to discover. Just how deeply personal and gripping this mathematical capacity can become is colourfully illustrated in the life of the twentieth century, largely self-tutored, Hindu mathematical genius Srinivasa Iyengar Ramanujan.[16] For him, as the great English mathematician John E. Littlewood is recorded to have said, "every positive integer was one of his personal friends". What is also noticeable in Ramanujan's work is the obvious isomorphism between his adherence to the Hindu Upanishadic concept of infinity and his contribution to the mathematics of infinity. For him mathematics was unquestionably a form of metaphysical expression which had its origins in the deepest recesses of the human self. And in Ramanujan's case the Self needs to be understood in the conceptual light of the classical Hindu Vedic literature. There are indeed some remarkable parallels between Ibn 'Arabi's conception of the Self and the Upanishadic world picture.

Whatever view we hold concerning the foundations of mathematics,[17] the constant production of significant and new mathematics (so well attested to in Ramanujan's work) – although, as a matter of course, subject to rigorous mathematical analysis – cannot itself simply be the outcome of such analysis. As Ramanujan himself was quite aware, its roots lie elsewhere. It is when we consider the human creative source of the mathematical enterprise that it is possible to glimpse the subtlety and richness of a philosophy, such as Ibn 'Arabi's, which endows an ontological and epistemological theophanic role to the creative imagination.[18] In other words, here is an understanding which conceives of the imagination as having a specific ontological reality capable of receiving ideas and images (that is, knowledge) directly from the Divine source, including mathematical inspiration. Ramanujan himself once said "an equation for me has no meaning unless it expresses a thought of God".[19] He would have had little difficulty in accepting Ibn 'Arabi's claim that "there is not one single thing that cannot be known through revelation or spiritual experience".[20] From such a viewpoint the roots of all knowledge are inextricably tied to the personal. But our epistemological understanding of the nature of this inextricability is metaphysically reconfigured when the individual is pictured as a unique and essentially infinite theatre of God's manifestation to Himself "from all eternity".

Under this metaphysical rubric all forms of knowledge potentially reflect a revivifying and transfiguring entanglement between the knower and the known. It was existentialists like Nikolai Berdyaev and Miguel de Unamuno who insisted that behind every effort to know stands the knower. For them (and for existentialism in general) philosophizing is not done by reason alone "but with the will, with the feelings, with the flesh and with the bones, with the whole soul and with the whole body. It is man that philosophizes."[21] Further aspects of this existentialist insight into the relationship between the knower and the known are carefully elucidated by John Macquarrie when he remarks:

> fundamental ... is the difference between knowing a fact and knowing a person – a difference so deeply felt that many languages have separate verbs for expressing the two kinds of knowing ... For the existentialist the paradigm of knowledge is not the objective knowledge of empirical facts sought by the sciences, but knowing persons. Such knowing may be either the subjective ... knowledge of self, or the knowledge of other persons gained through encounter with them ... What then is

peculiar about the kind of knowing which the existentialist takes to be paradigmatic? The answer would be that such knowing is characterized by participation. It is not obtained by observing something external to oneself but by immersing oneself in that which is known.[22]

The basic structure of Ibn 'Arabi's metaphysics of unity adds a new and extraordinary profundity to the conception of knowledge as a form of encounter, whether the encounter is within the deepest recesses of oneself, or the encounter with another human being, or with ideas or music or literature or even with the power, beauty and awesomeness of nature. For Ibn 'Arabi there is an important sense in which all knowledge is potentially a form of encounter. To understand this let us return to the metaphysical premise of *wahdat al-wujud* that there is only One Being and, thereby, only One Essential Knower. This One Being has in itself infinite modalities, some of which constitute the appearance of the phenomenal world as we know and experience it, including us. As the "theatre of manifestation" the phenomenal world is the place where the One Being reveals itself constantly and kaleidoscopically in an infinity of its own forms. Or as the Quran says: "Each day He is upon some task."[23] The only reality that the phenomenal world has is as a forever-in-the-making modality of the One Being. The phenomenal world is an apparently external-ized expression of the internal relationships of the One Being. The One Being manifests as apparently other and it may appear that this otherness implies a fragmentation of the original Unity. But this is not and cannot, in fact, be the case according to Ibn 'Arabi. There is only a perceived fragmentation or an apparent otherness or an apparent externalization. From our point of view it may appear as if the cosmos is inhabited by separate individual consciousnesses and separate objects of all kinds. The reason for such perceived fragmen-tation might be, as Izutsu argues,[24] that reality appears as a plurality of particulars because of the structure and nature of human cogni-tion itself and the finitude of human consciousness. Affifi[25] affirms a similar point when he rehearses Ibn 'Arabi's view that it is because our finite minds cannot grasp the whole as whole that we perceive it as a plurality of things. But, according to Ibn 'Arabi, in spite of this perceived fragmentation, what we are actually encountering is not many separate things or individuals but the infinite manifestations of the One and Only Being. It is the corner-stone of Ibn 'Arabi's mystical philosophy of knowledge that the *raison d'être* of human kind is to return to the vision of the original Unity and this is, to put it in existentialist terms, *the* fundamental human project. For Ibn 'Arabi, to return to this total vision of the original Unity (known as *tawhid* or Union) is the epistemological gold standard. It is the unalloyed awareness that there is Only One Being and Only One Knower.

Among the infinite modalities of being and knowing, not all encompass such a total vision. The scientific enterprise, whilst depicting the extraordinary wonder of the workings of the cosmos, can also, by its very modality as an empirical study, enclose its understanding of the cosmos within its own relatively circumscribed impersonal frame of reference. It can veil the cosmos as theophany or, in Macquarrie's sense, it can veil it as encounter. But clearly it need not, as Einstein reminds us:

> The most beautiful and profound emotion … is the sensation of the mystical. Those to whom this emotion is a stranger, who can no longer wonder and stand rapt in awe, are as good as dead. To know that what is impenetrable to us really exists, manifesting itself as the highest wisdom and the most radiant beauty … this knowledge, this feeling, is at the center of true religiousness.[26]

What Einstein alludes to here is expressed in the very language of personal encounter and in no sense is this insight diminished by scientific discovery. In fact, scientific discovery is one of the modes in which such intimations of a "most radiant beauty" can be discerned, or also ignored. In contrast to Einstein on this point Ibn 'Arabi cannot stress too strongly that what "really exists" is far from being "impenetrable to us". On the contrary, the source of "the highest wisdom" and the "most radiant beauty" constitutes the foundations of human reality and it would run counter to the Divine love to be known if it remained irrevocably impenetrable.

Metaphysics, historically positioned discourses and human aspiration

To proceed further with the exploration of the conceptual contours of Ibn 'Arabi's metaphysics of unity it is pertinent at this stage to revisit the question "Why does metaphysics matter?" The answer must be to do with the fact that metaphysical questioning has always been directed towards a comprehensive account of the nature of Being (as, for example, in Plato or Aristotle), or directed towards the nature of what it is possible for human beings to know (as in Kant or Hume), or what it is possible or desirable for human beings to become (as in Aquinas, Spinoza, Marx or Freud). It is arguable that there is not any major theorist in the Western intellectual tradition who was not forced to choose in matters of metaphysics. Whilst metaphysics itself has historically been seen as a branch of philosophy – sometimes considered a disreputable branch – it can also be said to distinguish itself from philosophy in its characteristic attempt to offer a comprehensive account of the whole as a whole. It is quite possible for a particular metaphysical account to engender, from its own inclusive perspective, a critique of the assumptions of the metaphysics behind such philosophies as rationalism, logical positivism or existentialism. Metaphysics, in this sense, does not deal piecemeal with the particular contents of our conceptual apparatus.

Traditional metaphysics, which has typically addressed itself to comprehensive questions about the whole as a whole, often postulates the existence of a reality which is unutterable, unknowable, incomprehensible, unqualifiable and unfathomable. This is undoubtedly the case with the metaphysics of Ibn 'Arabi, according to whom there is a dimension of "the Majesty of God"[27] which is beyond the grasp of human conceptualization. In Ibn 'Arabi's metaphysics this unknowable essence is described as the "Absolute Unknowable" and sometimes as the "First Presence". It remains essentially Unknowable (except to Itself) and conceptually unspecifiable. However, the magnitude of its presence as *Origin* is indicated by the "First Unveiling" or "First Individuation" and by all the further modalities and consequences which follow from this "Most Holy Effusion" (*al-fayd al-aqdas*).[28] He expresses this in such a way as to emphasize the simultaneity of the situation, as it is that we ourselves, in essence, signify our Origin. In the Quran one is frequently reminded in various ways that God is closer to us "than our jugular vein". In this context, we can now consider the enigmatic and paradoxical nature of Ibn 'Arabi's meeting with "the youth steadfast in devotion":

> I ... met the eagle stone of the youth steadfast in devotion who is both speaker and silent, neither alive nor dead, both complex and simple, encompassing and encompassed ... I grasped what he was and his significance ... that he was far beyond all considerations of space and time. When I had realized this ... I kissed his right hand ... and said to him, "O bearer of tidings, look and see how I seek your company and desire your friendship." Then he indicated to me by hint and sign that he was created to speak only by signs ... I begged him to reveal his secrets to me. He said "Behold the details of my structure and the order of my formation and you will find the answer to your question set forth in me, for I am not one who speaks or is spoken to, my knowledge being only of myself and my essence being naught other than my names. I am knowledge, the known and the knower."[29]

The questions which traditional metaphysics, such as Ibn 'Arabi's, address about the nature of Being require and imply a profound shift in our cognitive orientation. Such a shift opens up a vast spiritual and epistemological landscape hitherto hardly imaginable.

Ibn 'Arabi's doctrine of *wahdat al-wujud*, Oneness of Being, is inherently a *dispositional ontology*. What is clear is that the metaphysics of Ibn 'Arabi is not a personal intellectual construction of his own. To conceive it as such would be to misconstrue the fundamental idea that the metaphysics of *wahdat al-wujud* intends to convey. It is precisely because it is not a personal intellectual construction that it avoids the accusation of being based on the extravagances of the human intellect. If such metaphysical insights concerning the whole as a whole are left off the intellectual agenda or left unaddressed, one can never be sure that local, regional, cultural and intellectual preferences are not mistaken for a more universal point of view.

What can be said at this stage is that metaphysics suggests that piecemeal strategies are insufficient. The defence of metaphysics is usually located in the production of some "bold new vision of the nature of the world"[30] which naturally carries with it some degree of conceptual articulation. Such a universal point of view like that of Ibn 'Arabi's, can only be regarded as providing a revised view of the world, if what is meant by revised is seeing that the whole is more than the sum of its parts and that the parts can only be properly understood from the point of view of the whole. *Ibn 'Arabi's metaphysics is predicated on God's vision of Himself in the infinity of His own forms.* This extraordinary metaphysical picture does not entail that the ordinary stock of "fundamental concepts and categories of human thinking"[31] have to be abandoned. In fact, the revised picture of the world as expounded by Ibn 'Arabi is a picture in which these fundamental concepts and categories of human thinking have their place and value. But the acknowledgement of their relative usefulness is also an acknowledgement of their relative limitation. Human concepts and categories cannot penetrate the true nature of "the Real" as Izutsu indicates when he says "the ... world is real in so far as it is the absolute truth or Reality as perceived by the relative human mind in accordance with its natural structure."[32] Ibn 'Arabi's remarks on the incapacity of reflective thinking to uncover anything other than a profoundly limited and infinitesimal fraction of reality also alludes to this situation.

But let us make another general point about the nature of metaphysics. Very often developments in the physical sciences have encouraged metaphysical revision. In this regard it is noticeable that there is an increasing movement among many recent leading scientists towards a reconceptualization of the metaphysical foundations of modern science. Such theorists as Bohm, Sperry, Goodwin, Mae-Wan Ho, and others, advocate an account of scientific epistemology which encapsulates, as an indispensable premise, a more unitive understanding of the encounter between the knower and the known: the observer and the observed are seen to be inextricably interconnected.[33] When Rom Harré suggests "particularly in physics itself, philosophical considerations have always been very much to the fore in the thinking of the great physicists. Metaphysics, that is, critical reflection on the nature of the 'world' to be investigated, has played a central role not only in the formulation of theories, but also in the development of empirical methods,"[34] we can conclude that metaphysics and physics are far from being poles apart.

Finally, there is another general feature of Ibn 'Arabi's metaphysical outlook which it is necessary to hold in view. This feature is difficult to pin down but is extremely important: it is a kind of tolerance, openness and metaphysically inspired generosity of outlook. It is the kind of outlook which will have nothing to do with the petty and the mean-spirited, or the dogmatic and the intolerant. It is an outlook which continually reaffirms the great nature which God has essentially bestowed upon the human Self in creating man in His image. There is a vastness about Ibn 'Arabi's metaphysics which makes it antithetical to any narrow religious fundamentalism or a relative closedness and inflexibility of mind, secular or religious. In brief, Ibn 'Arabi's metaphysical writings reflect the strength, generosity and grandeur inherent in the vision of the original Unity alluded to in the description *wahdat al-wujud*.

In any comparison between traditional and modern thought it is a primary conceptual requirement that we are familiar with the metaphysical scaffolding of our own theoretical culture. As Robin Horton argues in his excellent article about the similarities and differences between traditional religious thought and Western science,[35] it is only familiarity with our own twentieth-century theoretical culture which will provide the "vital key to understanding" the nature of traditional cultures and thought. He suggests that social anthropologists, for example, have been blinded by the personal idiom utilized by traditional tribal cultures in their everyday explanations and general metaphysical views of their worlds (i.e. references to gods, spirits, ancestors and so on). Horton contends that because traditional thinking is couched in the personal idiom rather than in the impersonal idiom of modern science, anthropological studies have failed to take account of the important similarities of rational strategy between the two different approaches. He does, however, identify a number of important instances where they coincide, the most fundamental of which are the following: *both* enterprises exemplify (a) the quest for explanatory theory which is directed towards the quest for unity underlying diversity, order underlying apparent disorder, regularity underlying apparent anomaly and (b) in both cases, such explanatory theory places things in a causal context wider than that provided by common sense. In short, both traditional religious thinking and modern scientific thinking exemplify similar rational strategies but they are expressed in different linguistic idioms – the former in a personal idiom and the latter in an impersonal idiom. Horton then goes on to locate the major theoretical divergence, namely, that in traditional cultures "there is no developed awareness of alternatives to the established body of theoretical tenets". From this position he concludes that traditional cultures are relatively closed whereas modern scientific cultures are intrinsically open. How open modern Western scientific and technological culture actually is to "alternatives to the established body of theoretical tenets" is a moot point, particularly in relation to the question of what constitutes enlightened human progress. If we confine Horton's suggestion specifically to scientific research programmes then it seems largely true that scientific culture subjects its own theoretical productions to radical self-appraisal in the light of alternative theories. By comparison, some traditional religious metaphysics may seem to be relatively closed ways of viewing the world. If we were searching for contemporary illustrations of the radical closedness of some religious metaphysics it is probable that we would cite modern forms of religious fundamentalism. We know that religious fundamentalism is an increasing problem in the modern world. However, it may be, as Parekh[36] points out, that religious fundamentalism is "a specific kind of response to a religion facing a crisis of identity and authority". According to Parekh such a response to crisis involves the ignoring of tradition and the construction of "a highly simplified and ideological system of beliefs" which "radically reconstitutes the religion concerned". If we accept this view, then fundamentalism is an aberration of the original tradition it seeks to represent.

In relation to the metaphysics of *wahdat al-wujud* it is clear that such a concept does not constitute a "highly simplified ... ideological system of beliefs", nor does it involve any ideological simplification of Islam. One of the refreshing recommendations of Ibn 'Arabi's thought is "that the person of knowledge (*'arif*) does not get caught up in any one form of belief". This essential recommendation stems from a metaphysics which allows for the awareness that all human knowledge is, to some extent, perspectival, conditioned and relative. The '*arif*'s directive is to seek the "knowledge inherent in God" ('*ilm laduni*) and not to be imprisoned within ideologically closed ways of viewing the world. The '*arif* is advised to be the *hayula* or essence of all beliefs in the metaphysical sense conveyed by the famous line from Ibn 'Arabi's *Tarjuman al-Ashwaq* (The Interpreter of Desires), "My heart has become capable of every form". Here again we sense the sheer vastness of his metaphysics which makes it intrinsically antithetical to all forms of fundamentalism, cognitive or metaphysical.

It is historically true that, despite the more recent developments discussed earlier, the Western intellectual tradition (especially in the period of European intellectual history known as the Enlightenment) has tended to emphasize the hiatus between the knower and the known, between the object and the subject, between the mind and the body and between the creator and creation. For René Descartes the divorce between mind and body, whilst radical, did allow their alleged conjunction in the "pineal gland", but for those Enlightenment supporters of Deism, the divorce between Creator and Creation was more absolute. For the Deists there had to be an unbridgeable gulf between Creator and Creation in order to achieve the objective of excluding any form of knowledge by revelation. Deism presents the picture of a radically non-theophanic cosmos. For the Deists, God had created the Cosmos and then left it to run according to its own laws without any further interference. It was the conception of a distant, yet providential God whose only traces were to be discovered in the design and order and beauty present in the Universe. Isaac Newton, the central hero of the Enlightenment thinkers, favoured the "argument from design".[37] For the Deists, the "argument from design", which was so famously criticized by their contemporary David Hume, was persuasive and appealing precisely because it represented for them a rational proof of the existence of God which did not appeal to revelation. Classical Newtonian physics had demonstrated unequivocally that the universe was ordered and law-like. It seemed to them that the Newtonian picture of a deterministic universe regulated by immutable laws left no room for revelation, or divine intervention, or sent prophet, or revealed text, or miracle. The secrets of nature could only be discovered by human observation and reason: the universe was to be properly conceived of as an empirically and scientifically closed system. This was not Newton's own view – he remained deeply interested in the occult – but it was a view that became predominant among many of the *philosophes.*

Such newly emerging intellectual conceptions of the Cosmos, coupled with developing ideas about the scope of scientific and technical knowledge, soon became unalterable and unquestionable truths amongst some of the new and influential enlightened intellectuals (e.g. Diderot, D'Alembert, Voltaire). Such beliefs underwent, as a modern sociologist of knowledge might remark, a process of reification: they became taken-for-granted "facts".

Of course, there were many reactions against this intellectual entrenchment, notably encapsulated in the tenets of Romanticism and, much later, in the doctrines of Existentialism. The radical divide between knower and known was further challenged with the rise of twentieth-century quantum physics. But such entrenchment takes a while before it "melts into air".[38] All in all, the Enlightenment Project – as Habermas was later to call it – and the reactions it provoked, brought into new prominence the question of the nature and scope of knowledge and its relation to human subjectivity, progress and aspiration. This in itself is one of the crucial questions facing the twenty-first century: what is the nature of the relationship and responsibility between knower and known? The philosophy of Ibn 'Arabi has a direct and urgent relevance to this question.

It is because of the importance of, and the meaning that Ibn 'Arabi attaches to knowledge, that the present study attempts to elucidate his underlying conception of knowledge and compare it with the paradigmatic assumptions about the nature of knowledge that permeated much of twentieth-century Western theoretical culture. One might legitimately say that to traverse the intellectual landscape of modernity in the light of Ibn 'Arabi's *wahdat al-wujud* is a salutary and exhilarating exercise.

Before embarking on such an enterprise, it is perhaps necessary and useful to address another substantial general problem. This is the issue of understanding Ibn 'Arabi's metaphysical requirement of viewing the whole as a whole in relation to the issue of the relativism of the positioned discourses which constitute contemporary intellectual history. Clearly, such specific domains of knowledge as history, science, psychology, sociology and so on have their own frames of reference and their own intrinsic assumptions and methodologies.

To illustrate what is at issue here let us take the case of the academic discipline of modern history. Carr[39] remarks in his discussion of the historian and his information that "the facts speak only when the historian calls on them: it is he who decides to which facts to give the floor, and in what order and context." This observation implies that all history is inherently a historiographical enterprise which inevitably reflects the theoretical and ideological commitments of the historian. More recently the historian Keith Jenkins[40] insists that "the idea that somehow the past can be re-created objectively" (that is, *without bias*) is to ignore a major premise of modern historical scholarship that history is a "series of readings, all of which are positioned". For Jenkins there is no possibility of an "unpositioned center ... The only choice is between a history that is aware of what it is doing and a history that is not."[41]

In summarizing his case, Jenkins cites the work of another contemporary theorist Hayden White, to the effect that

> we should no longer naively expect that statements about a given epoch or complex of events in the past "correspond" to some pre-existent body of "raw facts". For we should recognize that what constitutes the facts themselves is the problem that the historian ... has tried to solve by the choice of metaphor by which he orders his world, past, present and future.[42]

It appears, therefore, that historians in the practice of their trade are dealers in interpretive, explanatory and ordering metaphors which are intrinsically positioned. As a result, all historical discourses are culturally and ideologically positioned discourses. This is no doubt why Carr reminds us first to "study the historian before you begin to study the facts."[43] However, these comments on the philosophy and methodology of modern history seem to run counter to any metaphysical requirement of viewing the whole as a whole.

What can be concluded from this – and it is an important point to make – is that it is not through positioned discourses that one can arrive at such a metaphysical vision as that proposed by Ibn 'Arabi. Two responses emerge: one is articulated in Henry Corbin's short monograph in which he argues, in effect, that there are two incommensurable and opposing paradigms of history: the ancient, oriental and sacred, and the modern, Western and secular. The second response, which is the one preferred in the present study, is to re-examine and reconceive this apparent dilemma in the light of Ibn 'Arabi's metaphysical principle of the immanencing of knowledge.

Let us first consider Corbin's argument. He identifies the hegemonic paradigm of the modern age as that historical paradigm which represents "man as being *in history*": human beings are seen essentially and fundamentally as historical and cultural beings. This historical model, he continues, defines history as "an exterior history of 'historical phenomena'" which posits "the mirage of a historical causality". In short, for Corbin there is an almost empiricist assumption operating in modern historical analysis which insists that not only do human beings live in the historical and cultural mode but they are no more than historical and cultural beings. One might usefully add here, although Corbin does not, that from such an historical perspective human beings are both the producers of history and culture and are, themselves, products of their own productions or those of their predecessors. Such a view allows for radical historical and social change, both intended and unintended. The central issue here is the closedness of this assumption which Corbin regards "as the great failing of so-called modern thought". It is the assumption that "... the state of society is ... the primary datum". Corbin summarizes his case thus: "the great failing of so-called modern thought ... is relentlessly set upon closing up all the outlets which could lead beyond this world. This is what is known as agnosticism. It has utilized for its purposes sociology, historicism, psychoanalysis and even linguistics."[44]

Whatever insight there undoubtedly is in Corbin's assessment, strategically it leads him to oppose the dominant epistemological presumptions of one era with those of another. In the adoption of such a strategy there is a clear tendency to construct a kind of judgmental impasse. Whilst certain readings of Ibn 'Arabi may seem to legitimize this impasse, nevertheless, in strict accordance with Ibn

'Arabi's doctrine of *wahdat al-wujud*, it will be argued, it must be treated with some caution. Corbin and Nasr both attest that much of modern Western theoretical culture involves a "desacralization" of knowledge and both authors acknowledge the necessity of what Nasr, in his Gifford Lectures,[45] calls the rediscovery of the sacred and the revival of tradition. There is little doubt that the notion of tradition that Nasr invokes is one in which teachings of the spiritual magnitude of Ibn 'Arabi would have some vital contribution to make. But the question which naturally arises is, how are we to view, in the light of Ibn 'Arabi's *wahdat al-wujud*, the alleged desacralized forms of modern theoretical culture?

Firstly, in order to save the "transcendent" meaning of cultural, historical and social phenomena, it is not strategically necessary to counter one era against another, or one paradigm of history against another, as Corbin seems to do. Ibn 'Arabi allows for "degrees of knowledge"[46] and levels of understanding and insight: he cites approvingly Junayd of Baghdad's saying "The colour of water is the colour of its container". Part of what is alluded to here is that everything has its place and value, even though it may represent a partial or limited point of view. Its limitation is in its being "coloured" by the nature of a particular human belief. On this view, the predominant colouring of "modern thought" (that is, assuming for the moment that there is a "predominant colouring") results directly from the degree of self-knowledge of the theorizers themselves. But we would not want to say, for instance, that a theorist who proposes some form of new mathematics or a new theory about the effects of unemployment or poverty is necessarily devoid of self-knowledge in the sense Ibn 'Arabi deploys the term. Academic theorizing does not imply self-knowledge or agnosticism or atheism or belief in the sacred, although in some individual cases such theorizing may take some such assumption as its premise or conclusion. It is more likely to be the case that much contemporary theoretical culture would simply not consider these assumptions relevant to their investigations or equally feel any need to pronounce on them. It is not, therefore, academic theorizing *per se* which is at issue. What is it then?

Degrees of knowledge: the principle of immanencing

According to Ibn 'Arabi the Real in its continuous and infinite Self-disclosure conforms "to the opinion" that "His servant has of Him". In this sense the Real conforms to the mental constructions or beliefs of the servant. The servants themselves can be regarded as unique loci which condition or colour the matter according to their particular and unique nature as individuations. The Real discloses itself continuously and infinitely to all and sundry. The servant's belief is the cognitive manner in which the Self-disclosure of the Real is understood or misunderstood, cognitively conceived or misconceived.[47] Or better still, it is the manner in which the Self-disclosure is received and conditioned by the human receptor. This ultimately depends, for Ibn 'Arabi, upon the established potentiality or essential predisposition of the human receptor. Accordingly, the predisposition of the servant crucially configures and determines the nature of self-experience. For most individuals, Ibn 'Arabi suggests, their predisposition is a most hidden thing which unconsciously structures their moral and aesthetic self-experience as well as their cognitive experience. In short, what Ibn 'Arabi intends, by the locution the belief of the servant, is the essential and unique predisposition of the person. It is these established potentialities which configure and condition the Self-disclosure of the Real. This is the principle of immanencing. And it is Ibn 'Arabi's treatment of the principle of immanencing which Corbin underestimates in his discussion of the problem he sets himself.

The principle of the immanencing of knowledge and the logical role it plays in the *weltanschauung* of Ibn 'Arabi offers a fascinating insight into a concern that, in one way or another, has haunted much contemporary theorizing: that is, the problem of relativism – moral, religious, cognitive, aesthetic and so on.

In addition, we can respond to this issue from another Akbarian direction. There is in Ibn 'Arabi's thinking an important role for the expression "secondary causes" – such as the economic, social, scientific, and cultural determinants characteristic of a particular era. For Ibn 'Arabi the primary and generally unseen cause of *all* phenomena is God, whereas the apparent or secondary causes are as many and varied as the things and processes of the universe such as biology, history, culture, economics, art, ideas, books, lectures, bank accounts, marriage, and so on. Secondary causes are mediating mechanisms or causes through which certain ends can be accomplished: they are, as Chittick[48] points out, fundamentally constitutive of the cosmos. They are the continually changing conditions which allow human life to exist and develop. According to Ibn 'Arabi they are the "outward forms of unseen realities" which "God did not establish ... aimlessly". They are also the working out of things at the level of phenomena and thereby accrue a certain veracity, causal influence, attraction and importance as lived human experience. This clearly and appropriately attributes to the study and analysis of social, historical, cultural and physical phenomena its due value. It is the kind of worth and value which any serious student of modern history, sociology or natural science would confirm. But Ibn 'Arabi says that secondary causes are much more than this. In one obvious metaphysical respect they act as a veil over their true nature as theophany. In another equally metaphysical respect they can act also as a constant reminder of our human dependence. Consider how intrinsic to modernity are economics, science, and technology and how much modern life depends upon, for example, the vicissitudes of the stockmarket and the reliability, security and privacy promised by computerized telecommunications. This dependency on secondary causes is, for Ibn 'Arabi, not only an external and literal dependence but is indicative of a more essential poverty and dependence. The "theatre of manifestation" which we experience and describe (from certain points of view and for certain purposes) as biological, physical, economic, historical, and cultural stands in indissoluble dependence on and poverty towards *wahdat al-wujud* in its non-manifested, transcendent origin, like that – to use one of Ibn 'Arabi's telling metaphors – of a shadow to its originator.

Because of these considerations the present strategy will be rather different from that proposed by Corbin. We will consider what is to be lost or gained in explaining and interpreting cultural and historical phenomena under differing theoretical assumptions and perspectives. This will not entail a presumption of an in-built agnosticism as Corbin assumes, but there will be a presumption of what I call differentiated seeing. This is a term which, I intend to show, reflects a rather different insight into the state of affairs than Corbin's term agnosticism, without negating it entirely. The process will be one of viewing human experience from a variety of paradigmatic settings in order to make apparent what each theoretical setting reveals and conceals, rejects or accepts, loses or gains. Each paradigm can be viewed as a particular mode of differentiated seeing bringing out certain aspects of the phenomena at the expense of concealing others. It is analogous to Junayd's "the water takes on the colour of the container". We have an illuminating example of this in the case of modern physics. Quantum mechanics reveals light as made up of particles, whereas wave-theory reveals light as wave-like. The problem, as Harré points out, is that if the physicist, using "particle-creating equipment", forces the world to display itself in one way then it loses at that moment the ability to reveal the properties it would have revealed had we not done so or had the physicist deployed "wave-creating equipment" instead.[49]

Such an analytical and comparative procedure facilitates an extraordinary glimpse into the diversity of modernity's intellectual productions: from modernist to postmodernist paradigms. These intellectual productions may themselves be regarded as a kind of "theatre of manifestation" which reveal *one* of the ways in which the Self-disclosure of the Real is "every day engaged in a different business". Academic theorizing itself can be viewed as a particular "theatre of manifestation" which can be amusing, silly, serious, engaging, misleading, insightful and sometimes riveting. Bearing all this in mind, we can take to heart Kierkegaard's advice not to review "all systems of philosophy … and show up the inconsistencies within each … and so construct a world in which I did not live but only held up to the view of others": this is not the intention of the present study.[50]

The purpose of these comparisons will be to explore the epistemological implications of Ibn 'Arabi's remarks on the principle of immanencing *vis-à-vis* contemporary theoretical culture, without necessarily denying the validity of the slant cast by any particular paradigm or theoretical perspective or even individual thinker. To insist, for example, that contemporary social and economic historians can only proceed professionally by basing their explanations on contemporary social and economic phenomena, is to make a point about the perspectival nature of the knowledge with which they deal: that is, about its boundaries and limits. Within such theoretically and empirically defined parameters a whole set of differently positioned discourses may co-exist, not always too happily, which colour the type and tenor of a particular theorist's explanation. Was it not that alleged inaugurator of modernity, Friedrich Nietzsche, who pointed out that, in this sense, all human knowledge is perspectival: "the *more* eyes, different eyes, we can use to observe one thing the more complete ... our 'concept' of this thing"?[51]

Ibn 'Arabi's w*ahdat al-wujud* allows for such differentiated seeing without, unlike Nietzsche, denying the reality of non-perspectival knowledge-in-itself. In so doing, Ibn 'Arabi can consistently hold that the Divine source of the "act of bringing to be" remains "unseen" and this applies to the theorizer and the theorizer's theorizing as well as to what is being explained and theorized about.

Ibn 'Arabi and modern thought: a reconfigured topography

With this in mind, the present study is essentially an analysis of the concept of knowledge deployed by Ibn 'Arabi with an examination of its possible bearing on some of the twentieth-century epistemologies prevalent in the industrial (and post-industrial) West.[52] To this end it will be necessary to sketch the main philosophical and intellectual traditions of Western industrial culture and the theories of the human self which inform them.

The genre of this study is an open discourse between the ancient and the modern, the traditional and the scientific, the industrial and the personal. Embracing recent developments in the natural and social sciences, there are three main areas of modern thought which are of primary concern: philosophy, sociology and psychology. All three disciplines have been strongly influenced by the trajectory and developments of science and technology within modern industrial culture. For example, how else is it possible to explain the rise and popularity of computational theories of mind in psychology? With an increasingly extensive literature available on the possible metaphysical implications of recent developments in physics and biology, these particular discussions will not be treated separately but will be integrated where and when relevant.

Pivotal to our present discussion is how the theoretical landscape of modern industrial technological culture (and perhaps postmodern culture?)[53] appears from the all-inclusive topography of Ibn ʿArabi. This is quite a complex question which cannot be settled prematurely by any form of theoretical dogmatism (say, for example, by assuming that the methods of modern science represent the only reliable foundations of knowledge) or by any over-eager doctrine of eschatology, such as the view that the tendency towards increasing secularization within industrial capitalism heralds a state of religious and moral bankruptcy and final collapse.

Our first task is to locate some trigonometrical and metaphysical co-ordinates. What becomes immediately apparent as we proceed is the unexpectedly and thoroughly modern nature of much of Ibn ʿArabi's thought. Clearly, some of the thematic preoccupations concerning the holistic nature of human aspiration, value and completeness to which Ibn ʿArabi constantly draws our attention are still present in contemporary culture, even when these themes are thoroughly secular or secularized.

Such recurring human, transcultural themes come as no surprise: perhaps what is surprising, though, are the forms these themes take in modern industrial culture and the light which Ibn ʿArabi's metaphysics throws on them. It is still, however, relatively rare in the history of European culture to locate thinkers who even begin to approach the breadth of vision and universality of Ibn ʿArabi's philosophy of Being. Two eminent figures in the history of Renaissance philosophy are worth mentioning in this respect: Giovanni Pico and Nicholas of Cusa. Both men, like Ibn ʿArabi himself, cannot be fitted neatly into the usual classificatory categories. Pico emphasizes, in strikingly Akbarian fashion, the fundamental dignity and central place of man in the cosmic scheme of things "against the increasing tendency of medieval religion to depreciate man's nature";[54] and, interestingly, Nicholas of Cusa's deployment of the concept of learned ignorance provides a parallel illustration of Ibn ʿArabi's insistence that it is beyond the power of human discursive reason to fathom the infinity of God, "in whom all opposites coincide".

In general, the main difference between Ibn 'Arabi's insights into the nature of the self and modern theories of the self reside not so much in matters of detail but precisely in the *universality* of the point of view from which the whole matter of the human self is viewed. Let us explore this further.

It is theoretically commonplace to modern analysts of culture and consciousness to say that human consciousness is, in some sense, self-reflexive. This means the human mind can ask questions about itself, about the origin and value of its own species and about its possible future, and in this self-reflexivity we have the roots and possibility of scientific, aesthetic, religious, ethical and technological knowledge. Or, at least, the roots of what has been commonly accepted as such knowledge. It is generally accepted that the self-reflexive capacity of the human mind is what distinguishes human consciousness from animal consciousness. This distinction is acknowledged, for instance, by Charles Darwin when he remarks that "It may freely be admitted that no animal is self-conscious, if by this term is implied that he reflects on such points, as whence he comes or whither he will go, or what is life and death and so forth."[55]

The capacity of the human being to ask questions about itself, about (and via) its own nature, rests on two vital and inter-related human dispositions and powers: linguistic competence and imaginative capacity. It may be that in the history of modern thought Ludwig Feuerbach's oft-cited formulation will suffice as a suitable example of the importance of this insight: "But only a being to whom his own species, his own nature, is an object of thought, can make the essential nature of other things or beings an object of thought."[56] Of course, the Feuerbachian enterprise essentially emphasizes the non-transcendent and strictly immanent nature of human-beingness, whereas for Ibn 'Arabi human reality expresses and synthesizes both the immanent and the transcendent in a unique and single reality described as *wahdat al-wujud*. Nevertheless, Ibn 'Arabi's philosophy would make perfect sense of Feuerbach's assertion that "in religion man contemplates his own latent nature",[57] but without the Feuerbachian limitation of reducing theology to anthropology. Ibn 'Arabi would certainly have seen the value of Feuerbach's attempt to cast aside the speculations of what had arguably become an almost Medieval dogmatic *dualistic* theological enterprise. Ibn 'Arabi had scant regard for theologians who, in the Islamic context of his day, he often characterized scathingly as "Doctors of Law". But equally Ibn 'Arabi would have insisted, unlike Feuerbach, that both the divine and the human are aspects of a Single Unique Reality, other than which there is not.

The truth or reality of this Single and Unique ontological situation is, for Ibn 'Arabi, what is experientially revealed to the knower in the contemplation of their own self-experience and in the contemplation, to use a Feuerbachianism, of their own latent nature.

For Ibn 'Arabi the full value and significance of the human subject can only be grasped *sub specie aeternitatis*, as Spinoza might have put it. There is a correct viewing distance; for instance, when using the analogy of viewing a painting, an incorrect viewing distance would be looking at it from too close a proximity. From such a viewing position any attempt to describe it, even when apparently veridic, would also be completely misleading. Such descriptions would be likely to involve a complete failure to recognize what it is that is really being seen. One central implication would be that the immediate and engrossing nature of each person's biological, psychological and cultural landscape (and the historical circumstances and events which define and constitute their particular era) provide too narrow a circumference when viewed solely from *within* the historical and theoretical co-ordinates which define them. Developing the analogy a little further we may say that the correct viewing distance entails a radical shift of viewpoint. It is not simply the intellectual possibility of such a shift of perspective which interests Ibn 'Arabi but the actual accomplishment of it.

The profound difference between the theoretical adoption of such a cognitive shift in consciousness and the complete realization of it is intimated in the account of the meeting between the great Andalusian philosopher Averroës (Ibn Rushd) and the young Ibn 'Arabi. In the conversation which ensues between them there emerges the first glimmerings as to what might be the nature of this profound difference: a difference which turns Averroës' cheeks pale and makes him doubt his own thought.

Consider the following:

I spent a good day in Cordova at the house of Abu al-Walid Ibn Rushd. He had expressed a desire to meet me in person, since he had heard of certain revelations I had received while in retreat and had shown considerable astonishment concerning them. In consequence, my father, who was one of his close friends, took me with him on the pretext of business, in order to give Ibn Rushd the opportunity of making my acquaintance. I was at the time a beardless youth. As I entered the house the philosopher rose to greet me with all the signs of friendliness and affection, and embraced me. Then he said to me "Yes!" and showed pleasure on seeing that I had understood him. I, on the other hand, being aware of the motive for his pleasure, replied, "No!" Upon this, Ibn Rushd drew back from me, his colour changed and he seemed to doubt what he had thought of me. He then put to me the following question, "What solution have you found as a result of mystical illumination and divine inspiration? Does it coincide with what is arrived at by speculative thought?" I replied, "Yes and no. Between the Yea and the Nay the spirits take their flight beyond matter, and the necks detach themselves from their bodies." At this Ibn Rushd became pale and I saw him tremble as he muttered the formula, "There is no power save from God." This was because he had understood my allusion.[58]

We begin to see that for Ibn 'Arabi the theoretical mind cannot adequately or imaginatively conjecture about the reality which is being alluded to even though the theoretical intellect can entertain the possibility of its existence. Averroës' personal intellectual matrix underwent a kind of "existential wobble" on hearing Ibn 'Arabi's reply: to "doubt his own thought" was to doubt the capacity of reflective thought itself to adequately deal with the domain and nature of mystical experience. Such a thesis does not suggest the irrationality of mystical experience but implies a view about the limits and reliability of human reason. For Ibn 'Arabi, some of the worst aspects of human speculative reason were to be seen in the work of theologians. But neither does the reality to which Ibn 'Arabi alludes present us with a case of "unverifiable metaphysics": quite the reverse

– for the whole *raison d'être* of human existence, for Ibn 'Arabi, is to reach that verifiable condition known as *tawhid* or Union.

Let us be clear also that the universality of perspective which Ibn 'Arabi advocates necessitates that the study of his philosophy cannot adequately be conceived of as merely a specialized study of some obscure medieval Arabic metaphysics to which only the classical Arabist has the proper means of access. This in no way negates the profound gratitude and indebtedness that non-Arabic speaking students of the writings of Ibn 'Arabi owe to the work of classical Arabists for the recent proliferation and substantial translations of his works into English, and also for much accompanying exegetical material. As mentioned above, there is enough translated material of sufficiently high quality available now in English to arrive at a rounded picture of the world-view of Ibn 'Arabi. Importantly, misdescriptions of his viewpoint and clear errors of understanding have been cleared up, or at least have been shown for what they are. We shall return to this point briefly towards the end of the present chapter when we examine Affifi's attempt to philosophically dismiss Ibn 'Arabi as a pantheistic monist guilty of systematically misusing the verb "to be".

The main point to be emphasized here is that Ibn 'Arabi's metaphysics are grounded in universal human social and personal experience which cannot be limited to particular cultural settings, although their expression may well take on the characteristics and idioms of particular times and places. Izutsu's classical comparative study of the mystical traditions of Ibn 'Arabi and Lao Tsu lends testimony to this point. In this sense the *wahdat al-wujud* of Ibn 'Arabi is and will remain thoroughly modern and universal, as it was and always has been thoroughly ancient and universal.

The metaphysical orientation of Ibn 'Arabi is the Oneness of Being, from whence it follows with impeccable logical precision that all human experience is, *ipso facto*, an expression of that inescapable metaphysical fact, whether it is recognized as such or not. This means that the universality already referred to includes cosmological as well as historical, cultural and psychological experience; nothing can be excluded. Neither can such universality be limited, or even confined to these types of phenomena: again this is a strict logical implication of Ibn 'Arabi's ontology. It is not an ontology of "many things" but, rather, an ontology of "a disposition to appear as" or, to put it in the language of Ibn 'Arabi, "a Love to be Known".

In abstract terms, Ibn 'Arabi's monumental and largely original contribution is to provide (in extraordinary and comprehensive detail) a dispositional ontology with which to view the matrix of personal, social, historical and spiritual experience, both ancient and contemporary. And this is not to take into consideration the immensely practical nature of that same ontological world-view. According to Izutsu, what I have signified as a *dispositional ontology* lies at the heart of all mystical traditions. In the case of Ibn 'Arabi its logical and inner structure is articulated with such completeness and magnificence that it is unsurpassed in the great mystical and religious literature of the world.[59]

As I have noted elsewhere,[60] Ibn 'Arabi's vision of reality as it is documented in the *Fusus al-Hikam* or the *Futuhat al-Makkiyah* cannot be appropriated to an ontological system. It is not an intellectually worked out axiomatic metaphysics along the lines of Spinoza or F. H. Bradley: it is a living metaphysics full of cadences, moods, modalities, and breath-taking vision, and imbued with a disarming and relentless logic. It reveals and unfolds, time and time again, its own shimmering ontological beauty. The mytho-poetic ambience of the *Fusus al-Hikam* is not the result of rational systematization. Ibn 'Arabi's writings, in general, do not exemplify any Hegelian system-building propensity. Nor are they an attempt to codify knowledge along the lines of the *Encyclopédie* of the eighteenth-century French Enlightenment. It is probably this apparent lack of rational systematization which has led some commentators, quite wrongly, to describe the *Fusus al-Hikam* as badly lacking both form and cohesion. A closer analytical scrutiny suggests that the unity of its structure resides in the consistency of its two main themes: the Oneness of Being and the *raison d'être* of Adamic kind, and also in its potential inner experiential effect on its reader. To use a metaphor of modern chaos theory, the deeper ontological unity of, for example, the *Fusus al-Hikam* of Ibn 'Arabi is configured by a hidden "attractor": the "Love to be Known". The variety of internal styles and modalities within the text itself conform to this order, cannot be separated from it, and constitute its essential unity. In this respect the ordinary discursive intellect is regarded as a relatively limited form of human consciousness unable to penetrate the experiential depths, cadences and beauty of such a "Love to be Known". It is only the inspired intellect, or inspired knowing, and various spiritually inspired[61] states or "tastes" which constitute the preparation for and the personal assimilation of the reality and nature of this Divine love to be known. A part of what is required, according to Ibn 'Arabi, is to empty the heart of discursive thinking: to develop a predisposition to a kind of uncluttered contemplative openness of being. Such meditative states of consciousness in which the activity of ordinary discursive thinking is suspended, hushed or subdued, constitute a state of spiritual poverty and receptivity in which the pendulum of discursive thought finally finds its point of rest and origin in its essential attractor. To state the matter more prosaically, the ordinary discursive intellect is accorded a profoundly subordinate role in Akbarian epistemology, but it is still accorded a role and a value. The reading of the *Fusus* itself cannot fail to engage and stimulate the rational critical faculty of the reader. In fact, part of the ambience of the *Fusus* is its intellectually fascinating and engaging diversity: consider the remarks on causality, time, contingency, necessity, epistemology, ontology, ethics, and aesthetics. These alone would be enough to entice modern philosophical intellects, even those of a quite different persuasion, as indeed Affifi's study corroborates. There is undoubtedly a philosophical vein running through the writings of Ibn 'Arabi which is frequently utilized in his penetrating assessment of a wide variety of philosophical terminologies prevalent in the cultural and intellectual heritage of his times. But such philosophical terminologies are always in the service of his main theme, *wahdat al-wujud*. For example, Ibn 'Arabi proposes, in the light of his central ontology of *wahdat al-wujud*, a unitive account of causality which implies (in the words of the *Fusus*) that "cause and effect are identical" – a judgment which he admits would be "pronounced impossible by the unaided Intellect". But one feels that it is also part of Ibn 'Arabi's strategy in stating the matter so stridently to engender in the reader a view of "what there is" which emphasizes phenomena not as a collection of separate causally interconnected individual things but rather as constituting part of the infinite expression of a Single Unique Reality. From this point of view Ibn 'Arabi's remarks on causality are rendered less apparently paradoxical and are logically consistent with the ontological vision of the *singularity* of the movement of Divine Love and Beauty. It is this seamless metaphysics of Beauty, in which there cannot be, in reality, a multiplicity of existents or things but only an apparent otherness to which Ibn 'Arabi is alluding when he talks about Being, or more accurately Oneness of Being.

It is to this conception of Being which Affifi turns his philosophical attention. He attempts to show that Ibn 'Arabi's treatment of the concept of Being is in danger of committing the error, to put it philosophically and technically, of "treating the existential proposition as a predicational one".[62] What Affifi means, following Kant, is that the concept of being or existence (which as we have seen is intrinsic to Ibn 'Arabi's whole metaphysical programme) is not like the concept of "an atom" or "a molecule" or "human anatomy". The concept of existence is not a kind of thing or process: it does not possess properties as do atoms and molecules which can be further investigated and explored. In the sentence "Atoms exist", so the argument goes, the word "exist" adds nothing whatsoever to the properties of what an atom is, it merely confirms, when it is true, that something possessing those properties actually exists. Existence is thus considered not to be a property or predicate at all. If Ibn 'Arabi could be shown to deploy the concept of Existence as a property, in the required sense, it would render philosophically illegitimate in its entirety the concept of *wahdat al-wujud*. Such a philosophical criticism, if it could be substantiated, would be analogous to holding the view, for example, that the whole of Upanishadic metaphysics[63] (including the sublimity of the famous *sachidananda*) is due to "following grammar beyond the boundaries of sense".[64]

But it becomes clear that it is a profound misconstruction to consider the *wahdat al-wujud* of Ibn 'Arabi as being based on the systematic misuse of the verb "to be". There is no such logical ambiguity or misuse in Ibn 'Arabi's metaphysics of Being. Quite the reverse, its logic is to direct attention to the *possibilities* inherent in being human and to document the universal spiritual landscape of such potential. This is much the same as a mother considering what the future holds for her child, or Plato considering the destiny of the human soul. Human existence, for Ibn 'Arabi, is to be understood as a potential which has an order, ground and meaning. For Ibn 'Arabi, at any rate, we have to find out and know who and what we are. One of the fundamental meanings of the Arabic *wujud* is "to find". And the way of finding is "to know ourselves" in order to know God, of which we are, Ibn 'Arabi insists, in reality, no other. This is the fundamental logic of Ibn 'Arabi's deployment of the concept of Being.

It is at this point that we begin to situate our discussion in relation to the domain of modern analytical philosophy, which affords us a useful starting point. Chittick[65] suggests that the relating of Ibn 'Arabi's metaphysics to the contemporary world is one of those fields which knows no limits, as indeed also is the relating of Akbarian teachings to other religious traditions and to intellectual authorities in general, both religious and secular. Fortunately, Chittick adds that "Perhaps others will be inspired to take up the obvious leads". The orienta-tion of this study is to take up one of these leads: the examination of Ibn 'Arabi's *weltanschauung* in relation to contemporary theoretical culture and its technological and industrial setting.

Notes

1 Plato, *The Collected Dialogues*, ed. E. Hamilton and H. Cairns (Princeton, 1961).

2 L. Wittgenstein, *Tractatus Logico-Philosophicus*, trans. D. F. Pears and B. F. McGuinness (London, 1961).

3 K. Kumar, *Prophecy and Progress* (Harmondsworth, Middlesex, 1983), pp. 300–1.

4 As William C. Chittick points out in *The Sufi Path of Knowledge* (Albany, NY, 1989), p. 79, Ibn 'Arabi does not employ this exact term but the idea permeates his work and is fundamental to it. Claude Addas adds in *Quest for the Red Sulphur*, trans. P. Kingsley (Cambridge, 1993), p. 232, that the term *wahdat al-wujud* seems to have been used for the first time by Sadr al-Din Qunawi, one of Ibn 'Arabi's closest pupils, and eventually, through the intermediary of others, it became the standard description designating Ibn 'Arabi's metaphysics. Whatever the case, this central term is an accurate and appropriate description of Ibn 'Arabi's ontology, which does no injustice whatsoever to Ibn 'Arabi's thought. Quite the contrary, it is such an apt description that we find Ralph Austin in his translation of Ibn 'Arabi's *Fusus al-Hikam*, entitled *The Bezels of Wisdom* (London, 1980), p. 26, suggesting that Ibn 'Arabi coined the term.

5 This is partly engendered by the different meanings such a term can bear in different Akbarian contexts. (The description *Akbarian* is the adjective derived from the title bestowed upon Ibn 'Arabi "Shaykh al-Akbar", which means "The Greatest Teacher".)

6 See S. A. Q. Husaini, *The Pantheistic Monism of Ibn al-Arabi* (Lahore, 1945). In relation to the inadequacy of this kind of description, see Chittick, *Sufi Path*, p. 79.

7 The term Oneness of Being embraces the 'whole as a whole', that is, both transcendence and immanence. Or, as Affifi expresses it, it embraces both *Haqq* (the Real or God) and *Khalq* (created beings, phenomenal world). This means that the term is not limited to the traditional understanding of the Oneness of God as referring exclusively to a transcendent Deity. *Haqq* and *Khalq* can be conceptually separated, but not ontologically. In fact, argues Ibn 'Arabi, 'transcendence' as asserted by the human intellect must always be accompanied by the assertion of 'immanence'. Therefore, the assertion of 'transcendence' alone has to be transcended if we are to not limit Oneness of Being by our human understanding. As Affifi affirms, for Ibn 'Arabi the term 'Unity has no other meaning than two or more things being actually identical, but conceptually distinguishable the one from the other; so in one sense the one is the other; in another it is not.' So Ibn 'Arabi can assert, without real paradox, that '"I am He and He is I"; "I am He and not He"; "*Haqq* is *Khalq* and *Khalq* is *Haqq*"; "*Haqq* is not *Khalq* and *Khalq* is not *Haqq*"; and so on' (*Twenty-Nine Pages*, p. 12). The real meaning of these distinctions (and the discrimination they involve) can only be fully accomplished by mystical realisation. The point to remember here is that the term

Oneness of Being alludes to the inclusiveness of the whole as a whole and as such cannot imply reductionism or dualism of any kind. This includes, of course, the fact that 'The absolute unity and simplicity of the Divine Essence is only known to the Divine Essence – there is no duality of subject and object, knower and known', and that this higher form of transcendence 'is independent of all assertion'.

8   Addas, *Red Sulphur*, p.293.
9   S. H. Nasr, *Knowledge and the Sacred* (Edinburgh, 1981), pp.160–88.
10 See note 21 for John Macquarrie's discussion and identification of this existentialist view of knowledge.
11 A. Abadi, "Ibn 'Arabi's theophany of perfection", *Journal of the Muhyiddin Ibn 'Arabi Society* (1982, Vol. I), pp.26–9.
12 M. Detlefsen, "Philosophy of mathematics in the twentieth century", in *Routledge History of Philosophy*, ed. S. G. Shanker (Vol. IX, London, 1996), p.50.
13 B. Russell, *My Philosophical Development* (London, 1985), p.156.
14 T. Irwin, *Classical Thought* (Oxford, 1989), p.95.
15 Russell, *My Philosophical Development*, p.157.
16 R. Kanigel, *The Man Who Knew Infinity* (London, 1993).
17 J. E. Tiles, "The truths of logic and mathematics", in *An Encyclopedia of Philosophy*, ed. G. H. R. Parkinson (London, 1989), pp.99–120.
18 H. Corbin, *Creative Imagination in the Sufism of Ibn 'Arabi*, trans. R. Manheim (Princeton, 1969), pp.216–20.
19 Kanigel, *The Man*, p.7.
20 Addas, *Red Sulphur*, p.105.
21 M. de Unamuno, cited in J. Macquarrie, *Existentialism* (London, 1972), p.15.
22 Macquarrie, *Existentialism*, pp.132–4.
23 Chittick, *Sufi Path*, p.101.
24 T. Izutsu, *Creation and the Timeless Order of Things* (Ashland, Oreg., 1994), pp.10–11.
25 A. E. Affifi, *The Mystical Philosophy of Muhyid Din Ibnul Arabi* (Lahore, 1979), p.12.
26 A. Einstein, quoted in *Journal of the Muhyiddin Ibn 'Arabi Society* (1984, Vol. III), p.1.
27 Muhyiddin Ibn 'Arabi. *The Wisdom of the Prophets*. Partial translation of the *Fusus al-Hikam*, from Arabic to French by T. Burckhardt, and from French to English by A. Culme-Seymour (Swyre Farm, Gloucestershire, 1975), p.10, n.15.
28 Ibn 'Arabi, *Wisdom*, p.10, n.15.
29 Ibn 'Arabi. *Sufis of Andalusia*. Partial translation of the *Ruh al-Quds* and *Durrat al-Fakhirah* by R. W. J. Austin (rep. Gloucestershire, 1988), p.37.
30 P. F. Strawson, "Metaphysics", in *The Concise Encyclopedia of Western Philosophy and Philosophers*, ed. J. O. Urmson and J. Rée (London, 1991), p.205.
31 Strawson, "Metaphysics", p.204.
32 Izutsu, *Creation*, p.10.

33 H. Harman and J. Clark, *New Metaphysical Foundations of Modern Science* (Sausalito, Calif., 1994).

34 R. Harré, "Reappraising social psychology: rules, roles and rhetoric", *The Psychologist* (January 1993), p. 24.

35 R. Horton, "African traditional thought and Western science", in *Rationality*, ed. B. R. Wilson (Oxford, 1970), pp. 131–71.

36 B. Parekh, *The Concept of Fundamentalism* (Leeds, 1991), p. 39.

37 M. Bartholomew, D. Hall and A. Lentin, *The Enlightenment*, Studies 2 (Milton Keynes, 1992), p. 6.

38 F. Engels and K. Marx, *Communist Manifesto*, intro. by A. J. P. Taylor (London, 1967), p. 83.

39 E. H. Carr, *What is History?* (2nd edn, London, 1961), p. 5.

40 K. Jenkins, *Re-thinking History* (London, 1991), p. 37.

41 Jenkins, *Re-thinking History*, p. 69.

42 Jenkins, *Re-thinking History*, p. 57.

43 Carr, *What is History?*, p. 17.

44 H. Corbin, *The Concept of Comparative Philosophy*, trans. P. Russell (Cambridge, 1981), pp. 11–13.

45 Nasr, *Knowledge*, see particularly pp. 1–64 and 65–159.

46 Ibn 'Arabi. *Ismail Hakki Bursevi's Translation of and Commentary on Fusus al-Hikam*, trans. B. Rauf (4 vols, Oxford, 1986–91), Vol. 4, p. 984.

47 Chittick, *Sufi Path*, p. 340.

48 Chittick, *Sufi Path*, p. 44.

49 R. Harré, "Ontology and science", *Beshara Magazine* (Issue 3, 1987), p. 12.

50 S. A. Kierkegaard, *Journals*, trans. A. Dru (New York, 1959), p. 44.

51 R. Schacht, *Nietzsche* (London, 1983), p. 9.

52 Izutsu, in *Creation and the Timeless Order of Things*, Chapter 3, analyses the concept of *wahdat al-wujud* and suggests that "the ... concept is something which, if structurally analyzed and elaborated in a proper manner, will provide a theoretical framework in terms of which we shall be able to clarify one of the most fundamental modes of thinking which characterizes Oriental philosophy in general – not only Islamic philosophy, but most of the historical forms of Oriental thought ... so that we might make a positive contribution from the standpoint of the philosophical minds of the East towards the ... development of a new world philosophy based on the spiritual and intellectual heritages of East and West."

53 The phrase in parentheses is put in the interrogative form because of the essentially contested nature of the term "postmodernism". See "Postmodernism and the social sciences", in *Contemporary Social Theory*, ed. R. Hollinger (Vol. 4, London, 1994), pp. 1–190.

54 B. P. Copenhaver and C. B. Schmidt, *Renaissance Philosophy* (Oxford, 1992), pp. 163–84.

55 C. Darwin, *The Descent or Origin of Man* (Britannica Great Books Series, Vol. 49 of 54, Chicago, 1987), p. 297.

56 L. Feuerbach, *The Essence of Christianity*, trans. G. Eliot (New York, 1957), p. 2.

57 Feuerbach, *Christianity*, p. 33.

58 Ibn 'Arabi, *Sufis of Andalusia*, pp. 23–4.

59 As Nasr, in *Knowledge*, p. 273, insightfully remarks, "The great masterpieces of Oriental metaphysics such as the works of Shankara or Ibn 'Arabi are also literary masterpieces ..."

60 P. Coates, review of Izutsu's *Sufism and Taoism: A Comparative Study of Key Philosophical Concepts*, *Journal of the Muhyiddin Ibn 'Arabi Society* (1986, Vol. V), pp. 69–71.

61 In Jami's *Lawa'ih*, trans. E. H. Whinfield (London, 1978), p. 57, we read "Thus as we talked and yearned after the eternal life, we touched it for an instant with the whole force of our hearts. We said, then, if the tumult of the flesh were hushed; hushed these shadows of earth, sea, and sky; hushed the heavens and the soul itself, so that it should pass beyond itself and not think of itself: if all dreams were hushed and all sensuous revelations, and every tongue and every symbol; if all that comes and goes were hushed ... turning their ear to Him who made them, and that He alone spoke, not by them, but for Himself ... suppose we heard Him without any intermediary at all ... might not eternal life be like this moment of comprehension?"

62 Affifi, *Mystical Philosophy*, p. 6.

63 In this respect Austin, in *Bezels* (p. 26), remarks that the Hindu term *satchidananda* (which is usually translated as Being-Consciousness-Bliss) is similar, in crucial respects, to Ibn 'Arabi's *wahdat al-wujud*. The whole question of the influence of Hindu and Buddhist ideas on the work of Ibn 'Arabi is an interesting one.

64 A. J. Ayer, *Language, Truth and Logic* (London, 1987), p. 58. In its most virulent form this type of argument was used by logical positivists to eliminate metaphysics in its entirety from the legitimate realm of philosophy and to denigrate the existentialism of Sartre and Heidegger.

65 Chittick, *Sufi Path*, p. xx.

2 Ibn 'Arabi: philosophy and reason

Ibn 'Arabi, Averroës and philosophy as demonstrative science

Two central senses of the term philosophy can be identified in the writings of Ibn 'Arabi: philosophy as *love of wisdom* and philosophy as *reflective thinking*. These two meanings of philosophy are differentiated primarily by the authority on which they rely rather than by any specific difference in the content with which they deal. It is philosophy as "love of wisdom" (as the word itself implies) which constitutes its original and, for Ibn 'Arabi, its ultimate meaning.[1]

For Ibn 'Arabi, Plato was the example *par excellence* of the philosopher devoted to the love of wisdom. Plato, in this respect, is firmly aligned by Ibn 'Arabi with "men of revelation and contemplation".[2] In the context of Ibn 'Arabi's metaphysics wisdom (Greek, *sophia*; Arabic, *hikma*) is to be understood as a divine gift which is instantiated in certain individuals who are its "settings" or "bezels", such as prophets, saints and those who know. These are the human exemplars of wisdom and the only people to whom the title philosopher can properly be applied in its original meaning. This meaning of philosophy is perfectly reflected in the lexicological appropriateness of the title of Ibn 'Arabi's famous synoptic work, the *Fusus al-Hikam*, or, The Bezels of Wisdom.

By contrast, the concept of philosophy depleted of its original meaning and used simply as a synonym for "reflective thinking" can mean, by implication, either (1) that the philosopher is one who takes human reason as the only reliable avenue to truth, or, (2) that the

37

philosopher is one who assumes that, whilst truth can be arrived at by processes of rational investigation, this is not the only avenue to such truth.

The eighteenth-century European Enlightenment movement exemplifies this first sense of reflective thinking, a view which is well-encapsulated in Diderot's strident epistemological recommendation:

> All things must be examined, debated, investigated without exception and without regard for anyone's feelings ... We must ride roughshod over all ancient puerilities, overturn barriers that reason never erected, give back to the arts and the sciences the liberty that is so precious to them.[3]

In contrast to this is Averroës (whose meeting with Ibn 'Arabi we discussed earlier), who adheres to the second sense of reflective thinking which he extensively defends in *On the Harmony of Religion and Philosophy*. These two views on the epistemology of reflective thinking need to be carefully separated for it is only this latter view which can countenance the truths of revelation.

These two fundamentally differing meanings of philosophy – either as love of wisdom or as reflective thought – are distinguished for Ibn 'Arabi by their contrasting epistemic authorities. For him, philosophy as love of wisdom entails that the only certain ground for the "knowledge inherent in God" (*'ilm laduni*) is God's revelation. The main epistemic access to this knowledge is, as Niffari points out, "in the contemplation of ... self-experience"[4] and it is this self-knowledge which is the foundation of the contemplative and spiritual life. The meeting between Ibn 'Arabi and Ibn Rushd (Averroës)[5] illustrates unambiguously the distinction between philosophy as love of wisdom and philosophy as reflective thinking. It equally illustrates the difference between the eighteenth-century *philosophes'* view and the Averroësian view of the scope and legitimacy of reason.

Let us explore this matter a little further bearing in mind Ibn 'Arabi's caveat that "reflection can only roam in its own specific playing field, which is one of many fields. Each faculty in man has a playing field in which it roams and beyond which it should not step."[6]

For Averroës, philosophy (*falsafa*) was conceived as a demonstrative science. It was viewed as a rational activity based on indubitable premises from which the truth of certain conclusions logically follow. As Hourani[7] points out philosophy "is thought of by Ibn Rushd and his Arabic predecessors not as speculative in the modern sense, but as yielding knowledge of reality which is demonstrative according to the Aristotelian conditions: conclusions drawn from flawless logic from indubitable premises. ... It shares with other sciences the authoritative name of *hikma*." Averroës defines philosophy as "the systematic application of demonstrative reasoning to the world."[8] This broad conception of philosophy as a form of demonstrative reasoning applied to the world would include, for Averroës, what we now call natural science. Averroës' fundamental commitment to philosophy as a form of demonstrative reasoning, in the manner of a sound Aristotelian syllogism,[9] enabled him to conceive of the study (*nazar*) of philosophy as being immune from any "connotations of uncertain methods".[10] It was because of this assumed immunity of philosophy to methodological error that he came to believe in the possibility of philosophical reasoning achieving a knowledge of the "content of the *inner* world"[11] as well as encompassing a knowledge of the *outer* world. The locution, "content of the inner world", refers to the world of spiritual realities as described within the context of Islam. Averroës clearly sought a role for philosophy that was legally permitted by the Islamic religion and in harmony with it. He thought, as a Muslim, that to reflect upon the external natural world and inner human experience was to reflect upon God and that such rational reflection was in perfect accord with Quranic injunction.

The difficulty was that Averroës committed himself, at least philosophically, to a rather narrow form of Aristotelian deductive rationality. From the perspective of Ibn ʿArabi this commitment underestimates the necessary and vital role of direct epistemic access to ultimate spiritual realities. Philosophy, as demonstrative science, is simply incapable of grasping the experiential domain of the mystical. Equally, from the perspective of modern philosophy, scientific knowledge of the empirical world is far from being based on "indubitable demonstrative premises" as Averroës presumed. Averroës' belief in the epistemological adequacy of Aristotelian rationality to deal with the matters to which he was deeply committed was his Achilles heel: it can neither account for the nature of mystical knowledge, nor does it constitute an adequate account of the logic of science.

For modern philosophers of science such as Popper, Kuhn and Feyeraband,[12] Averroës would be regarded as simply failing to recognize the conjectural, conceptual and contingent grounds of the scientific enterprise. For contemporary theorists science does not rest on the indubitable basis which Averroës seemed to wish for it. Of course, this is not to deny the logic and rationality of science but this does not make science indubitable in the way it was considered it to be by Averroës.

As we have noted, Ibn 'Arabi categorically insists that it is not reasoning (demonstrative or otherwise) which leads to knowledge of the Real but, rather, divine inspiration. Ibn 'Arabi's response to Averroës' question – "What solution have you found as a result of mystical illumination and divine inspiration? Does it coincide with what is arrived at by speculative thought?"[13] – raises the more general question of what Ibn 'Arabi considers speculative thought can come to know about God.

The most positive aspect of reflective thinking derives from the fact, according to Ibn 'Arabi, that it is a divine gift found only in human beings. But it is also a test and a trial. It can at most lead to the acknowledgement that knowledge of God cannot be attained through one's own rational resources. Reflective thinking, in this respect, *positively* attests to the impotence and incapacity of human beings to reach the knowledge of the Real via unaided reason. Reflective reason can recognize not only its own limitations but also the manner in which it limits – it can discover its own unsatisfactoriness when it comes to the knowledge inherent in God and of God. What reflective thinking can establish is the incomparability of God through the method of *via negativa*, that is, the method of attempting to show what God is not; for example, God is not corporeal, He is not temporal, and so on. And yet even this would lead to an overly transcendent view of God, ultimately incompatible with Ibn 'Arabi's *wahdat al-wujud*.

Summarily, reflective thinking is regarded by Ibn 'Arabi as unreliable in a number of inter-related senses: firstly, rather than being the means by which spiritual realities can be achieved, it is, simply, an inappropriate method; secondly, it is unreliable because reason acts as a "veil"[14] which constricts and binds reality within its own rational schemas and often preoccupies the thinker with other than the Real; thirdly, reason is unreliable because reason for the men of rational faculties becomes the ultimate arbiter of truth and the episte-mological gold standard; fourthly, cognitive acts are generally thought to imply the separate ontological identity of the thinker from God and thereby they implicitly deny *wahdat al-wujud* and, fifthly, human reason can only accept what is consistent with its own canons, and its canons deny the existence of what is self-contradictory or logi-cally impossible.[15] This last point is a crucial one which needs further clarification.

When the knowers of God enter the universe of spiritual mean-ings they are in the presence, Ibn ʿArabi informs us, of a reality in which what is hidden to the rational faculty, and therefore some-times deemed impossible by it, actually occurs and is witnessed. This world is referred to in Ibn ʿArabi studies as the intermediate objec-tive world of the divine creative imagination.[16] As James Morris carefully points out, Ibn ʿArabi draws a decisive distinction "between each individual's 'self-deluding imagination' and the ongoing Divine 'Imaging' underlying all creation".[17]

Nevertheless, in whatever way we may wish to describe the divine imaginative presence, a central feature of it, according to Ibn ʿArabi, is that it is a spiritual reality teeming with the impossible and the coincidence of opposites. The unaided rational faculty has no direct access to this world and cannot countenance its true reality. It is the world where "the impossible is given form". Ibn ʿArabi tells us: "sense perception is the nearest thing to the imagination, since imagi-nation takes forms from sense-perception, then it discloses meanings through those sensory forms". In this way, continues Ibn ʿArabi, "it sees knowledge in the form of milk, honey, wine, and pearls. ... It sees religion in the form of a cord ... the Real in the form of a human being or a light."[18]

Ibn ʿArabi paints this extraordinary picture of an ontological realm in which spiritual meanings are given tangible form and tangible forms become subtle spiritual meanings. This is the reality where the substrata of phenomenal forms are forever newly created with profound spiritual meanings. It is in this presence that the foundations of the cosmos reveal themselves to have essential spiritual meaning and foundation. This essential theophanic dimension of all phenomenal existence invites the reader to an awareness of the extraordinary nature of the ordinary, rather than to a separate realm of the extraordinary.

In the normal way of things Ibn ʿArabi recognizes that "The *sensory thing* cannot be a meaning, nor can the *meaning* be a sensory thing" but in the domain of the Imaginative Presence meanings are literally embodied and sensory things subtilized.[19] This is the realm of archetypal contemplative experience to which William Blake,[20] for example, alludes when he declares, "A fool sees not the same tree that a wise man sees," and the same archetypal realm informs Blake's description of his visionary London when, as a child, he sauntered along on Peckham Rye by Dulwich Hill. An unexpected confirmation of the rational unfathomability of the relationship between sensory things and meanings occurs in Jaegwon Kim's defence of the computational theory of mind when he remarks "How meaning and understanding could arise out of molecules and cells is as much a mystery as how they could arise out of strings of zeroes and ones."[21]

In his discussion of "the manifestation of the impossible thing" in the *Futuhat al-Makkiyah*, Ibn ʿArabi clearly conveys the vastness and width of the Presence of the Imagination.[22] He records, "Within it becomes manifest the existence of the impossible thing. Or rather, nothing becomes manifest within it in verification except the existence of the impossible thing. For the Necessary Being – who is God – does not receive forms, yet He becomes manifest in forms in this presence."

In the history and development of scientific thought there are some well-documented accounts of knowledge being conveyed via the human imagination in some extremely unusual ways. Take the case of the German chemist Kekule[23] who recounts what led him to discover the carbon ring:

> I was sitting writing at my textbook but the work did not progress; my thoughts were elsewhere. I turned my chair to the fire and dozed. Again the atoms were gambolling before my eyes. This time the smaller groups kept modestly in the background.

My mental eye, rendered more acute by repeated visions of the same kind, could now distinguish larger structures of manifold conformation: long rows, sometimes more closely fitted together all twining and twisting in snake-like motion. But look! What was that? One of the snakes had seized hold of its own tail, and the form whirled mockingly before my eyes. As if by a flash of lightning I awoke; and this time also I spent the rest of the night in working out the consequences of this hypothesis.[24]

In relation to Ibn 'Arabi's treatment of the impossible thing the canons of reflective reason are likely to deem such experience impossible. It is not surprising then that Averroës trembled when, in answer to his question, Ibn 'Arabi replied: "Yes and no. Between the Yea and the Nay the spirits take their flight beyond matter, and the necks detach themselves from their bodies."[25] It seems, therefore, that either human reason can accept its own impotence in these matters and simply acknowledge what it receives from God; or it can classify such experiences as hallucinatory or delusory. For Ibn 'Arabi, this is always the dilemma of human reason: it either asserts itself as ultimate judge or it acknowledges the existence of a quite different epistemic order. When reason does assert itself as sole epistemological arbiter of truth it steps beyond its own specific playing field. Normally, says Ibn 'Arabi, the manifestation of the impossible thing, in the ontological domain of the imaginative presence, is found only in the hereafter because the "imagination stands in a degree which is posterior to sense perception". In this domain the levels interpenetrate and "the property of the Real in creation and creation in the Real" produce the actual manifestation of the impossible thing in the "here before".[26]

Philosophy, reason and metaphysics

The Akbarian notion of reason having its own specific domain beyond which it must not, or cannot, profitably roam is at the heart of much contemporary theorising about the proper and legitimate role of metaphysics. It is Ibn 'Arabi's view that, with the exception of the inspired intellect, human reason can uncover only a profoundly infinitesimal fraction of reality and that reason acts as a veil binding and constricting reality (and the thinker) within its own rational schemas. It was those twin intellectual pillars of the European Enlightenment, David Hume and Immanuel Kant, who, in their determined attempt to curb the excesses and extravagances of speculative reason, constructed their own version of what constituted the proper playing field of rational activity. Both Hume and Kant wanted to eliminate from the realm of legitimate rational discourse transcendent metaphysics. For Kant, there could be no rational knowledge of what is beyond nature: there could be no knowledge of the supersensible, supernatural or super-empirical. Kant contended that when human reason (what he called pure reason) strayed into these speculative areas, it transgressed its proper boundary. Such a transgression resulted in "a dialectic of illusory inferences"[27] and contradictions. It is still consistent with Kant's position that there could exist a transcendent realm of things-in-themselves but human reason cannot know it. The human mind is so cognitively constituted that human thought cannot have knowledge of objects that transcend possible experience. Kant insists that all we can have knowledge of is the way things appear to us as phenomena; he is adamant that we can have no knowledge of things-in-themselves as noumena. There may exist noumenal realities but we can have no knowledge of them. Such a profound, intrinsic, unalterable and ubiquitous human ignorance of the noumenal had as its corollary the Kantian assumption that human reason itself is the only "ultimate touchstone of truth".[28] What we cannot know by human reason we cannot know. Kant's sense of knowledge here would also include knowledge acquired through the senses. Two brief Kantian remarks will convey his general understanding of the situation: "Without sensibility no object would be given to us, without understanding no object would be thought" and "What objects may be in themselves, and apart from all this receptivity of our sensibility, remains completely unknown to us".[29]

Kant recognizes, therefore, a boundary beyond which human reason cannot progress. In this crucial respect Ibn 'Arabi and Kant (and, for that matter, David Hume) are in complete agreement. The fundamental difference between Ibn 'Arabi and Kant is that the doctrine of *wahdat al-wujud* allows for epistemic access to the thing-in-itself via an ontological presence in which "the impossible takes form". Epistemic access to mystical visionary experience is not through the unaided human intellect. The human intellect is regarded as an indirect and comparatively restricted form of knowing which should be confined to its own proper playing field. Reflective thinking is, for Ibn 'Arabi, an epistemologically inappropriate means of approaching or embracing the grandeur and infinity of the "knowledge inherent in God" ('ilm laduni).

In spite of this caveat there is a more positive function attributed to human reason in the metaphysics of Ibn 'Arabi. We can locate a clue to this more *metaphysically oriented quality* of human reason by further examining Kant's discussion of the demarcation between reason's legitimate and illegitimate role. As we have seen, for Kant, speculative metaphysics arose when reason transgressed its proper boundary. When it did this, he argued, it resulted in forms of "confusion and contradictions".[30] The question naturally arises therefore as to why, in the history of human intellectual endeavour, human reason has so persistently attempted to transgress its proper domain? Why has it insisted on the persistent production of so much of what Kant would regard as metaphysical nonsense?

Kant's answer to this question[31] is perhaps the most illuminating of all. His response is that pure reason has a natural disposition towards metaphysics: that is, a "feeling of need" to construct some kind of all-inclusive metaphysical world-view. Kant identifies "a deep, but insatiable, need of human reason for the complete explanation of experience".[32]

This view largely coincides with metaphysics conceived characteristically as the attempt to offer a comprehensive account of the whole as a whole. In this respect, human reason (both for Ibn 'Arabi and for Kant) has an inbuilt totalizing orientation. Human reason cannot, however, ever complete this task without transgressing either its proper playing field (as Ibn 'Arabi suggests) or issuing in confusion and contradictions (as Kant intimates). Kant recognized the ambivalent nature of human reason which, in its desire for comprehensive explanation, strays into areas in which no intellectual progress is possible. From this it followed, at least for Kant, that the intrinsic tendency of reason itself to seek a "complete explanation of human experience" had to be guarded against and dismissed as a form of intellectual extravagance and unwarranted speculation. This reminds one of the famous line at the end of Wittgenstein's *Tractatus Logico-Philosophicus*: "What we cannot speak about we must pass over in silence".

Ibn 'Arabi's metaphysics of *wahdat al-wujud* throws an entirely different light on this matter. The metaphysically oriented desire of human reason to seek a comprehensive explanation of human experience is to be regarded as positive in the sense that reason may come, by its own self-examination, to realize its own impotence in dealing with such questions. It can "come to understand that the only way to know God is for God to give it knowledge".[33] Ibn 'Arabi categorically denies that which Kant affirms: that is, that human reason is the "*ultimate* touchstone of truth". But even here Kant recognized that human reason is impotent in its attempts to provide knowledge of the existence of God or the immortality of the soul. In making reason the ultimate judge of truth, however, Kant allows reason to dictate its own sovereignty as judge and jury. This is indeed curious as he to some extent accepts human reality to be profoundly embedded in noumenal realms without entertaining the possibility that there may be, as it were, noumenal ways of knowing. Kant's philosophy presents us with a metaphysical picture of the world as a collection of individual, knowing, human subjects who can only know the world as it *appears* to them via their human aesthetic, moral, cognitive and physical constitution, but, they can never know it as it really is in-itself. Kant's philosophy contains the seeds of a profound ineliminable agnosticism. It postulates an unbridgeable gulf between human subjective knowledge and the unknowable "thing-in-itself" and at the same time promotes a view of the epistemological privilege of human reason. At best this results in the idea of a totally unknowable God (at least in this life), an idea which is itself premised upon a radical dualism between the human and the divine. Kant argued that in freeing human reason from its speculative extravagances regarding questions of God, freedom and immortality, he was making room for faith uncluttered by the confusions engendered by rational speculation. But, in effect, Kant's faith was in *human reason*, as indeed was the faith of the Enlightenment movement generally. In his essay "What is

Enlightenment?", Kant reaffirms his faith in human reason as the sole arbiter of truth when he advocates that the enlightened "emergence ... from self-incurred immaturity" requires the "freedom to make *public use* of one's reason in all matters".[34]

Kant's plea was the "call to reason" to undertake its own self-examination. If we view this plea in the light of Ibn 'Arabi's instruction to the *'arif* to seek the "knowledge inherent in God", we begin to see its logical topography radically transformed. Firstly, there is clearly a marked tendency for Kant's self-examination of reason by itself to act as a veil which constricts and binds reality within the parameters of its own self-examination. On the whole one or more of the deficiencies of the epistemology of reason already identified by Ibn 'Arabi would be the fate of Kant's metaphysical construction. For what is Kant proposing but a metaphysical theory of knowledge of his own?

However, in spite of Ibn 'Arabi's caveats on the epistemological limits of human reason, he carefully insists on its intrinsic place and value: "employ reason as it should be employed and 'Give to each that has a due its due.'"[35]

So why is it that Ibn 'Arabi almost compels us to recognize the limitation of *any* intellectually constructed metaphysics, even when such a metaphysical system, for example that of Spinoza, has many thematic affinities with the doctrine of *wahdat al-wujud*? We have not yet quite answered this question thoroughly enough, and to do so we should now consider the case of Spinoza.

Spinoza, in his monumental work *Ethics*, employs a system of definitions, axioms and propositions to erect a kind of geometric architecture of proofs to demonstrate that God's "essence involves existence" and to establish that there is only one substance or being in existence. This rather abstract formulation implies, for Spinoza, that there is only one Being who is infinite in nature and that all things (like bodies and people) are a determinate expression of the essence of God – a doctrine in perfect accord with Ibn 'Arabi. Spinoza would have had no difficulty in accepting the metaphysical picture expressed in the line from the Turkish folk poet Yunus Emre "I wrapped myself in flesh and bones and appeared as Yunus."[36]

For Spinoza and for Ibn 'Arabi the fundamental human obligation is to strive for that view of ourselves and the world which is God's view of ourselves and the world: this vision constitutes for Spinoza the highest kind of knowledge. He designates this as "the third kind of knowledge", or intuitive knowledge, and carefully contrasts it with knowledge obtained through the more usual processes of sense perception, imagination and reason.[37] Through intuitive knowledge lies the attainment of the human self's ultimate state of blessedness. Much of the logical scaffolding of Spinozian metaphysics is isomorphic with the general metaphysical outlook of *wahdat al-wujud*, with the qualification that for Ibn ʿArabi the doctrine of *wahdat al-wujud* is intrinsically and inescapably Quranic in its viewpoint. There is no counterpart to this in Spinoza's *Ethics*. The isomorphism therefore does not apply to revealed content. It is precisely these logical similarities which invoked for Ibn ʿArabi and Spinoza the erroneous description of their work as a form of pantheism.[38]

However, Spinoza's *Ethics* does illustrate that human reason, from Ibn ʿArabi's point of view, is sometimes capable of sketching approximately the right scaffolding and that "the science of the philosopher is not totally in vain".[39]

What is undeniably apparent is that reading Ibn ʿArabi's *Fusus al-Hikam* is a profoundly different experience from reading Spinoza's *Ethics*. The difference rests in the incapacity of an intellectually constructed metaphysics to capture the richness, diversity and intimacy of the spiritual dimension it seeks to systematize. Spinoza's *Ethics* lacks the multi-dimensionality, experiential veracity and sheer comprehensiveness of the *Fusus*. By comprehensiveness is meant the essential and often detailed narrative concerning the spiritual and mystical significance of the twenty-seven prophets with which the *Fusus* is concerned. It is a book of spiritual meanings and revelations aimed at the inner response of the reader. Reading Spinoza's *Ethics*, in spite of the sublimity of its subject matter, is literally like following the intricacies of a geometric proof.

The *Fusus*, the content of which Ibn ʿArabi states was received in a veridic dream, exhibits a variety of internal styles and semantic modalities which endow it with a freshness and direct intimacy which evokes the taste of (and, perhaps, for) its place of origination. For Ibn ʿArabi theoretically constructed metaphysical enterprises do not (and cannot) possess the capacity to convey to the reader a taste of the

experiential depths and cadences and movement of mystical experience. It may be better to see Spinoza's *Ethics* as the systematization
of what was, by his own confession, a form of intuitive knowledge.
Its strictly geometrical demonstrative structure seems antithetical to
the intuitive forms of perception which probably inspired it. Perhaps
Spinoza adopted an axiomatic deductive structure to directly reflect
the result of his metaphysical belief that it is "logically impossible that
events be other than they are".[40]

Whatever Spinoza may have meant by this strong claim, for Ibn
'Arabi human actions can be said to belong to us or to God, depending
on the point from which they are viewed. "People of the heart", we
are told, understand this existential ambiguity and they know in which
way and when and to whom to ascribe the origin of human acts. As
Affifi points out there is no real paradox involved, for the possibility
of the ascription of human acts both to us and to God follows from
the fact that the One Unique Being possesses the two fundamental
aspects of transcendence and immanence. Nevertheless, Ibn 'Arabi
insists that courtesy demands "that only good and beautiful acts
be ascribed to God, while evil and ugly acts must be ascribed to
the servants".[41] From the point of view of immanence human acts
can be ascribed to man as created in God's image. From the point
of view of transcendence the freedom of the Original belongs to
God alone as unmanifested Source. This matter of the ascription of
human freedom to the human subject is fundamental to Ibn 'Arabi's
metaphysics. He relates, with some force, a conversation he had with
his student Ismail Ibn Sawdakin, who said: "Which proof of the attri-
bution and ascription of the act to the servant and of self-disclosure
within him is stronger than the fact that his attribute is that God has
created man in His own form? Were the act to be disengaged from
him, it would no longer be correct for him to be upon His form and
he could not accept the assumption of the traits of the names."[42] This
statement by Ibn Sawdakin has, as Ibn 'Arabi himself was at pains
to point out, momentous implications for understanding the actual
ontological situation of the *insan-i-kamil*. It means that the *insan-i-
kamil* images and expresses perfectly the freedom of the Original. This
is the fundamental freedom to which human beings can aspire and,
perhaps paradoxically, they must be free to desire this.

This extended comparison between examples of theoretically constructed forms of metaphysics (like those of Kant and Spinoza) and the revealed metaphysics of *wahdat al-wujud* illustrates fairly clearly, as Addas[43] points out, why Ibn ʿArabi insists that unaided reason cannot lead to decisive certainty concerning the Real.

We can further examine Ibn ʿArabi's point about the incapacity of human reason to lead to decisive certainty by examining what W. B. Gallie characterizes as "essentially contested concepts". "Metaphysics" itself would be an example of an essentially contested concept as would "democracy", "art", "religion", "power", "education", "philosophy", "morality", and "politics".[44]

Reason and essential contestability

Gallie identifies a range of concepts which have been, and are, in varying degrees central to the historical development and trajectory of Western theoretical culture, about which there have been endless irresolvable disputes. He remarks

> that there are disputes, centered on the concepts [such as works of art, democracy and Christian doctrine] …,[45] which are perfectly genuine: which, although not resolvable by arguments of any kind, are nevertheless sustained by perfectly respectable arguments and evidence. This is what I mean by saying that there are concepts which are essentially contested, concepts the proper use of which inevitably involves endless disputes about their proper use on the part of their users.[46]

The concept of essential contestability has been widely utilized in academic culture for it accurately characterizes a central and intrinsic feature of theoretical disputes about education, politics, religion, art, sociology, psychology and even philosophy. Essential contestability is endemic in academic culture. If one delves into the history of almost any of the previously mentioned academic disciplines one is likely to uncover theoretical disputes of an essentially contestable nature. If we take the case of academic history which we discussed in the preceding chapter and we accept Jenkins' view that it is a major premise of modern historical scholarship that history is a "series of readings all of which are positioned", it is clear that each particular reading is likely to be essentially contestable from another reading's point of view. Hence, we have different ideological readings of history – marxist, conservative, socialist, religious, and so on. Many of these "positioned discourses" may agree on the main historical facts that are under critical scrutiny but there is likely to be permanent disagreement on what the facts mean and how they are to be explained. The important characteristic of essentially contested issues is that they are not conclusively resolved by factual means though they are "sustained by perfectly respectable arguments and evidence". These issues are intrinsically value-laden and are essentially matters of value-preference and value-conflict. This distinguishes essentially contestable disputes from merely factual disputes, such as "What is the cause of AIDS?". In the latter case such disputes are capable of being, in principle at least, resolved by factual or scientific means. In the case of issues, such as "What constitutes a good education?", "How ought we to live?", and "What is knowledge?", the history of human theoretical culture often indicates an outcome of permanent intellectual disagreement and deadlock. In this sense, these issues lack rational progress. We are no nearer agreeing about these issues than we were when they were first raised in ancient Greece and before. Such disagreements seem to rest ultimately on different value-systems or paradigms or theoretical frameworks. The possibility of permanent disagreement in these areas does not imply that such disputes are irredeemably subjective: each positioned discourse appeals to its own tradition of argument and evidence in defence of its claims. It is not possible for the individual to argue in any way he or she chooses; rather, the individual appeals to the tradition of argument and evidence typically invoked by the positioned discourse being advocated. It is also an important feature of such traditions of discourse and ways of life that they are open to revision in the light of new experience. They are not in this sense, therefore, closed or unalterable forms of discourse but they are quite definitely located within particular ways of seeing. Two examples will provide an illustration of these points: one from the history of psychology and another from the area of moral philosophy.

First, let us look at psychology. The founder figure of behaviourist psychology, J. B. Watson, proposed a reconceptualization of the nature and scope of psychology along the lines of what he took to be "purely objective natural science". Watson described his proposed new paradigm as behaviourism. He said "its theoretical goal is the prediction and control of behaviour. Introspection forms no essential part of its methods, nor is the scientific value of its data dependent upon … interpretation in terms of consciousness."[47] The implication is clear: the matter of human subjective conscious experience is no longer to figure in the scientific psychological study of human behaviour. Only that which is externally observable and measurable is to be taken into consideration and that solely for the purposes of prediction and control. Of course, Watson's psychology arose, in part, as a reaction against the subjectivism of and a dissatisfaction with earlier introspective methods. But, in effect, Watsonian behaviourism excluded from the realm of legitimate scientific enquiry that vital and defining area of human experience and identity known as subjective consciousness. And this was done in the name of objective natural science. In brief, behaviourism exemplifies a preference for a certain understanding about the nature of science and its scope and the preference for an almost veterinary view of the human animal. It aims "to externalize the internal" and thereby ignore or by-pass the reality of the internal worlds or cognitive states of the individual. For quite some time behaviourism effectively excluded the arena of human consciousness from the legitimate agenda of scientific psychology. It self-professedly ignored what is arguably a defining feature of human kind, that is, self-reflexive conscious experience. Of course, much has happened in the development of psychology since then. But even so it is only recently that there has been a movement within the British Psychological Society for the establishment and recognition of a Consciousness and Experiential section.[48] That it has taken so long for consciousness studies to re-assert itself as a legitimate area within professional psychology indicates the power of essentially contestable paradigms, like behaviourism, to be presented, by their advocates, as unassailably objective explanatory frameworks. This example from the history of modern psychology is a clear reminder that such rationally constructed paradigms rest upon presuppositions of an essentially contestable kind and that they are often presented not simply as a paradigm but as the paradigm. There is a noticeable tendency among paradigm-makers to universalize their claims and ascribe to their own paradigms an epistemologically privileged status. This tendency reminds one of Ibn ʿArabi's view that in the matter of theory-construction the advocates of particular theories "make the mistake of believing they are absolute".[49]

Secondly, let us take the case of disputes in moral philosophy. In "On morality's having a point", the co-authors Phillips and Mounce offer the following analysis of moral disputes using the example of an argument between a scientific rationalist and a Catholic housewife over the question of birth control:

> the so-called scientific rationalist ... stressed the harm which
> could result from having too many children. He obviously
> thought that the reference to physical harm clinched the matter.
> The housewife, on the other hand, stressed the honour the
> mother has in bringing children into the world ... How would
> the scientific rationalist and the housewife reach the agreement
> which some philosophers seem to think inevitable if all the facts
> were known? It is hard to see how they could without renouncing
> what they believe in. Certainly, one cannot regard their respective
> moral opinions as hypotheses which the facts will either confirm
> or refute, for what would the evidence be? For the rationalist, the
> possibility of the mother's death or injury, the economic situation
> of the family, the provision of good facilities for the children, and
> so on, would be extremely important. The housewife too agrees
> about providing the good things of life for children, but believes
> that one ought to begin by allowing them to enter the world. For
> her, submission to the will of God, the honour of motherhood,
> the creation of a new life ... are of greatest importance. But
> there is no settling the issue in terms of some supposed common
> evidence called human good and harm, since what they differ
> over is precisely the question of what constitutes good and harm.
> The same is true of all fundamental moral disagreements.[50]

We soon recognize this issue as one of essential contestability in which, even though the disputants present respectable arguments in defence of their position, the result is one of moral deadlock. In this example it is also clear that such deadlock does "not entail the liberty to argue as one chooses":[51] a point mentioned earlier in our discussion.

Reason and commitment[52]

These examples from psychology and moral philosophy suggest that a whole range of essentially contestable concepts co-exist within academic, industrial and technological culture. Such concepts involve appeals to argument and evidence embedded in particular traditions of social, religious, aesthetic and political discourse. It is the crucial role, though not ultimately a decisive one, which reason and argument play in the defence of these concepts which differentiates them from unargued expressions of strong feeling or matters of personal opinion. But, whilst the contribution of reason and argument is crucial, it is not the decisive criterion in theory-choice: reason alone is not the deciding factor. This is not necessarily because other factors, such as aesthetic, emotional or practical considerations, are more important (though for some they may be) but because rational strategies tend to articulate particular insights and intuitions rather than originate them. Many of these essentially contestable perspectives exemplify a preferred picture of the human self and its possibilities, views which have their roots in imaginative vision rather than in strictly empirical or logical processes of reasoning. In *Feminists Rethink the Self* the co-authors cite, as a prelude to their critique of it, the doctrine of *homo economicus*. This is the view that the individual is a "free and rational chooser and actor whose desires are ranked in coherent order and whose aim is to maximize desire satisfaction."[53] Their purpose in doing this is not only to show that such a view is "incomplete and fundamentally misleading" but that it could only have arisen in a society where the self is identified with the calculative rationality of the market-place. Such an imaginatively impoverished account of human beings as *homo economicus*, if taken as true or valid, can have direct effects upon the ways in which human beings consider it acceptable to treat one another, and it can also direct human aspiration and personal self-image in general. The equation of *who you are* (that is, your worth as a human being) with *what you do* (that is, your job in the market-place) is a familiar one in industrial capitalism and constitutes a very particular ideological view of work. That we *ought* to make this equation and predominantly assess people and ourselves in these terms is, of course, the essentially contestable issue. But to insist that such a judgmental equation is imaginatively impoverished is to head towards an alternative vision of the nature of human possibilities: perhaps towards a more complete metaphysical picture. In this respect it is worthwhile contrasting the performative-assessing ethic of the market-place with the primordial human obligation contained in the *Futuhat al-Makkiyah* of Ibn 'Arabi:

> God never commanded His Prophet to seek increase of *anything except knowledge*, since all good (*khayr*) lies therein. It is the greatest charismatic gift. Idleness with knowledge is better than ignorance with good works ... By knowledge I mean only knowledge of God, of the next world, and of that which is appropriate for this world, in relationship to that for which this world was created and established. Then man's affairs will be "upon insight" wherever he is, and he will be ignorant of nothing in himself and his activities.[54]

So one might say that for Ibn 'Arabi it is incumbent upon the individual to seek knowledge, in the primordial sense that Ibn 'Arabi intends, even *in* the market-place. We may grasp a little more of what Ibn 'Arabi had in mind here by exploring this matter further.

Let us summarize some of the main points covered so far: we have seen that disputes over deeply held human values, be they secular or religious, are not decisively resolvable by empirical or rational means. This is because such issues are as much about how the human self is to be intellectually conceived and investigated as they are about empirical evidence. These debates characteristically presuppose different concepts of the human self. In Meyers we note that the "implications of one's account of the self reverberate throughout one's worldview, opening up social, intellectual and aesthetic possibilities and concomitantly limiting imagination and action".[55] The predominant views of the self inherent in any particular theoretical discourse or historical milieu are important cultural determinants

of the aesthetic, imaginative and practical human possibilities enter-
tained by those committed to (or directly influenced by) such views.
Historically predominant views of the self may, as some sociolo-
gists of knowledge have suggested, prevent people from even imagining alternative conceptions of the self. In this way, as the feminist
philosophers cited above suggest, views of the self can limit human
"imagination and action". This suggests that any preferred view of the
human self is multi-dimensional in its impact upon the individual
and capable of affecting cognition, emotion, imagination, action
and social relations: in short, potentially affecting every facet of the
person. At the purely intellectual level it seems that there is nothing
approaching what we might call a one hundred percent intellectual
certainty about any particular preferred view. This does not imply
that such narratives of the self are embraced by their advocates as
being only probable truths, or that they regard such narratives as
hypotheses which can be assigned a probability value or that they
can easily be cast aside. Such preferred topographies of the self are
often constitutive of the person and their identity and not lightly
relinquished. What can be said is that such discursively constructed
views of the self, whilst not intellectually unassailable, are generally
held onto with tenacity and certitude. By certitude is meant that
such culturally functional narratives are adopted *as if* they are true:
theoretically, imaginatively, socially and practically. This is perhaps the
deeper meaning behind Kierkegaard's remarks:

> What would be the use of discovering so-called objective truth
> and of being able, if required, to review all systems of philosophy
> and show up the inconsistencies within each … and so construct
> a world in which I did not live but only held up to the view of
> others. … I certainly do not deny that I still recognize an *impera-
> tive of understanding* and that through it one can work upon men,
> *but it must be taken up into my life*, and *that* is what I now recognize
> as the most important thing. That is what my soul longs after, as
> the African desert thirsts for water.[56]

As Kierkegaard's statement suggests, fundamental human values
involve and entail much more than cognitive or rational assent: they
most often require whole-hearted existential commitment. Ibn

'Arabi's remarks on the nature of this commitment are superbly brought to our attention in the account given of him by Nunah Fatimah bint Ibn al-Muthanna, one of his teachers who was in her nineties when he met her:

> She used to say, "Of those who come to see me, I admire none more than Ibn al-'Arabi." On being asked the reason for this she replied, "The rest of you come to me with part of yourselves, leaving the other part of you occupied with your other concerns, while Ibn al-'Arabi is a consolation to me, for he comes to me with all of himself. When he rises up it is with all of himself and when he sits it is with his whole self, leaving nothing of himself elsewhere. That is how it should be on the Way."[57]

The undivided attention of the whole person is a pivotal require-ment, according to Ibn 'Arabi, of following the mystical path of knowledge. It is only in this way that the *salik* (or seeker) can hope to become "aware of facts he could not otherwise be aware of".[58] One way of describing what happens here is that when human reason becomes aligned with and directed towards spiritual development it has the possibility of coming under direct and divine guidance. Ibn 'Arabi puts this view unambiguously at the very beginning of the *Ruh al-Quds* in the memorable statement of the advice he was given by one of his teachers: "If you will shut out the world from you, sever all ties and take the Bounteous alone as your companion, He will speak with you without the need for any intermediary."[59] When this happens the human intellect begins to serve the spiritual aspiration of the seeker and not other traits of character. Such sincere aspiration is, by its very nature, capable of embracing and affecting the whole of a person, including one's cognitive insights and the cognitive apprecia-tion of certain truths. In this way reason is capable of becoming aware of facts that it otherwise would not have the means to be aware of. The facts one becomes aware of are not those "obtained by observing something external to oneself but by immersing oneself in that which is known".[60] The ontological fact of *wahdat al-wujud* also implies that in taking "the Bounteous alone as your companion", the *'arif* increas-ingly recognizes that God is capable of communicating directly to the *'arif* by or through any situation whatsoever, and by or through any of the human faculties, including intellectual cognition. Or, even, communicating through no faculty whatsoever. Both the objective external world and the subjective internal states of the *'arif* are experienced as being impregnated through and through with spiritual meaning and significance. Both external and internal worlds are to be properly understood as expressing the Oneness of Being in its love to be known and witnessed. In short, *all* human experience, both the apparently objective world and the apparently subjective world, is experienced by the *'arif* as intrinsically unitary and theophanic. The *'arif* recognizes the world and all that there is in it, including themselves, as theophany. To have been transported to such a universal theophanic perception is to be in proximity to the Divine consciousness, and constitutes, according to Ibn 'Arabi, the Station of Proximity.

It needs to be carefully pointed out at this juncture that whilst the beatific vision of God is a central and recurring motif in the writings of Ibn 'Arabi, the term "vision" is usefully put in quotation marks to remind us that the term "is not relegated only to the sensory eye but to *all* [my italics] that evokes a 'taste' (*dhawq*) of gratifying, nevertheless, overwhelming beauty or beatitude, be it a person, a sunset or a poem, etc., etc."[61]

We need now to contextualize this matter in relation to developments in contemporary Western philosophy regarding the nature of knowledge. In contemporary European philosophy two distinct philosophical tendencies can be discerned: one which gives priority to an epistemology of the objective, the quantitative and the factual, and the other which gives epistemological primacy to the subjective, the qualitative and the experiential. A clear example of the former would be the logical positivism of the Vienna Circle and of the latter that European style of philosophy known as existentialism. Philosophy is of such an encompassing nature and scope that one might expect that the metaphysical preferences of individual philosophers will play a large part in the history and development of philosophy itself.

The Oxford philosopher P. F. Strawson expresses this point succinctly:

> Agreement among experts in the special sciences and in exact
> scholarship may reasonably be hoped for and gradually attained.

But philosophy, which takes human thought in general as its field, is not thus conveniently confined; and truth in philosophy, though not to be despaired of, is so complex and many-sided, so multi-faceted, that any individual philosopher's work, if it is to have any unity and coherence, must at best emphasize some aspects of the truth, to the neglect of others which may strike another philosopher with greater force. Hence the appearance of endemic disagreement in the subject is something to be expected rather than deplored; and it is no matter for wonder that the individual philosopher's views are more likely than those of the scientist or exact scholar to reflect in part his individual taste and temperament.[62]

We shall now consider further these remarks in relation to two contemporary and influential philosophical schools already cited: logical positivism and existentialism.

Scientific philosophy

Logical positivism, which originated in the Vienna Circle during the period 1926 to 1938, encapsulates a view of philosophy as the hand-maiden of modern science. In this sense it rests upon an unambiguous preference for the world as revealed through the methods and findings of the natural sciences. The Vienna Circle consisted of a number of eminent scientists, mathematicians and philosophers including Moritz Schlick, Rudolf Carnap, Otto Neurath, Friedrich Waismann, Kurt Gödel[63] and Philip Frank. There were also some visitors to the Circle who were to become famous later, such as A. J. Ayer, W. V. Quine and Karl Popper, although both Quine and Popper, unlike Ayer, did not endorse the doctrines of logical positivism. Moritz Schlick, who occupied the chair of the philosophy of the inductive sciences at the University of Vienna, was the founder of the Circle and remained a central and organizing figure. The Vienna Circle had a deep reverence for science and the efficacy of its methods. One of the most influential texts read and discussed at their meetings was Ludwig Wittgenstein's *Tractatus Logico-Philosophicus*; however, Wittgenstein himself was not a member of the Circle. Even so, Schlick "regarded the *Tractatus* as a decisive turning point in philosophy."[64] The Circle, in spite of their general agreement with the view of science and philosophy contained in the *Tractatus*, tended to utilize only the ideas expressed in it which concorded with their own emerging viewpoint. For example, Ayer notes the following:

> In Wittgenstein's *Tractatus* where the exclusion of metaphysics is effected very sharply, there is none the less a slight suggestion that the metaphysician may be grasping at truths which only the limitations of language prevent him from describing. Its famous last sentence ... "Whereof one cannot speak, thereof one must be silent", seems to imply that there *are* things that one cannot speak about. The Vienna Circle rejected this suggestion.[65]

The basic doctrines of logical positivism are reasonably easy to discern. They held the view that the propositions of the natural sciences (e.g. physics, biology, chemistry, psychology, and so on) aim to describe and explain what Bertrand Russell was to call "the furniture of the world". That is, they describe the world revealed to us through observation and experimental reasoning. Logical positivists held the hope that the whole corpus of the natural sciences would eventually provide a unified and complete scientific description and explanation of what there is. This is what Wittgenstein means when he asserts in the *Tractatus* that "the totality of true propositions is the whole of natural science". If this task of the natural sciences were to be completed we would have at our disposal "the totality of true propositions"; in effect, there would remain nothing else left to be described or explained. Of course, it could readily be admitted that the natural sciences were far from accomplishing such a task. Nevertheless, according to their doctrine, the methods of science, based on observation and reason, were regarded as the cornerstones of all legitimate empirical knowledge and the engine of scientific progress. Epistemologically the claim was that it is only through the processes of confirmable observation and replicable experimental reasoning that the empirically true propositions of the natural sciences can be successfully secured. The gold standard of science, for the logical positivists, was its procedures of verification. In a general sense the doctrines of the Vienna Circle can be regarded as continuing the tradition of the Enlightenment project of the eighteenth-century *philosophes*. It became *the* maxim of the Circle that the meaning of a proposition is its method of verification. This famous "verification principle" of logical positivism was therefore, in part, a theory of meaning which was used to demarcate sense from nonsense, to separate meaningful discourse from the meaningless kind and to differentiate science from non-science. The fundamental axiom of logical positivism and its essential orientation is summed up in Carnap's phrase: "there is no question whose answer is in principle unattainable by science".[66]

Carnap's assertion, taken at its face value, inclines one to ask what has become of the Kantian-type questions, "What ought I to do?", "How ought I to live?", "What kind of human being ought I to be?" The belief that science can provide answers to questions concerning fundamental human values seems wildly naive and conceptually eccentric. But Carnap's remark clearly indicates, at the very least, that logical positivism was intrinsically a scientific world-view. Even if we interpret his remarks as meaning that only those questions which can, in principle, be answered scientifically are questions that can be asked at all, it still leaves unresolved the distinction between questions of fact and questions of value: that is, questions of what is the case and questions of what ought to be the case. In this connection one of the dominant claims of scientific discourse is that its truths are independent of political, moral or religious values – in this sense, it is maintained, scientific propositions are value-free. There were some logical positivists (excluding Ayer) who advanced a utilitarian view of ethics suggesting that the way we ought to live is to pursue the doctrine of the greatest happiness for the greatest number. If you adopt such a view then it becomes a factual and empirical matter as to whether or not a particular way of life produces the greatest happiness for the greatest number. But utilitarianism, in all its varieties, suffers from the problem of equating happiness with goodness and completely ignores the essentially contestable nature of what constitutes "the good life". Utilitarianism may be a plausible theory of ethics but it is an essentially contestable one and, therefore, can only beg the question of the is/ought issue and cannot resolve it. In this matter it may be useful to remind ourselves of the earlier discussion of the work of Phillips and Mounce, in which they remark: "Sometimes philosophers seem to suggest that despite the moral differences which separate men, they are really pursuing the same end, namely, what all men want. The notion of what all men want is as artificial as the common evidence which is supposed to support it."[67]

Let us return to the main thread of the present discussion. The Vienna Circle, having outlined, to their satisfaction at least, what they considered to be the essential characteristics of the modern scientific world-view, were then faced with finding a role for philosophy concomitant with their scientifically inspired outlook. They concluded that philosophy was not to be considered as an empirical discipline on a par with the natural sciences. Philosophy, they contended, did not deal directly with matters of empirical fact. It was not the job of philosophy to produce empirical propositions, neither true ones nor false ones. In short, philosophy was not in the business of proposition production. Its new role was conceived as primarily an activity of clarification. It was redefined as an activity of conceptual and logical investigation; an investigation into, among other things, the arguments and assumptions and methods of the empirical sciences themselves. In Wittgenstein's *Tractatus* the matter is succinctly formulated thus: "Philosophy aims at the logical clarification of thoughts. Philosophy is not a body of doctrine but an activity." This, then, was the revolution in philosophy so admired by Moritz Schlick. Part of what was meant by "the logical clarification of thoughts" was the clarification of our concepts about the world. It was contended, by Ayer at least, that our concepts had an important bearing on what we regard the nature of the world to be, for it is through our concepts about the world that we comprehend and view the world. It follows from this that the elimination of certain conceptual confusions, in the name of "the logical clarification of thoughts", may well result in an alteration of what we take the world to be. And this meant that when we actually undertake such a process of logical clarification we will come to see that the discourses of metaphysics and religion rest on the production of "pseudo-propositions".

Ayer states this case clearly in the first chapter of his famous *Language, Truth and Logic*, which is entitled "The elimination of metaphysics". He argues that *all* propositions about the world, both those of common sense and those of science, have either to be empirical or analytical but not both, and using this distinction he goes on to demonstrate that the propositions of traditional meta-physics and religion are neither empirical propositions nor analytical propositions and, therefore, can only be regarded as pseudo-proposi-tions. The pseudo-propositions of the metaphysician are factually meaningless and literally non-sensical. This view of religion and metaphysics resulted in a form of logical agnosticism which asserted that it is as meaningless to deny the claims of religion as it is to assert them. The claims of transcendent metaphysics are as nonsensical as the claim that "the cube root of three is having a nice day". The sentences used by the metaphysician were deemed to have no literal or factual meaning: they were neither true nor false. Therefore, they could not figure in arguments either. This attempted elimination of metaphysics from the realm of legitimate discourse was regarded by the Circle as complete and irrefutable: a *fait accompli*. Ayer puts the matter as follows: "We may accordingly define a metaphysical sentence as a sentence which purports to express a genuine proposi-tion but does, in fact express neither a tautology nor an empirical hypothesis. And as tautologies and empirical hypotheses form the entire class of significant propositions, we are justified in concluding that all metaphysical assertions are nonsensical."[68]

Why then, one might ask, is the history of human culture so persistently impregnated with metaphysical assertions? The answer is, according to Ayer, that metaphysicians have been misled by the superficial grammatical similarity between such sentences as "The houses of parliament exist" and "God exists", into assuming that the latter statement is as factually meaningful as the former. In short, it is a "consideration of grammar" that has led to metaphysics. In this way Ayer seeks to eliminate in its entirety the metaphysical concept of Being from the realm of legitimate discourse.

Of course, the logical positivists, even in their heyday, never succeeded in adequately formulating their beloved verification prin-ciple to their satisfaction. Further, when it was pointed out to them that the verification principle itself was neither an analytical truth nor an empirical truth and, thereby, according to their own doctrine, it must be a metaphysical principle of the kind they openly disavowed, they responded by saying that the verification principle was to be regarded as a fruitful methodological recommendation. But for whom was it fruitful? Certainly not for the metaphysician. And why accept it when it ruled as nonsense so much that had been of such value to so many? And again we can ask, why accept it when it denied that reason and argument had any part to play in metaphysics (and, for Ayer, any part to play in ethics)? There were serious problems with all the central doctrines of logical positivism from which it never recovered. At any rate in the 1990s we find such critics as Rom Harré referring to the doctrines of logical positivism as moribund.[69] There are no longer any self-styled logical positivists on the philosophical scene. Perhaps its empiricist spirit lingers on, but in a much modified manner. One of the most potent philosophical critiques of logical positivism was Quine's "Two dogmas of empiricism".[70] Quine himself continued to support, however, a form of empiricism (devoid of the two dogmas, one may add) and he still embraced the scientific philosophy which lay behind logical positivism.

There are, however, one or two features of the rise and fall of logical positivism which will bear further consideration, particularly in relation to Strawson's point that the "individual philosopher's views are more likely than those of the scientist or exact scholar to reflect in part his individual taste and temperament". Firstly it is abundantly clear that logical positivism in its whole-hearted defence of the scientific attitude and the scientific world-picture was a philosophy of the tangible.[71] Reason served as much to articulate this preferred view as to originate it. The way in which logical positivism was presented by its advocates was that it was following reason "wheresoever it leadeth". Reason was regarded as the neutral arbiter of paradigm-preference. This is a somewhat naive and spectatorial view of both scientific and philosophical reasoning, and is a view which fails to give due weight to the historical circumstances in which logical positivism had its roots – that is, in a technological and scientific industrial culture. Logical positivism mirrored the scientific ethos of such a culture and refracted its predominant interests and aspirations about knowledge and progress. The logical positivist's appeal to the neutral arbitration of reason was far from being value-free. We might say that the Vienna Circle's search for – to borrow a phrase from Quine – "an

organized conception of reality" reflected a very particular and historically located organized conception of reality. Again, if we look at the
rise and fall of logical positivism from the point of view of its individual contributors, it provides an example of the way in which, as
Strawson suggests, individual taste and philosophical temperament
can come to exercise a considerable influence on the search for such
preferred conceptions of reality.

Some of the factors contributing to the emergence of differing
philosophical views of reality may be those cited by Hao Wang
when he says that "philosophers of different schools are interested
in different aspects of human activity and talk about different things.
They set out with different goals to attain, tasks to accomplish, and
problems to solve. Those who are interested in ethics, aesthetics,
or political theory may find Carnap or Quine disappointing because
they say so little in these areas."[72] But, as the history of logical positivism so obviously testifies, philosophy is not always a case of live
and let live: certain philosophical goals were ruled out of court and
certain branches and conceptions of philosophy were denounced. For
example, Ayer's emotive theory of ethics as presented in *Language,
Truth and Logic* argued that ethical discourse consisted solely in
expressions of feeling which had no propositional content and could
neither be true nor false. If this is so, moral philosophy has no future.
What we might conclude, then, is that what philosophy is is itself
a controversial and essentially contestable question. By specializing
in certain areas of philosophy (say, the philosophy of mathematics,
or the philosophy of logic) one might avoid directly dealing with
the issue of the essential contestability of different conceptions of
philosophy, but in other areas (say, the philosophy of religion, or
politics, or education, or moral philosophy, or metaphysics) the issue
soon becomes apparent. Any precursory reading of the history of
philosophy soon reveals evidence strongly in favour of the insight
contained in Hume's dictum that "Reason is the slave of the
passions", in the sense that different schools of philosophy reflect to
a considerable extent the temperamental predispositions, passions and
tastes of their advocates.

To Ibn 'Arabi this conclusion would come as no surprise, for not
only is reason incapable of leading to decisive certainty about the

nature of the Real but, following Ibn 'Arabi, the Self-disclosure of the Real varies according to the predisposition of the receptor. As the Shaykh al-Akbar reports, "knowledge of God takes on the measure of your view, your preparedness and what you are in yourself."[73] The Self-disclosure of the Real conforms to the mental constructions or beliefs of the receptor and such preferred pictures of reality issue from the fundamental predisposition of the person.

In the light of Ibn 'Arabi's view we might usefully reconsider certain comments in Carnap's short autobiography of his connection with the Vienna Circle, particularly the anecdotes about Wittgenstein. Carnap records the following:

> When I met Wittgenstein, I saw that Schlick's warnings were fully justified. But his behaviour was not caused by any arrogance. In general, he was of a sympathetic temperament and very kind; but he was hypersensitive and easily irritated. Whatever he said was always interesting and stimulating, and the way in which he expressed it was often fascinating. His point of view and his attitude towards people and problems, even theoretical problems, were much more similar to ... a creative artist than ... a scientist; one might almost say, similar to those of a religious prophet or a seer ... the impression he made on us was as if his insight came to him as through a divine inspiration, so that we could not help feeling that any sober rational comment or analysis of it would be a profanation ... I sometimes had the impression that the deliberately rational and unemotional attitude of the scientist and likewise any ideas which had the flavour of "Enlightenment" were repugnant to Wittgenstein. ... Once when Wittgenstein talked about religion, the contrast between his and Schlick's position became strikingly apparent. Both agreed of course in the view that the doctrines of religion in their various forms had no theoretical content. But Wittgenstein rejected Schlick's view that religion belonged to the childhood phase of humanity and would slowly disappear in the course of cultural development. When Schlick, on another occasion, made a critical remark about a metaphysical statement by a classical philosopher (I think it was Schopenhauer), Wittgenstein surprisingly turned against Schlick and defended the

philosopher and his work. ... Neurath was from the beginning very critical of Wittgenstein's mystical attitude, of his philosophy of the "ineffable", and of higher things.[74]

If one wanted a clear illustration of reason being guided by individual predispositional preference, in the manner suggested by Hume's dictum, one could not find a clearer illustration than the difference in attitude to the "mystical" between Wittgenstein and central members of the Vienna Circle like Schlick, Carnap and Neurath.

Perhaps one final point ought to be made about logical positivism and the philosophy of Ibn 'Arabi. Logical positivism was clearly a "philosophy of the tangible": this is nowhere more obvious than in its central emphasis on procedures of verification. But what is really at issue is the narrowness of its conception of verification in terms of sense-data; there is nothing intrinsically amiss with the notion of verification itself. In fact, verification is central to Ibn 'Arabi's doctrine of *wahdat al-wujud*. There is a strong sense of what could well be described as scientific probity running throughout the *Fusus al-Hikam* and the *Futuhat al-Makkiyah*. The knowledge that Ibn 'Arabi conveys always has its foundation in directly verified spiritual experience, either his own or other trustworthy sources. Henry Corbin cites the following statement by Ibn 'Arabi: "I know ... of no degree of mystic life, no religion or sect, but I myself have met someone who professed it, who believed in it and practised it as his personal religion. I have never spoken of an opinion or doctrine without building on the direct statements of persons who were its adepts." And Corbin concludes, "This visionary master provides an example of perfect scientific probity".[75] Scientific probity or verification has, therefore, its analogue in mystical experience.

We can now turn to an entirely different conception of knowledge and philosophy which could be described as the antithesis of the scientific philosophy of logical positivism: that is, existentialism.

Philosophy of the subject

Existentialism, in all its varieties, is a philosophy of the human subject. Its orientation is rooted in an account of the nature and structure of human potential. Unlike logical positivism, it is not concerned with the truth of propositions but with the truth of what it *means* to be an authentic and fully developed human being. The logic of existentialism explores the possibilities open to the human subject as a sentient, conscious being.

Within the paradigm of existentialist thought human existence is radically differentiated from other forms of existence such as that of trees, stones, plants, stars, animals and, for Heidegger, even angels. As Jaspers so carefully expresses it, human *Existenz*[76] is not a type or category of being (like animal, vegetable or mineral), but potential being. Human beings are born unfinished and have to define and create themselves by what they do and what they become. Decision is a fundamental existentialist category. Behind and in the midst of the vast array of all human decision-making lies the fundamental choice of what kind of human being we wish to be or to become. The decisions which the existentialists are generally interested in are those which determine the direction and quality of the individual's life – like the choice of vocation or marriage. It is decisions of an intensive kind rather than an extensive kind which carry the most telling existential import and depth. It is not so much the decision to buy a new car or new house which interests existentialism, it is more those decisions which determine the quality and depth of human authenticity. As Kierkegaard puts it, authenticity requires finding "the idea for which I can live and die". Kierkegaardian existentialism, as MacQuarrie notes, is an individualism which puts "the single individual" in a higher category than "fellowship".[77] For Kierkegaard, who is often regarded as the father of modern existentialism, we must become our unique authentic selves; we must become "the single individual, which everyone can be and should be." Kierkegaard says adamantly that "the crowd is untruth". Part of the engaging incisiveness of Kierkegaard's *Stages on Life's Way* lies in the extraordinary psychological veracity of his typology of human potential: a typology concerned ultimately with what is involved in becoming that single individual. There are noticeable affinities between Kierkegaard's conception of the single individual and Ibn 'Arabi's exhortation to "Know thyself" in order to know God.

Pre-eminently existentialism is a philosophy of human becoming. Existentialists themselves describe the special and unique nature of human existence by a variety of terms. Sartre says, for instance, that the human subject is a "being-for-itself" (*pour-soi*) rather than "in-itself" (*en-soi*). *Pour-soi* roughly corresponds to Heidegger's term *Dasein* and to Jaspers' term *Existenz*. They all use the word "existence" in a special sense: primarily to denote the dynamic potential and nature of human consciousness. The basic human project (a favourite term of Sartre) which faces every individual is to choose, or to fail to choose, the kind of human being we want to become. The responsibility is ours. To say that existentialism is a philosophy of human becoming is also to recognize that it is a philosophy of human freedom. The great and monumental existentialist themes are *freedom, decision, authenticity, commitment,* and *being-with-others-in-the-world.* As Jaspers points out, we can *flee* from our freedom as well as embrace it. Sartre puts the matter memorably when he says we can "hide behind excuses". For existentialism, human identity is a continual act of self-creation and self-projection into an open future. The fundamental tense of existentialism is the future – we are what we become. We are not inextricably locked into what we are now. Summarily, human *Existenz* is intrinsically dynamic, future-oriented and profoundly open in its possibilities.

A corollary of the existentialist view of human freedom and choice is that we always find ourselves in particular concrete historical and cultural circumstances. These circumstances are not of our own choosing – they are what Sartre calls *facticities* or givens. Human freedom and decision is necessarily, by its very nature, located in the concrete particularities of our everyday lives. Human freedom and human decisions are not free-floating. What we can choose is our attitude towards, or perspective on, or reaction to, the historical, cultural and psychological and even biological contingencies in which we inevitably find ourselves: the particular attitude(s) we choose to adopt reflect, or define, the kind of person we are. It is in this sense that existentialists argue that what we are, or are to become, is the result of our decisions and choices.

Nevertheless, in spite of the emphasis on the historical positioning and facticity of the human subject, the individual is equally conceived of as an irreplaceable and unique centre of consciousness. As Sartre puts it "we are not manufactured objects" and cannot be cloned. This affirms one of the great existentialist themes which is the insistence that human subjects cannot be reduced to components in ideological systems: whether such systems be industrial–technological, scientific or religious. The human subject cannot be reduced to an ideological subject; nor should they be treated as one. Existentialism is a profoundly moral project. It reasserts the intrinsic dignity of the human subject over and against all those industrial, technological, and social processes which tend to dehumanize and diminish the value of the individual.

Two distinct aspects of modern existentialism present themselves: existentialism as an investigation into the universal logic of human subjectivity and consciousness, and existentialism as a reaction against the dehumanizing propensity of industrial capitalism. Existentialism constitutes a historically rooted reaction. The real crux and value of existentialism lies in the assertion that the human subject is not a thing and that human subjectivity can transcend social or historical ideological reifications of its nature. Human subjectivity is capable of going beyond the mental packages of its time. Consider, for example, the ways in which women in the later part of the twentieth century (and earlier) transcended the ideological stereotypes into which many of them were born. The most enduring aspect of existentialism is likely to be its investigations into the more universal trans-historical potentialities of human consciousness. It is this aspect which has a direct ontological bearing on the *wahdat al-wujud* of Ibn 'Arabi.

The most important features of human consciousness as delineated by existentialist topography of the self are, firstly, that human subjectivity is a process and potential, not a thing: it is neither a biological thing, nor a cultural thing, nor an economic thing, nor an ideological thing. Secondly, that human consciousness is an imaginative consciousness in which resides the possibility to imagine a new future for ourselves, that is, to imagine what we "not yet are" but may strive to become. Thirdly, and fundamentally, human consciousness is self-reflexive. Human consciousness is not only aware of its own contents (e.g. thoughts, situations, feelings, desires, physical states, and so on) but is also aware that it is aware. It is aware of its own awareness. Because of this intrinsic self-reflexivity, human awareness is also capable of engendering radical self-alteration. Human consciousness, for the existentialist, possesses an inherent disposition to direct and reconfigure its own contents – it is not fixed or unalterable.

This point concerning the possibility of self-generated change is the key to understanding Kierkegaard's insistence on the profound leaps of faith necessary to accomplish new ways of being-in-the-world. Of course, for Kierkegaard the primordial relationship was between the single individual and God.

The fundamental existentialist axiom is, therefore, that the human subject is more accurately described as an *existence* rather than an *existent*. Izutsu documents this ontological preference very well when he remarks:

> Thus, if Heidegger ... so proudly declares that he is accomplishing a revolutionary break with the whole ontological tradition of Western philosophy comparable in importance to the Copernican revolution of Kant, it is due to his conviction that he, of all Western philosophers, has at last discovered a new key to an authentic ontology by his discovery of the significance of "existence", *das Sein*, as distinguished from "existent", *das Seiende*.[78]

Such a paradigm contrasts quite vividly with the logical positivist's pre-eminent concern with the truth of propositions. The existentialists directly explore the internally experienced worlds of human subjectivity, intersubjectivity and encounter; the logical positivists confine their operations to the observable, external empirical world. For theistic existentialists, like Kierkegaard, the primary human existential encounter is with the spiritual.

All in all, existentialism has important affinities with the philosophy of Ibn ‘Arabi. They both emphasize the sheer givenness, variety and primordiality of existence: for both, the primary datum is *existence*. Again, both world-views engender an astonishing freshness

of vision into the overwhelming immediacy and meaning of existence. For Kierkegaard, such freshness of vision is paradoxical or
bewildering for it testifies to the truth that "the eternal has come
into being in time". This is equally true for Ibn 'Arabi, except for Ibn
'Arabi time has only a perspectival reality, not an ontological one.
But we should remember "I wrapped myself in flesh and bones and
appeared as Yunus". In a similar manner both world-views recognize
that *existence* is prior to *thought* and not its product. For Ibn 'Arabi
only the Divine Self-consciousness could have ever conceived of the
ubiquitous plenitude and primordial vastness of existence; human
thought can only be astounded by its sheer givenness and variety.
Kierkegaard himself remarks that "the only thing-in-itself which
cannot be thought is *existence*".[79]

The idea that we *are* existence, and that we cannot therefore ever
step outside it but can only encounter it and seek to understand it, has
semantic resonances with one of the meanings of Ibn 'Arabi's term
"*wujud*", which is "to find".

Ibn 'Arabi's remarks on the Unity of Existence add a further dimension to the general ontology of existentialism. The unity alluded
to by Ibn 'Arabi is not the unity of a collection, but the unity of a
Single, Unique Existence appearing in an infinity of its own forms.
Fundamentally, following the metaphysics of unity, it is the possibility of returning to the original vision of existence as a unity which
distinguishes Ibn 'Arabi's position from all forms of European existentialism. For Ibn 'Arabi, as an objective for the accurate understanding of one's existence, our path is not to seek God but to seek
God's vision of Himself as us. The existential possibility of this
realization depends on the receptivity (*qabul*) and preparedness
(*isti'dad*) of the locus of manifestation, which is ourselves. The *insan-
i-kamil* alone has the receptivity to display the consciousness of
God in Its fullness.[80] Quite clearly, this Akbarian ontology lends an
infinitely vaster and richer ontological texture to human possibility
than the individualism of much modern European existentialism.
From the point of view of Ibn 'Arabi's metaphysics, much modern
existentialism radically misdescribes and excludes the true nature of
human potentiality and closes off the extraordinary domains of
human possibility to which Ibn 'Arabi's writings testify. Ibn 'Arabi's

ontology has no recourse to the Sartrian image of the solitary individual locked in a hostile universe. The assessment of Kierkegaardian existentialism *vis-à-vis* Ibn 'Arabi's perspective is more complicated because the high value Kierkegaard sets on the single individual does not necessarily imply individualism. Kierkegaard undoubtedly held the view that the dignity of the human subject resides in the fact that he is made in the image of the One God. In some respects, Kierkegaardian existentialism sails very close to a unitive ontology: for instance when he observes that "the eternal has come into being in time" and when he views the human subject as embracing both the finite and the infinite, the temporal and the eternal, and when he characterizes the deepest inward striving of the human soul as a desire to go beyond the finite self to the infinite self. Whether ultimately Kierkegaard recognized the indissoluble identity between the One and the Many as constituting two aspects of a Single Unique Existence remains an open and interesting question which cannot easily be prejudged. If we were permitted to view Kierkegaard's deliberations from an Akbarian perspective there might be more in his metaphysics than would otherwise be apparent.

It is sometimes said in criticism of European existentialism that its individualism pays insufficient conceptual attention to the social and political nature of the human animal. Many theorists in the Western tradition have testified to the intrinsically social nature of the human subject, including such influential figures as Aristotle and Karl Marx. Human subjects exist in the historical mode and inhabit prevailing material, cultural and ideological conditions which largely define their individuality and self-conceptions. European existentialism was itself the product of an industrial and industrializing Europe. Such circumstances constitute the larger cultural canvas against which the existential human drama is enacted. But even if we accept the historicity of the human condition, this is still too narrow a perspective on human life for Ibn 'Arabi. He takes the matter much further by suggesting that a person's biological, psychological and cultural landscape (and the historical circumstances and events which define and constitute their particular era) provides too narrow a compass from which to judge human existential possibility. It is only from the point of view of the Unity of Existence that the true nature of human potential can be properly appreciated. Ibn 'Arabi's writings provide the reader with a universal spiritual cartography: an account for the *salik* of the spiritual terrain ahead, a glimpse into what otherwise would remain largely an unenvisaged human possibility. The *Fusus al-Hikam* itself constitutes just such a summary, and an announcement and an invitation concerning the all-inclusive nature of existence and an esoteric exposition of its landscape. It invites the would-be aspirant to reorient their attention to the Quranic and Socratic imperative "Know thyself" as the key to this more universal epistemic realm.

There is nothing comparable to this in European existentialist writing, not even in the writings of Kierkegaard. The "open horizons of being" (so loved by much contemporary existential philosophy) undergoes, in the hands of Ibn 'Arabi, a radical reconfiguration in its theophanic comprehensiveness and depth. Ibn 'Arabi's unfoldings of the "domain beyond reason" provide glimpses of an extraordinary existential and primordial human possibility. As Ibn 'Arabi says, "No one knows the dignity of Man and his place in the universe except those who know how to contemplate God perfectly."[81] Ibn 'Arabi's metaphysical picture exhibits a deep and compelling rationality which, in default mode (to deploy a computational term), realigns the findings of modern thought itself.

Wahdat al-wujud, wisdom and reason

One of the apparent paradoxes of Ibn 'Arabi's account of the limits of human reason is that it seems eminently reasonable. It is perhaps not so difficult for many to accept that an intuitive immediate experience of the truth is possible, which is not available to reflective thinking.[82] Sense perception would appear to be something of this kind and our perceptions of people may sometimes possess such a quality. Generally, we are not bereft of basic personal experiential anchorage when reading even the most difficult parts of Ibn 'Arabi. But there is much more to the reasonableness of Ibn 'Arabi than this.

But first a note about the basic Arabic term *kashf*, often used by Ibn 'Arabi in connection with his epistemological analysis. The term means an immediate and direct unveiling, a bit like the scales falling from one's eyes. Training and discipline may sometimes provide a conceptual background for such flashes of intuition but, as Stephen Hirtenstein remarks,

> One notable feature of Ibn 'Arabi's illumination was the lack of any formal preparation or study. He was a young man without any specific training or discipline, and appears not to have known any spiritual teachers at the time. However, we should beware of judging readiness in terms of actions or purification or preparation. It is a transformation that takes one out of the temporal successions of ordinary life.[83]

Training or no training, *kashf*, when regarded as an immediate perception of the truth, carries with it "decisive certainty" regarding God's knowledge in relation to the matter which it unveils. A good example would be the legendary Wisdom of Solomon. We might say that Solomon speaks with Divine Intuition (*al-kashf al-ilahi*). In the chapter on Solomon in Ibn 'Arabi's *Fusus al-Hikam* we are informed that in the being in whom the spiritual intuition is more vast "the Divine Principle is more apparent". This telling remark gives us a sense of the nature of the kind of compelling reasonableness which imbues Ibn 'Arabi's metaphysics and which can undoubtedly leave a lasting impression on any serious reader. The content of Ibn 'Arabi's work always issues from a view of the whole as a whole. It is the universality of this perspective which demands that the reader exercises his or her *reason* in regard to such a universal vision. It is as if the work contains a request to the reader to extend their rational appreciation into areas to which we are unaccustomed and yet which in no way taste of intellectual speculation or mere personal cognitive construction. Ibn 'Arabi's works, particularly the *Fusus* and the *Tarjuman al-Ashwaq*, exemplify what Plato may have had in mind in his axiom that "Philosophy begins in *wonder*", a wonder which realigns human reason with what, following Plato and Ibn 'Arabi, we already innately know to be universally true. It is this process of *anamnesis*, to use the technical term Plato gives it, which enables the penny to drop so that the reader can begin to appreciate Ibn 'Arabi's own "admiration for the sheer beauty and magnitude of such an exalted and all-inclusive ontological arrangement".[84] The organ of such direct perception is generally designated by Ibn 'Arabi as the heart. He says:

We empty our hearts of reflective thinking, and we sit together with God (*al-Haqq*) on the carpet of *adab* and spiritual attentiveness (*muraqaba*) and presence and readiness to receive whatever comes to us from Him – so that it is *God* who takes care of teaching us by means of unveiling and spiritual realization. So when they have focused their hearts and their spiritual aspirations (*himam*) on God and have truly taken refuge with *Him* – giving up any reliance on the claims of reflection and investigation and intellectual results – then their hearts are purified and open.[85]

Ibn ʿArabi's presentation of *wahdat al-wujud* engenders a profound sense of the rationality of reality itself: that is, of its unity and uniqueness and the *raison d'être* of human kind. As Affifi comments, Ibn ʿArabi sees that "the whole creation is a rational structure from the lowest mineral to the highest type of man ... Everything manifests the universal Rational Principle in a measure proportionate to its capacity ... even inanimate beings ... obey their own inner laws". It is abundantly clear that for Ibn ʿArabi the universe is permeated by the rationality of God. God is regarded as "the creative and rational Principle" of the universe.[86]

Human beings instantiate this rational principle in proportion to their capacity. Ultimately it is the rationality of God's love to be known, the rationality of divine mercy, of divine love, of divine beauty and essentially the rationality of divine communication. When human reason is aligned, even for a moment, to this vision it is capable of becoming the inspired intellect in which cognitive appreciation is extended to areas and domains of a deeper epistemic and universal order where the knower, the knowledge and the known are one. It is the compelling reasonableness of such a universal point of view, and the necessity for adopting it, to which the work of Ibn ʿArabi invites us. This is the wisdom of its logic and the logic of its wisdom.

We can note at this juncture a growing recognition that the multivalent nature of reality is, as Tarnas expresses it, "beyond the grasp of any one intellectual approach" and that "only a committed openness to the interplay of many perspectives can meet the extraordinary challenges of the postmodern era".[87] Chaos theory would be a very good example of such an emerging viewpoint which demonstrates that changes in our conceptual understanding of nature reflect prior changes in our general metaphysics. In order to see nature afresh, we first need the right metaphor or perspective which allows us to do this, otherwise we remain blind.

For most Western students of Ibn 'Arabi the study of his work initially exhibits a somewhat unfamiliar cognitive architecture, akin to the study of an unfamiliar world-view. One problem which such comparative studies raise, as Steven Lukes points out,[88] is the question of what constitutes an adequate account of rationality, particularly if the set of beliefs we are investigating seems at odds with a Westernized scientific view of things. Generally, for social anthropologists there is a cognitively prudent desire to avoid any form of intellectual ethnocentricity (or superiority) in dealing with other cultures and unfamiliar systems of belief. But the problem of understanding and rationally assessing other cultural systems of belief is further compounded by those Western intellectual authorities, like Karl Popper and others professionally familiar with the metaphysical scaffolding of Western theoretical culture, who conclude that the best we can hope for rationally, even in science, are interesting falsehoods.

One way of looking at Ibn 'Arabi's metaphysical strategy is, if we may employ a favourite semantic item of much postmodern theorizing, that it deconstructs and re-evaluates such intellectual findings and constructions from a more universal ontological vantage point. That is, from a universal viewpoint from which the whole creation is seen as possessing a perfectly rational structure in which everything has its allotted place, including human reason itself.

We are now in a position to turn to the broader canvas of how we may regard the lived-experience of a technological, scientific, and industrial world in the light of *wahdat al-wujud*. To accomplish this we must delve a little into the contours of the modern era.

Notes

1 W. C. Chittick, *The Sufi Path of Knowledge* (Albany, NY, 1989), p.203.
2 C. Addas, *Quest for the Red Sulphur*, trans. P. Kingsley (Cambridge, 1993), p.105.
3 M. Bartholomew, D. Hall and A. Lentin, *The Enlightenment*, Studies 1 (Milton Keynes, 1994), p.12.
4 Al-Niffari, *The Mawaqif and Mukhatabat*, trans. A. J. Arberry (London, 1978), p.131, line 8.
5 Ibn 'Arabi's account of this meeting is documented in Chapter 1, p.27 of this study.
6 Chittick, *Sufi Path*, p.165.
7 G. F. Hourani, *Averroes: On the Harmony of Religion and Philosophy* (London, 1976), p.20
8 Hourani, *Averroes*, p.20.
9 For example, the syllogism "All men are mortal, Socrates is a man, therefore, Socrates is mortal."
10 Hourani, *Averroes*, p.20.
11 Averroes, *Tahafut al-Tahafut*, trans. S. Van Den Bergh (London, 1978), p.xxxvi.
12 See A. F. Chalmers, *What Is This Thing Called Science?* (3rd edn., Milton Keynes, 1999).
13 Muhyiddin Ibn 'Arabi. *Sufis of Andalusia*. Partial translation of *Ruh al-quds* and *Durrat al-fakhirah* by R. W. J. Austin (Gloucestershire, 1988), pp.23–4.
14 Addas, *Red Sulphur*, p.105.
15 See Chittick, *Sufi Path*, p.123.
16 Chittick, *Sufi Path*, p.117.
17 J. W. Morris, "Seeking God's Face", *Journal of the Muhyiddin Ibn 'Arabi Society* (1995, Vol. XVII), p.5.
18 Chittick, *Sufi Path*, p.122.
19 Chittick, *Sufi Path*, p.123.
20 P. Ackroyd, *Blake* (London, 1995), p.34.
21 J. Kim, *Philosophy of Mind* (Oxford, 1996), p.101.
22 Chittick, *Sufi Path*, p.124.
23 C. G. Jung, *Man and His Symbols* (London, 1990), p.38.
24 O. T. Benfey, "Chains and rings: Kekule's dreams", in *Faber Book of Science*, ed. J. Carey (London, 1996), pp.137–8.
25 Ibn 'Arabi, *Sufis of Andalusia*, p.24.
26 Chittick, *Sufi Path*, p.124.
27 L. W. Beck, ed., *Kant: Selections* (London, 1988), p.11.
28 L. W. Beck, "From Leibniz to Kant", in *Routledge History of Philosophy*, ed. R. C. Solomon and K. M. Higgins (Vol. VI, London, 1993), p.32.
29 A. J. Ayer and J. O'Grady, eds., *A Dictionary of Philosophical Quotations* (Oxford, 1995), pp.219–20.
30 I. Kant, *The Critique of Pure Reason*, trans. J. M. D. Meiklejohn (Britannica Great Books Series, Vol. 42 of 54, Chicago, 1987), p.1.

31 Kant, *Critique*, p.19.
32 Beck, *Kant Selections*, p.11.
33 Chittick, *Sufi Path*, p.163.
34 I. Kant, "What is Enlightenment?", in *The Enlightenment*, Texts 2, ed. S. Eliot and K. Whitlock (Milton Keynes, 1992), p.305.
35 Chittick, *Sufi Path*, p.179.
36 B. Rauf, *Addresses* (Gloucestershire, 1986), p.10.
37 B. Spinoza, *Ethics* (Britannica Great Books Series, Vol. 31 of 54, Chicago, 1987), p.388.
38 For a discussion of the term see: A. MacIntyre, "Pantheism", in *The Concise Encyclopaedia of Western Philosophy and Philosophers*, ed. J. O. Urmson and J. Rée (London, 1988), p.227.
39 Addas, *Red Sulphur*, p.105.
40 B. Russell, *History of Western Philosophy* (London, 1961), p.554.
41 Chittick, *Sufi Path*, p.209.
42 Chittick, *Sufi Path*, p.209.
43 Addas, *Red Sulphur*, p.104.
44 W. B. Gallie, "Essentially contested concepts", *Proceedings of the Aristotelian Society* (Vol. 56, 1955–56), pp.167–98.
45 Gallie, "Essentially contested concepts", p.168; here he refers to "work of art", "democracy", "Christian doctrine".
46 Gallie, "Essentially contested concepts", p.169.
47 J. B. Watson, "Psychology as the behaviourist views it", *Psychological Review* (1913, Vol. 20), pp.158–77.
48 J. Henry, *et al.*, "Towards a psychology of experience", *The Psychologist* (March 1997), pp.117–20.
49 Addas, *Red Sulphur*, p.104.
50 D. Z. Phillips and H. O. Mounce, "On morality's having a point", in *The Is/Ought Question*, ed. W. D. Hudson (London, 1969), p.239.
51 Phillips and Mounce, "On morality's having a point", p.239.
52 For a well-informed discussion of the relationship between reason and commitment see B. Mitchell, *The Justification of Religious Belief* (London, 1973), pp.117–34.
53 D. T. Meyers, ed., *Feminists Rethink the Self* (Boulder, Colo., 1997), p.2.
54 Ibn 'Arabi, *Futuhat al-Makkiyah*, trans. Chittick, *Sufi Path*, p.148.
55 Meyers, *Feminists Rethink the Self*, p.1.
56 S. A. Kierkegaard, *Journals*, trans. A. Dru (New York, 1959), p.44.
57 Ibn 'Arabi, *Sufis of Andalusia*, p.143.
58 Mitchell, *Justification*, p.131 (see note 50 above).
59 Ibn 'Arabi, *Sufis of Andalusia*, p.63.
60 J. Macquarrie, *Existentialism* (London, 1972), p.134.
61 B. Rauf, "Universality and Ibn 'Arabi", *Journal of the Muhyiddin Ibn 'Arabi Society* (Vol. IV, 1985), p.3.
62 P. F. Strawson, "Scepticism and naturalism: some varieties", *A Dictionary of Philosophical Quotations* (Oxford, 1995), p.435.
63 Gödel, however, never held to the central doctrines of logical positivism.

64 S. Brown, *Verification and Meaning* (Milton Keynes, 1976), p.21.
65 A. J. Ayer, "The Vienna Circle", in *The Revolution in Philosophy*, ed. G. Ryle (London, 1956), p.74.
66 Brown, *Verification and Meaning*, p.21.
67 Phillips and Mounce, "On morality's having a point", p.239.
68 A. J. Ayer, *Language, Truth and Logic* (London, 1987), p.56.
69 R. Harré, "Reappraising social psychology: rules, roles and rhetoric", *The Psychologist* (January 1993), p.25.
70 W. V. O. Quine, *From a Logical Point of View* (2nd edn., New York, 1961), pp.20–46.
71 H. Wang, *Beyond Analytic Philosophy* (Cambridge, Mass., 1986).
72 Wang, *Beyond Analytic Philosophy*, p.192.
73 Chittick, *Sufi Path*, p.342.
74 Brown, *Verification and Meaning*, p.72.
75 H. Corbin, *Creative Imagination in the Sufism of Ibn 'Arabi*, trans. R. Manheim (Princeton, 1969), p.46.
76 Macquarrie, *Existentialism*, p.68.
77 Macquarrie, *Existentialism*, p.279.
78 T. Izutsu, *Creation and the Timeless Order of Things* (Ashland, Oreg., 1994), p.180.
79 Ayer and O'Grady, *Dictionary of Philosophical Quotations*, p.233.
80 Chittick, *Sufi Path*, p.91.
81 A. E. Affifi, *The Mystical Philosophy of Muhyd din Ibnul Arabi* (Lahore, 1979), p.80.
82 Affifi, *Mystical Philosophy*, p.105.
83 S. Hirtenstein, *The Unlimited Mercifier* (Oxford, 1999), p.52.
84 P. Coates, "Review of Izutsu's Sufism and Taoism: a comparative study of key philosophical concepts", *Journal of the Muhyiddin Ibn 'Arabi Society* (Vol. V, 1986), pp.69–70.
85 J. W. Morris, "Listening for God: prayer and the heart in the *Futuhat*", *Journal of the Muhyiddin Ibn 'Arabi Society* (Vol. XIII, 1995), p.28.
86 Affifi, *Mystical Philosophy*, p.85.
87 R. Tarnas, *The Passion of the Western Mind* (London, 1996), p.404.
88 S. Lukes, "Some problems about rationality", in *Rationality*, ed. B. Wilson (Oxford, 1970), pp.194–213.

3   Ibn ʿArabi and the era

The metaphysics of the era: creation and change

Towards the end of *The Passion of the Western Mind* Richard Tarnas identifies an important aspect of the modern era when he notes, "As the twentieth century draws to its close, a widespread sense of urgency is tangible on many levels, as if the end of an aeon is indeed approaching. It is a time of intense expectation, of striving, of hope and uncertainty. Many sense that the great determining force of our reality is the mysterious process of history itself, which in our century has appeared to be hurtling toward a massive disintegration of all structures and foundations, a triumph of the Heraclitean flux."[1]

There can be little doubt that the momentous events of the latter part of the twentieth century made its inhabitants acutely aware that "everything in the world (and therefore the world itself) is constantly changing".[2] The ancient Heraclitean metaphor of the flowing river into which, according to Plato's report on Heraclitus, "you cannot step twice; for fresh waters are ever flowing on you" depicts the world-process as a dynamic movement transforming itself "kaleidoscopically from moment to moment".[3] Such a view fits well with the ontology of *wahdat al-wujud* and with Ibn ʿArabi's cosmology of the perpetual Self-disclosure of Being. In the twentieth century "global village" (as Marshall McLuhan describes the transformation of life in the modern world), one of the most potent icons for capturing the cinematographical quality of the ever-increasing rapidity of historical and technological change was television. Nothing demonstrates so clearly and intimately as television the spectatorial and global witnessing of the act of change and creation.

Ibn 'Arabi's account of perpetual new creation (*al-khalq al-jadid*) presents us with a fundamental metaphysics of the perpetual creation and transformation of phenomenal reality. For Ibn 'Arabi the basic logic of this ontology is clear: the Absolute in its love to be known is continuously disclosing Itself and manifesting Itself as and in the infinity of possible things. Human consciousness can witness this constant movement of creation both internally within itself and externally in nature, in history, and in culture. What largely goes unnoticed, according to Ibn 'Arabi, is that this constant flux of life, at all levels, is actually an act of ever-new creation. Phenomenal existence is a never-ending process of annihilation and recreation at every moment. Literally, nothing repeats itself: it is a constantly new creation. Things are being born freshly all the time. In so far as human beings are unaware of the constant freshness of existence they lag behind the moment. What is more, according to Ibn 'Arabi, the perpetual disclosure of Being to the particular human receptor is in accordance with its archetypal essence (called *'ayn al-thabita*) in the Divine knowledge.

As Al-Qashani records "all the modes of the archetypes are things that have been known to God (from eternity) … and God brings them out to actuality incessantly and perpetually. And so He goes on transforming the possibilities that have been there from the beginning-less past and that are (therefore) essentially uncreated, into infinite possibilities that are actually created."[4] Perpetual new creation is in accordance with the archetypes and these archetypes act as a kind of potential or pattern which determine the unfoldments of the phenomenal world, although they themselves always remain in their archetypal state in the Divine Consciousness. What God knows of the archetypes in the Divine knowledge, Ibn 'Arabi informs us, is what they (the essences or archetypes) have given to God of themselves as specified and particular possibilities. The archetypes exist in the Divine Consciousness as unique possibilities, analogous to the manner in which ideas exist in the human mind. As ideas in the Divine Consciousness and as modes of the One Being such possibilities are never repeated and reside essentially for ever in the Divine knowledge.

At the microcosmic and individual level, the perpetual renewal of creation renews the entity of the individual at each instant. As Ibn ʿArabi says "the creation of individual human beings is in fact infinite ... shown by the diversity of properties ... in every state."[5] As human beings, therefore, we directly witness something of the infinity of the ever-newly created within ourselves, within the era in which we live and within the cosmos generally. As the Quranic verse says, "Each day He is upon some task", and one of those "tasks" is *ourselves*.

At a more macrocosmic level, the general term era (and its analogues times, days, epochs, moments) refers to particular configurations of the Divine Self-disclosure as it unfolds as a "theatre of manifestation" in the infinity of the world-process. The term era denotes the primary fact of Divine activity. It must be remembered that the vastness of these tasks embraces both the macrocosmic and the microcosmic: from the historical and cultural contours of a particular civilization to the "rejoicing at the repentance of His servant";[6] to the "stars, planets, and mansions of the moon; earth, air, water, and fire; animals, plants, and inanimate objects";[7] to life and death, heaven and earth and the journey from Him and the journey to Him. All these things and more are embraced by the term era.

God appears *in* the era, and He appears *as* the era. According to the hadith, "God is called 'Time'",[8] we are advised not to be disappointed by time, or curse time, for God is time. In another rendering, we are cautioned to "Revile not the era for I [God] am the era." This account of the metaphysical structure of the era is further elaborated by Ibn ʿArabi in the following way. In respect of Him being called time, the whole of existence is "God's Day". It is always God who is perpetually revealing and concealing Himself without beginning and without end. The term God's Day consequently reaffirms the Oneness, Uniqueness and Universality of Being and reminds us of the affirmation of Divine Self-disclosure as no other than the movement of His love to be known and its binary opposite affirmation that "God was and nothing was with Him", this latter locution denoting God's pre-temporal existence without time or things, or change, or movement. The former affirms apparent process, multiplicity, immanencing, causation and so on, whilst the latter reaffirms non-process, singularity, transcendence, and non-causality. For Ibn 'Arabi both immanence and transcendence have to be simultaneously asserted of reality as a whole, if you are, he says, "to follow the right course".

Within God's beginningless and endless Day there are differentiated modalities identified as particular "Days of God". We learn that "Having let us know that He is time, God mentions to us that He possesses days" and that these are the Days of God where there is differentiation into eras and epochs. For instance, there are the epochs of pre-modernity (like the days of Moses, and Jesus, and Muhammad) and the epoch of modernity itself. Chronologically, the modern era is situated somewhere along the continuum between the time of Muhammad and the second coming of Jesus at the end of time.

Each time comes under the ruling of particular properties or, what Ibn 'Arabi calls in their Quranic context, the Names of God, or the Divine Names. These Divine Names, or attributes or qualities, constitute lines of Divine action or influence which have tangible effects in the world. In fact, for Ibn 'Arabi, everything that exists in the phenomenal world is not only under the ruling of a particular Divine Name but is intrinsically constituted by a Divine Name or configuration of the Divine Names, including the era. Consequently, there are as many Divine Names as things: that is, they are infinite in number. The traditional Islamic summary of this bejewelled ontology is codified and known as the Ninety-Nine Most Beautiful Names of God and, in summary, these cover them all. In general, Ibn 'Arabi tells us:

> Just as God gave the cosmos the name *wujud*, which belongs
> to Him in reality, so also He gave it the Most Beautiful Names
> through its preparedness and the fact that it is a locus of mani-
> festation of Him. Every name in the cosmos is His name, not the
> name of other than He. For it is the name of the Manifest in the
> locus of manifestation.[9]

And, in particular, we learn that "Every person is a place for the manifestation of one or other Name and he is under the dispensation of that Name", such as, the names "Majesty (*jalal*), Beauty (*jamal*), Guidance (*hadi*) and Misguidance (*mudill*)."[10] Other Names include *khaliq* (the Creator who gives to each its own nature); *badi'* (The Most Beautiful Scientific Constructor); *'adl* (The Extremely Just); *musawwir* (The One Who gives Form) and *rahman* (The All-Compassionate). These are just a few. The dynamic logic of the shifting matrix of Divine influence accomplished by these names is illustrated rather well in relation to what Ibn 'Arabi tells us about the structure and meaning of the term era.

The overall dynamic of the term era follows the general formula that "Each name possesses days, which are the time for the ruling property of that name". Such days "commingle, interpenetrate and cover each other" and this constitutes the "diversity of properties that is seen in the cosmos at a single time".[11] The picture is one of each era being constituted by a set of interpenetrating names (some covering others and some being more visible than others) which have their "day" in which and through which certain ruling properties are evident. In effect this means that certain properties or identifying characteristics are seen to be predominant at particular times. An era is, therefore, a unique co-mixture of the Days of God bearing the determining imprint of certain governing qualities.

In addition, each era has an inward and outward aspect: an unseen and a visible dimension. Ibn 'Arabi carefully points out that each era contains that which is hidden and remains "unseen by us", and that which is obvious, visible, corporeal and tangible. The overall meta-physical picture is a bird's-eye view of the Days of God perpetually unfolding their inherent qualities in accordance with the axiomatic truth, "Each day He is upon some task."

As Izutsu points out, these perpetual unfoldings conform to three stages, "(1) the 'most holy emanation', (2) the 'holy emanation', and, then (3) the appearance of concrete individual things – going on being actualized one after another like successive, recurrent waves."[12] Each successive stage carries the imprint of the prior stage. In one sense, therefore, what we call concrete individual things are images of images – somewhat like pictures on a television screen or the shadows projected on the wall in Plato's Cave. One of Ibn 'Arabi's favourite metaphors for describing this situation is that of a mirror. He reports that the cosmos is a mirror within which God sees His own form.[13] The images in a mirror both correspond to and yet differ from the original: the shape of the mirror determines the type of inversion and the condition of the reflective surface of the mirror determines the quality of the image. Regarding the logical status of such images it appears that they have a certain kind of existence but do not possess any substantial reality of their own, analogous to a shadow. In short their status is somewhat ambiguous: the person's image in a mirror is both them and not them. So, according to Ibn 'Arabi, although there is an inherent isomorphism, unity and a continuity of meaning between the three stages of the Self-disclosure of the Real, the succeeding stage has the status of an image of the one preceding it. That is, it resembles it in some ways but not in others. This is why Ibn 'Arabi can assert that everything is inverted in this world.[14] It is not untypical of Ibn 'Arabi to seek to illustrate profound spiritual insights with everyday examples like that of the mirror, just as in the Quran it is said that God is not afraid of using the similitude of a gnat to convey spiritual meaning. Perhaps one of the most unusual similitudes used by Ibn 'Arabi is that of the chameleon.[15] It is the chameleon which, he says, most obviously symbolizes the constant transmutation of the cosmos through the action of the Divine names "since there is no animal that shows more clearly that the Real possesses the property of transmutation". The chameleon is, as it were, not only an evident spiritual symbol but a tangible physical instantiation of the principle of constant transmutation.

The non-stop transformation of the cosmos, what the poet Edmond Spenser called "the ever whirling wheels of change" is, Ibn 'Arabi tells us, "a reminder of the Root, for him who has a heart". And, he continues, "for the heart possesses fluctuations from one state to another ... If man examines his heart, he will see that it does not remain in a single state. So he should know that if the Root were not like this, this fluctuation would have no support."[16] And the Root, that is, God Himself, is called the "Turner of Hearts". Ibn 'Arabi records that the heart dwells between the "two fingers of the Merciful". Its nature is nothing less than tremendous. The heart is all-comprehensive, all-inclusive, and all-pervasive. It is in its "Root" co-extensive with the Mercy of God Himself; is free from all limitation and embraces "all things in mercy and knowledge".[17] It is the seat and root of the Divine Vision of Himself, and the *insan-i-kamil* (the Perfect Man) shares in its freedom and knows the secret of the famous verse from Ibn ʿArabi's *Tarjuman al-Ashwaq*, "My heart has become capable of every form". The *insan-i-kamil*, who is created in God's image, mirrors perfectly the Original and is himself named by God as "mercy to the universes". As such the *insan-i-kamil* possesses the Divine Identity to such an extent that, Ibn ʿArabi tells us, he (the *insan-i-kamil*) can and logically must assume the Divine attribute of Self-subsistence (*qayyum*). In a profoundly metaphysical sense, for Ibn ʿArabi, the constant transmutation of the cosmos is literally the "Breath of the Merciful" in His love to be known and is fully instantiated only in the Perfect Man. Each age, each culture, each historical epoch, each new era contains the possibility of its own zenith and aspiration; of producing or realizing its own "highest specimen" (to use a Nietzschian term), that is, the *insan-i-kamil*.

Finally, this outline of the metaphysics of creation and change in the writings of Ibn ʿArabi needs to include a further examination of the status and role of secondary causes (*asbab*) if for no other reason than that the language of secondary causes is another way of describing the action of the Divine Names in their tangible effects.

Chittick, in his discussion of the Arabic etymology of the plural secondary causes (*asbab*, literally meaning ropes, or cords), points out that by extension (and, I would add, by implication) the term refers to "*connecting things or factors*", to "*means of access*", or to "*means of accomplishment*". In the history of Islamic mystical literature the term has also come to mean the causes at work in the cosmos and, even more generally, has been taken to refer to all phenomena and existing things.[18] In one sense, therefore, the term secondary causes can be understood as a description of certain of the ways in which the tasks of God are accomplished. They constitute essentially the means by which God accomplishes His love to be known. Further, in so far as *existent things* are necessary for that primordial accomplishment, they too, in this respect at least, can be regarded as secondary causes. The human body itself is a means without which human subjects as we know them would simply not exist and certain possibilities would therefore be cut off at the phenomenal level.

Secondary causes are ubiquitously "constitutive of the cosmos" and provide a framework of links, connections or concatenations.

Situated in the context of Ibn 'Arabi's remarks on the cosmology of constant change, secondary causes – although they may be understood as forming some kind of concatenated structure (or apparent cause and effect relation) – cannot ultimately possess any ontological independence of their own. As far as human beings are concerned our dependence, for example, on the secondary causes governing the universe (like gravity and climate) is taken, by Ibn 'Arabi, as fundamentally indicative of our essential dependence on, and poverty towards, the transcendent origin of these causes. The *insan-i-kamil*, according to Ibn 'Arabi, recognizes the One cause operating in everything and is aware that there is no temporal priority between God and the Universe or between God *and* the era. There can be no such gap in the Oneness of Being. There are, of course, internal modalities of the One Being which can reveal themselves simultaneously and without fissure as a prophet, or an era, or a cosmos. They constitute the ever-changing outward expression of the One and Unique Being.

Given Ibn 'Arabi's ontology of Divine Names and his metaphysics of change and creation, perhaps we can venture into asking what might constitute the governing names of our own era: that which contemporary intellectual authorities have called modernity. This is not so speculative or presumptuous a task as it may seem, for modernity undeniably exemplifies a set of identifying characteristics. The three most obvious and inter-related characteristics identified by contemporary intellectual authorities in their analysis of modernity are the culturally dominant forms taken by *Science*, *Technology* and *Economics*. This is the back-drop within which, and against which, the human drama of modernity is being played out. They are the defining parameters of modernity and form the topographical co-ordinates of our era. Let us go on to examine this matter in line with the aim of the present study.

Social science and the emergence of the modern era

As the historian Eric Hobsbawm remarks about the beginnings of Industrial Society, "If the sudden, qualitative, and fundamental transformation, which happened in or about the 1780s, was not a revolution then the word has no common sense meaning".[19] And to this he adds that such a revolution "forms the greatest transformation in human history since remote times."

Thus began the modern era: the era of the Industrial Revolution, of industrial capitalism, of science and of technology. There had, of course, been forms of science and technology long before this but it never constituted a central defining characteristic of the era. And, even more significantly, the adamantine alignment of science and technology with the rationality of industrial capitalism was unique in its history and strategic to its prodigious development. The qualitative re-organization and reorientation of much of nineteenth- and twentieth-century Western society, which is often described as the "Great Transformation", gave birth also to the science of sociology – that is, the emergence of a new kind of intellectual authority.

It was an intellectual authority whose original aim was twofold: (1) to establish itself as a legitimate science, and, (2) to take as its object of analysis the emergence and distinctive characteristics of industrializing society. Its main theoretical architects were the classical founder-figures, Karl Marx, Emile Durkheim and Max Weber. There were some precursors, like Comte and Saint-Simon, but none possessed the analytical stature and calibre of the classical triumvirate. Many of the defining contours of modernity were brought into clear focus in the work of Marx (1818–83), Durkheim (1858–1917) and Weber (1864–1920). Each constructed a conceptual map of modernity. These intellectual constructions have profoundly influenced all subsequent sociological discussion and analysis. For our purposes it is useful to delineate some of the characteristics which Marx, Durkheim and Weber saw as distinguishing modernity from traditional societies. Their respective analyses share, of course, some historically agreed core material: "the movement from the land to the cities, the massing of workers in the new industrial towns and factories, [and] the separation of work and family life".[20]

In addition to this, as Kumar remarks, there was also at work a "powerful *image of industrialization* as a social system and a way of life".[21] Kumar goes on to point out that this image permeated the cultural consciousness of the time and itself began to constitute a *defining* co-ordinate of the emergence of modernity. This rather important reflexive process, which had its roots in the literary and artistic presentation of images of industrialism in the novels of Charles Dickens, George Eliot and others (and later in sociological theorizing), illustrates a crucial feature of all human social action which is that it has an in-built reflexive capacity to define and constitute social reality. This is a sociological analogue to the self-reflexive capacity of human consciousness spoken of earlier in our discussions of Feuerbach and existentialism. But it is a feature which takes on a new and particularly radical dimension in modernity: what Giddens calls "the presumption of *wholesale* reflexivity", that is, the view that

> only in the era of modernity is the revision of convention radical-
> ized to apply (in principle) to all aspects of human life ... What
> is characteristic of modernity is not an embracing of the new for
> its own sake, but the presumption of wholesale reflexivity – which
> of course includes reflection upon the nature of reflection itself
> ... the equation of knowledge with certitude has turned out to
> be misconceived. We are abroad in a world which is thoroughly
> constituted through reflexively applied knowledge, but where at
> the same time we can never be sure that any given element of that
> knowledge will not be revised.[22]

Before progressing further we must explore the idea of "wholesale reflexivity" more fully. To do this we need to revisit what Habermas later christened "the Enlightenment project." The *philosophes* of the European Enlightenment sought to replace traditional established forms of knowledge based on religious authority with new forms of knowledge based on observation and experimental reasoning. Observation and reasoning were the two essential methodological requirements held to be the hallmark of genuine science and the gold standard of all acceptable knowledge. The publication of the initial volumes of the *Encyclopédie* in 1751 heralded their new secular bible. The Enlightenment's epistemological preference for a scientific world-view also had important implications for the religious legiti-mation of the absolute claims to power exercised by enlightened despots like Frederick the Great and Catherine the Great. The Enlightenment project, in so far as it captured, codified, and legiti-mated the emergence of a new intellectual authority (based on reason and observation *alone*), was rather like an intellectual time-bomb waiting for the right conditions to explode the dogmas of tradition, particularly religious tradition. The early growth of industrial society, of machine technology and science lent considerable support to the Enlightenment idea of the achievement of human social progress through the application of rationally based strategies. Such an image was central to early modernity and the aspirations of much early sociology. This central commitment to the idea of human progress through the application and development of science and technology, although perhaps not quite as unsullied as in its original optimistic form, is still a very prevalent one today and promises to be so in the twenty-first century and beyond.

The presumption of the Enlightenment project was that human reason offered greater certitude than traditional religious authority and that rationally founded strategies were to be regarded as the antithesis of any form of authoritarian dogma, either social, political or intellectual. As Giddens puts it, "the claims of reason replaced those of tradition".[23]

With the further unfolding of the contours of modernity in the twentieth century, the presumption that the application of observation and experimental reasoning gave epistemic access to indubitable knowledge came itself under rational scrutiny. The Enlightenment equation of knowledge with certainty, and the privileged status accorded to scientific knowledge, came to be radically questionable through the realization, brought about by the later phases of modernity, "that we can never be sure that any given element of that knowledge will not be revised".[24] The increasing awareness of the conjectural and provisional nature of *all* forms of knowledge, both social and scientific, has itself become a hallmark of modernity. When reason reflects upon itself (as Kant prompted it to do at the beginning of the Enlightenment period) it becomes increasingly aware of the provisional and ever-changing nature of its own rational productions. This is nowhere better illustrated than in Karl Popper's reflections on the nature of modern scientific theorizing, when he asserts "We cannot identify science with truth, for we think that both Newton's and Einstein's theories belong to science, but they cannot both be true, and they may well both be false".[25]

When we turn from the natural world to the modern social world, that is, from natural to social science, the phenomenon of self-reflexivity is further compounded. The increasing and "chronic revision of social practices"[26] (say, in education or health) characteristic of much contemporary post-industrial culture, makes old social certainties seem mutable, relatively less stable and ultimately deconstructable. And, more importantly, what passes for knowledge about these practices is a constitutive feature in determining the revision and alteration of such practices. For example, if divorce or single parent families or widespread non-marital cohabitation become common practice, the general availability of this information itself can tend to accentuate such practices without any reference to past practice or legitimation: it is just accepted as what *is*.

This intrinsically reflexive feature of social practices means that the generation of such practices emphasizes the contingent and replaceable discursive nature of these very practices themselves. It is a social reality in which there are few, if any, uncontested certainties and an ever-increasing amount of information about differential practices. It is this information itself which can help to reconfigure the cultural landscape, in that what passes for knowledge about a particular social practice at any given moment feeds back into the very perception of the practice's status, and its future. The whole process is fundamentally one of a constant reconfiguration of reflexive positioned discourses, each claiming its own validity, either on the grounds that that is how it is *now* or by invoking tradition. Giddens suggests that the role of tradition[27] is significantly less than is sometimes supposed and has always to be justified in the light of the reflexivity of the present.

It is necessary to introduce a serious caveat to this particular formulation of Giddens, particularly when considering the tradition on which Ibn 'Arabi's metaphysics of unity draws. There is a sense in which traditions, although they may sometimes have to be abandoned or reflexively reconfigured, can also be reflexively rediscovered. In relation to the self-monitoring and self-changing capacities of modernity, there is equally a need to re-discover (and perhaps reconfigure) the value of certain 'traditions' and incorporate this into its view of itself.

This would certainly be an important reflexive possibility when considering the re-emergence of Ibn 'Arabi's metaphysics of unity at the beginning of the twenty-first century. From this standpoint Ibn 'Arabi's ontology of the ever-new process of creation recasts the concept of reflexivity in terms of a cosmology of continuously renewed secondary causes. It is possible to regard the concept of reflexivity as another appellation for, or redescription of, the term secondary causes. This does not imply that modernity recognizes its own reflexivity under this description. If there were such a recognition then modernity would be beginning to view itself *sub specie aeternitatis*, to use Spinoza's expression. From the universal point of view of *wahdat al-wujud*, the reflexivity of modernity is the result of "Each day He is upon some task." Without this point of view the significance and status of modernity's wholesale reflexivity remains locked into a kind of unresolved relativity. This is partly why Ibn 'Arabi says that the world is its own veil. The theophanic grounds of modernity are likely to remain opaque to modern social theory if the analytical concentration focuses solely on the intricacies of the self-reflexive entanglements of modernity. Regarding the opacity of the world, he remarks "(The world) is to itself its own veil and thus cannot see God, due to the very fact that it sees itself."[28]

The ontology of the constant transmutation of phenomena locates the reflexivity of the modern era as essentially indicative of the Divine Self-reflexivity itself. To grasp the essential significance and reality of what we call modernity requires, for Ibn 'Arabi, a complete alignment to the Oneness of Being and the abrogation of any lesser point of view.

But to return to the domain of modern social theory. The overall impact of the constant (social) reconfiguration of modern social life alters the view of the validity of validity itself. It is often taken for granted, in line with the pro-scientific view of the Enlightenment, that it is natural science and technology which are the calling cards of modernity. But if Giddens is right and a central defining characteristic of modernity is its wholesale reflexivity, then "the social sciences are more deeply implicated in modernity than is natural science".[29] It is the social sciences, not physics or chemistry or biology or mathematics, that have thrown up the problems posed for the search for certainty by the processes of human and social reflexivity.

There is a sense in which sociology's central founding-figures – Marx, Durkheim and Weber – each portrayed their own particular image of industrial society. These views fed into the general socio-logical imagination and determined its trajectory, at least for while. Very broadly, the emergence of the modern era was influenced by the growth of industrialism, capitalism, urbanism and liberal democracy. Industrialism and capitalism are not necessarily, nor historically, co-extensive but their conjunction in the emergence of the Industrial Revolution, and the alignment of science and technology with the values of industrial commodity culture and the market profit economy, were crucial factors.

There are ongoing debates among the intellectual authorities of social science as to whether or not industrial society has given way to postmodernity. The intellectual strategies of the protagonists involved in these debates are relatively straightforward, in principle, at least: there are those who argue that the fairly recent qualitative social reconfigurations of modernity are no more than later phases of modernity and not qualitatively discontinuous from it, and there are those who deny this.

Of course, there have certainly been some quite radical and significant developments in the recent history of industrial and industrializing societies. There have been important consequences and changes which were not, and perhaps could never have been, envisaged by the classical triumvirate in their theorizings about what has been described as the birth of "a terrible beauty". A number of important developments in the modern era have become obvious to us in the twenty-first century in a way that the early analysts of modernity could not have readily conceived or predicted. Following Giddens,[30] we may agree that two of the most important developments are: (1) the sheer rapidity of change observed, amongst other things, in the ubiquitous pervasion of technology in all spheres of modern life, and (2) the global nature of social transformation, communication and capital.

Other writers, such as Stephen Hill, have identified additional aspects of this process in the location of a widespread commodification of human consciousness. Hill argues that people tend to become profoundly identified with the industrial, educational, and technological organizations they serve and, as consumers, are constantly seeking happiness in the commodity market. And, even more pervasively, he suggests that commodity culture "mediates our consciousness of self" in an analogous manner to the way technology "mediates our relationship with, and engagement in, nature".[31] Hill's thesis, whilst having some affinities with Marx's concept of commodity fetishism, associates these developments with the danger of a reduction in the quality of our private internal worlds. He refers to the mirroring of human subjectivity in the "technological frame".

There are many other consequences of modernity which might be characterized as *unintended*. Perhaps the most obvious unintended consequence is the ecological crisis. This crisis itself demonstrates that the industrial free-market paradigm of calculative rationality, profit and maximizing efficiency may be a somewhat irrational and counter-productive paradigm when viewed from an ecological perspective. And one might add to this list of unintended consequences the far-reaching and unforeseen effects of reproductive technology on women's lives, choices and relations. What we have is a kind of catalogue of the intended and unintended consequences of the great transformation to modernity: its promises, dangers, and present condition.

Of the three classical founders, Weber was the most ambiguous regarding the benefits of material progress; whilst Marx and Durkheim clearly acknowledged the human costs, they hoped they would only be temporary. Weber alone seems to have envisaged a great (and seemingly permanent) human price that had to be paid for the benefits of industrial progress. He describes this human price as a new "iron cage"[32] of serfdom. By this he meant the meteoric rise and permeation of bureaucratic rationality in all facets of modern life. Weber suggests that the impersonal logic and power of bureaucracy meant the rise of "specialists without spirit, sensualists without heart". For Weber, modernity was the age of the rule book – of predominantly instrumental forms of rationality which he called *Zweck-rational*. Abstract, calculable and impersonal procedures increasingly replaced sentiment and tradition in all areas of modern life. Modernity, then, came to be pre-eminently characterized by the omnipresence of bureaucratic rationality. Whatever the degree

of truth there was – or still is – in Weber's prediction of the consequences of bureaucratic rationality in modern industrial culture, what
is clear is the force of his distaste of such a prospect. In spite of
his vitriolic criticisms of "soulless" bureaucracy, he also thought it
was equally futile to give oneself up to a posture of mere emotional
opposition to capitalism and its bureaucratic structures. According to
Weber one had inevitably to put up with the "disenchanted world"
increasingly engendered by modern capitalism and science and
technology.

But there is an equally important point to be made. As Kumar[33]
remarks, the characterizations of industrial capitalism given by Marx,
Durkheim and Weber are not simply scientific accounts: they are,
equally, exhortations. One must add, I think, that they are *moral*
exhortations. Their theorizings are as much moral projects as they are
scientific. In this way all three were following the Baconian and the
Enlightenment precept that the only justification for scientific and
technological knowledge was that it was socially beneficial to human
kind. Kumar further notes that their respective theorizing about the
nature of the industrializing process, for whatever reason, "put upon
it a peculiar colour, bias and pressure". And, he continues, that at their
source such an interpretation:

> seems to lie as much in artistic intuition, and particular glimpses
> and insights, as in the scientific accumulation and examination
> of evidence. No one can avoid that impression when reading,
> say, Max Weber on the rise of the Protestant ethic in Europe,
> George Simmel on "the metropolis and mental life", Marx on
> the alienating and dehumanizing effects of the capitalist economy,
> or Emile Durkheim on the disturbing state of *anomie* produced
> by the transition to the industrial society.

As well as being reminiscent of our earlier discussion concerning
the importance which Ibn 'Arabi attaches to the predispositional
refraction of reality through the eyes of the theorizer, Kumar's
statement, whilst not denying the important role that imagination and
intuition play in scientific theorizing, recognizes also that such images
of industrialism are partial viewpoints. It is perhaps this recognition of the relativity of *all* such theoretical viewpoints which is at the

source of the reflexivity of modernity. The reflexivity which Giddens cites as a defining characteristic of modernity is radical and wholesale because, in the history of modernity, it has penetrated *all* domains of human intellectual and social knowledge. It is essentially another version of Nietzsche's dictum that all human knowledge is perspectival, with the addendum that such perspectival points of view are in constant creation, co-existence and reconfiguration.

This matter can be approached from another sociological direction – that of sociological theories of history and historical change. Weber (unlike Marx) did not hold to a theory of history, or a theory of historical inevitability, or overall causality; his was a theory of *historical change*, not a theory of *history* in Marx's sense. Marx's theory of history usually revolves round two theoretical positions: scientific marxism and praxis marxism. Scientific marxism implies a view of the inevitability of historical change and direction, whereas praxis marxism implies that human agents make history under given cultural conditions which may take advantage of existing cultural trends. Either way, marxism implies a theory of the *direction* of history. This is not so for Weber. For him, the direction of history can be changed radically, initiated by the emergence of charismatic individuals such as a Buddha-figure, or a Jesus-figure, or a Hitler. History remained, for Weber, forever open to changes of value and redirection. For him it was not, nor could it be, wedded to a permanent universal value-system. As any first-year student of sociology quickly learns, Weber placed a primary importance on the efficacious role of values and ideologies in any analysis of cultural phenomena. He radically rejected any mono-causal explanation of industrial capitalism in terms of its economic base or structure. Weber asserts emphatically that cultural phenomena cannot simply be deduced as a product of material and economic constellations. In other words, value-laden ideals, as well as economic factors, are intrinsic to explaining the rise of modern industrial capitalism or, for that matter, in explaining any historical era. He also rejects, as antiquated and simplistic, any mono-causal explanation of the rise of modernity. The heart of Weber's view regards the world-process as intrinsically a meaningless infinity upon which human beings project a "polytheism of values". In this way he reasserts the value-openness of the historical universe.

This is the basic Weberian metaphysic. The world-process, for Weber, is in a constant state of flux and potential value-conflict and, construed empirically as a polytheism of values, it is ultimately inexplicable: it just is. Social science, using rational methodologies, achieves at best a partial understanding of specific cultural segments in the history of that polytheistic process. Whilst it is clear that Weber's is a theory of historical change, it is not a theory of history. From his sociological studies of ancient Chinese, Hindu, Buddhist, Judaic and Christian cultures it is likely that he gained a lasting sense of the kaleidoscopic variety of cultural formations: a sense of the infinity of the world-process.

In summary, of the three founder-figures of classical sociology it is Weber who saw most clearly and was probably most theoretically affected by the vast Heraclitean flux of cultural phenomena. It is also interesting to note that Weber thought that the "eternally onward flowing stream of culture" which "perpetually brings new problems", granted the cultural sciences an "eternal youth".[34] Like the undertaker, the cultural scientist may never be out of a job – but then, neither were the followers of shadows in Plato's Cave.

The reorientation of the self: science, technology and industrialization

As we have seen, sociology was a new intellectual authority which emerged in nineteenth- and twentieth-century Europe. In an effort to establish its scientific status it needed to differentiate its subject matter from both biology and psychology. It also needed to establish the nature of its empirical methodology and the logic of its theory construction. As originators of a new emerging science the classical triumvirate of Marx, Durkheim and Weber all sought in their own ways to deal with the question of religion. Marx identified religion as a form of false or illusory consciousness which constituted "the opium of the people". Emile Durkheim attempted to reduce religion to morality, and to establish that morality was the social force which held society together. He saw religion properly as a symbolic representation of society itself: a kind of disguised or metaphorical way of talking about society. Sociologically, Durkheim regarded society as that on which we totally depend and from which we receive all that is best in ourselves; religions indirectly and symbolically represented this dependence in their allusions to the Sacred. On the other hand, Max Weber's immense contribution to the comparative study of civilizations – in such areas as society and religion in China, society and religion in India, Buddhism, Judaism, the social organization of ancient Palestine – reveals a more thorough and complex sociological understanding of the place of religion. He considered religions as systems of value, or world-views, intrinsically providing accounts of what human beings are, what they ought to be, and how they ought to live. Weber insists that the validity, or otherwise, of such world-views cannot be decided by empirical science, particularly social science, making an important theoretical distinction between questions of moral or religious *values* and questions of scientific or empirical *fact*. As Eldridge[35] points out, Weber quotes Tolstoy's words with approval: "Science is meaningless because it gives no answer to our question, the only question really important for us [is]: 'What shall we do and how shall we live?'" For Weber, then, science, including social science, can offer no guidance on questions of fundamental value-preference; science remains a strictly empirical discipline. This insistence by Weber on the radical distinction between questions of fact and questions of value, or questions about what *is* and questions about what *ought* to be, is clearly reflected in his famous essay *Science as Vocation* when he asserts, "What man will take upon himself the attempt to 'refute scientifically' the ethic of the Sermon on the Mount?"[36] Weber envisaged social life as a "polytheism of values" always in potential conflict: for him this was the only empirically or scientifically correct position for a sociologist to take. Weber's view of science can take him no further than this conclusion; given his epistemological assumptions regarding the meaningless infinity of the world-process, there cannot be any view other than this. For Weber, there is no possibility of viewing the whole as a whole. As W. G. Runciman asserts, it is a basic assumption of Weberian metaphysics "that reality cannot be grasped by the human mind as a meaningful whole".[37] And, for Weber, there is no other epistemic means available.

It is pertinent to recall here what was said earlier concerning the basic epistemological orientation of Ibn 'Arabi's *wahdat al-wujud*, namely, that the basic question becomes "Who is known?" rather than "What is known?" Such an epistemological redirection of emphasis situates contemporary empirical science rather differently from Weber. Rather than science being impotent *vis-à-vis* "the only question really important for us", modern science (and we can equally include modern technology) would be envisaged as part of the Self-disclosure of the One Unique Being in Its love to be known. In this sense it would not be epistemologically correct to divorce science from the fundamental meaning and value of human existence: it is inextricably entangled in human possibility and already determines for the modern era many aspects of how we should live and what we should do. Science is thoroughly embedded in the matrix of modernity: it is clearly one of the defining and governing determinants of the era. The neat, perhaps over-neat, distinction between facts and values is epistemologically inverted when it is recognized that the whole as a whole has intrinsic meaning and value and that all the known and knowable facts which constitute the cosmos (including its atomic structure, its geology, its civilizations) reflect and constitute that very same meaning and value.

In the particular case of the *history* of science and technology (and its production, development and use) it is impossible to disentangle its trajectory from questions of human aspiration and value. In his brilliant study, *Technics and Civilization*, Lewis Mumford remarks:

> the fact is that in Western Europe the machine had been developing steadily for at least seven centuries before the dramatic changes that accompanied the "industrial revolution" took place. Men had become mechanical before they perfected complicated machines to express their new bent and interest; and the will-to-order had appeared once more in the monastery and the army and the counting-house before it finally manifested itself in the factory. Behind all the great material inventions of the last century and a half was not merely a long internal development of technics: there was also a change of *mind* [my italics]. Before new industrial processes could take hold on a great scale, a reorientation of wishes, habits, ideas, goals was necessary.[38]

For Mumford, science and technology had its roots in a new, emerging form of human consciousness which ideologically and cognitively paved the way for its future scale and development.

By about the seventeenth century, Mumford argues, "the power of the technical imagination had far outstripped the actual capacities of workmen and engineers" – but this was soon to change. Even so, at this earlier stage in the development of technics, this profound reorientation towards the development of *technical imagination* and technological consciousness was a crucial precursor of the later eighteenth-century European Enlightenment belief that science and technology heralded the human conquest of nature itself. According to Mumford, the idea of the perfection of the world through the machine was deeply rooted in human consciousness. He summarizes this part of his argument by pointing out that "the machine was the substitute for Plato's justice, temperance and courage, even as it was likewise for the Christian ideals of grace and redemption. The machine came forth as the new demiurge that was to create a new heaven and a new earth; at the least, as a new Moses that was to lead a barbarous humanity into the promised land."[39] From the hindsight of the twenty-first century we may well give a more sober estimate of what has been accomplished of the "promised land". But what cannot be denied is the irreversible change and reorientation of ideas that occurred, amounting to a qualitative and climatic change in human consciousness and aspiration. It was the emergence of a new scientific and technological attitude towards nature, towards knowledge, and towards the world in general. Mumford interestingly reports that:

> The machine itself, however, is a product of human ingenuity and effort: hence to understand the machine is not merely a first step toward re-orienting our civilization: it is also a means towards understanding society and towards *knowing ourselves* [my italics].[40]

This attitude and intellectual reorientation of the self was codified in the publication of the *Encyclopédie* in 1751. With the emergence of industrial society in the 1780s and the eventual wholesale alignment of science and technology with the values and economics of industrial capitalism, the modern era was born out of conditions prevalent and confined to the West. Science, technology, and economics became the calling cards of modernity. Associated with industrialization was, of course, a massive increase in the world population in general and in nineteenth-century Europe in particular. As Kumar points out, up until about 1750, citing Heckscher's phrase,

> "Nature audited her account with a red pencil". Then, from about 1750 onwards, there was a population revolution. Between 1650 to 1850 the annual rate of increase of the world's population doubled, and doubled again by the 1920s. From the 1940s and 1960s there was another great acceleration ... an increase, in the space of just over twenty years, of more than the *total* estimated population of the world in 1800.[41]

There is the view that in the case of Europe the demographic revolution and the industrial revolution were "intrinsically connected".[42] But as Max Weber observes in his studies of society and religion in China (mainly concerned with Confucianism and Taoism), there was also between the late 1500s and the early eighteenth century a doubling of the population from 60 million to 120 million. This explosion, according to Weber, was coupled with other factors which favoured the development of a Chinese capitalist economy. But, he argues, the prevailing mind-set of the Chinese *literati*, the patriarchal structure of the state and the powerful tradition of the extended family, strongly mitigated against any such development. If Weber's analysis is correct then the profound "change of mind, the reorientation of wishes, habits, ideas, goals necessary before new industrial processes could take hold on a great scale" (to which Mumford refers) was not strongly enough present, if it existed at all, in this period of Chinese history.

One may say, in general, that the existence of science and technology alone is not an intrinsic condition of the modern era. It is the *alignment* of science and technology with the social values and economics of industrial capitalism which further characterized the "Great Transformation". The European demographic transition clearly should be included when assessing such cultural transformation, but in itself this did not constitute a sufficient condition. Also, as Kumar insists, "whether population growth itself forced on economic development, or was a consequence of that development" is a moot point.[43]

But let us return to the question of technology. Although science and technology are clearly inter-related, their development has often been asymmetrical. In the mid-eighteenth century, for example, Newtonian physics contributed virtually nothing to the developing technologies of the day, at least not to those technologies recorded in the engravings of the *Encyclopédie*. The relationship between science, technology and society are historically and conceptually complex. It is sometimes the case that "technology determines further technology": "Given the boat and the steam engine, is not the steamboat inevitable?"[44] Alternatively, the so-called inspirational theory of technological invention – in which a particular invention is categorically assigned to a time, place and individual inventor – often underestimates that "existing technology is … an important precondition of new technology" and that much "technical change … is often a 'perpetual accretion of little details' … a process Gilfillan saw at work in the gradual evolution of the ship."[45] Most contemporary arguments about technology are usually decidedly sceptical about the thesis that changes in technology cause social change. The objections are that such a thesis is conceptually naive and fails to see the crucial *shaping* of the development of technology by the political, social and economic values of particular societies. Technological determinism seems to imply the view that technology can be viewed as a sovereign causal factor in social change and such a view is held to be conceptually inadequate. Advocates of the thesis of technological determinism, in its futuristic mode, make such causal claims as that the microchip will force us to "change our ideas of work and leisure" or that "it is changes in technology that are bringing about the new leisure society".[46] Perhaps, in the popular imagination, the ubiquitous nature of modern technology and our apparently crucial dependence on computerized technological systems seems to confirm the causal inevitability of technology and technological advance: there is no turning back. What is often overlooked, though, is that technology is essentially a human product and its future direction depends on human decisions and values: personal, political, economic and educational. This crucial dependence of the trajectory of technology on human decisions and values is apparent in all the main areas of technology: industrial, military, reproductive, medical and domestic. The development and use of technology – and, similarly, science – reflects the values of society. Which technologies and which aspects of science are promoted will, in general, be determined by their alignment with the aspirations and values of modern industrial and post-industrial society. In this respect, many feminists have noticed that the future development of science and technology will inevitably be affected by the gendered nature of the scientific, educational and political institutions of modernity. As Ruth Cowan points out,

> The indices to the standard histories of technology … do not contain a single reference, for example, to such a significant cultural artefact as the baby bottle. Here is a simple implement … which has transformed a fundamental human experience for vast numbers of infants and mothers, and has been one of the more controversial exports of Western technology to under developed countries – yet it finds no place in our histories of technology.[47]

These remarks on the nature of technology indicate unambiguously that technology is always ideologically aligned and never value-neutral: it always serves some perceived human need or aim. Any purely instrumental definition of technology as a means to an end implicitly locates technology in a number of value-laden contexts: the context of human power (for example, the technology which allows multi-national companies to function outside democratic control), the context of social life (that is, technology as a form of industrial and post-industrial life) and, finally, it locates technology in the context of human ideals (for example, technology as the key to freedom from toil). This is what the existentialist Heidegger is partly referring to in his enigmatic statement that "the essence of technology has nothing to do with technology". For Heidegger, modern technology is "a revealing" and "a representing", and what it reveals and represents is a human mind-set, or a set of values and attitudes towards the world. In particular, modern technology reveals a human attitude towards nature. It is an attitude which treats nature, according to Heidegger, as a particular kind of "standing reserve". As he puts it, the "earth now reveals itself as a coal-mining district, the soil as a mineral deposit".[48] Such is the case that the technological mind-set of modernity increasingly "enframes" our view of the world to the relative devaluation of other forms of "revealing", as can be seen in the devaluation of self-knowledge as an epistemology for revealing and understanding the nature of the world around us.

The general and recurring theme which informs much sociological discussion of modern technology is, therefore, that of its propensity to enslave or liberate. Such an either/or strategy, whilst it needs to be treated with some caution, does recognize a symbiotic connection between the modern technological frame and the quality of human subjectivity. This point is interestingly brought out in Stephen Hill's *The Tragedy of Technology*, and David Cooper's opening contribution to a series of essays called *Philosophy and Technology*. As we have already mentioned, Hill contends that the sense of self is increasingly becoming mediated by the technological frame. Cooper, in similar vein, talks about the fragmenting of the resources of the self. He says, for example, that "within a society geared to technological progress, and honouring the faculties which contribute to it, moral conviction, religious sense, taste and sensibility play only bit parts". Taste, morality, and religion tend to be regarded as optional, secondary and non-essential aspects of the human subject: the essential characteristics of a person, in this technological age, are seen as "reason and knowledge". But "regrettably, the person is unable to live by these alone" suggests Cooper.[49]

Such remarks concerning the nature and effects of modern technology, whatever we may make of them, are variations on the Weberian thesis that modern society is increasingly dominated by instrumental forms of rationality (*Zweck-rational*) rather than value-rationality (*Wert-rational*). For Weber, the decreasing status of value-rationality and the increasing status accorded to means-end rationality is part of the general "disenchantment of the world" associated with the rise of modern science, technology and industrialization.

If Weber is right in his thesis about the "disenchantment of the world", then perhaps it is opportune that the works of Ibn ʿArabi are becoming increasingly available to English-speaking cultures at the beginning of the twenty-first century. It is interesting to note in this respect that one of the titles bestowed upon Ibn ʿArabi was "revivifier of religion". The *wahdat al-wujud* of Ibn ʿArabi reveals a re-enchanted picture of the world as the ever-renewed Disclosure of Being. In this context, science and technology – rather than negating this world-picture – reveal, almost in a Heideggerian sense, the extraordinary potentiality and possibilities of Being. The metaphysics of *wahdat al-wujud* invites us to see the technological, scientific and economic contours of the modern era from a different and more universal vantage point. And the metaphysics of unity of Ibn 'Arabi is undoubtedly capable of revivifying and reconfiguring the quality and epistemology of human subjective experience: of enframing it in a universal perspective.

It is curious that Weber himself felt compelled to adopt a metaphysical stance (i.e. the meaningless infinity of the world process) which precluded him from adopting a more universal point of view. This is even more curious as Weber, by his own admission, was acutely aware of the limitations of sociological knowledge and very much affected by what his sociological findings revealed to him about the future prospects of industrial society and human destiny. In almost Akbarian fashion, he recognized the constant transformation of the cosmos and observed that "as soon as we attempt to reflect about the way in which life confronts us in immediate concrete situations, it presents an infinite multiplicity of successively and coexistently emerging and disappearing events both 'within' and 'outside' ourselves. The absolute infinitude of this multiplicity is seen to remain undiminished even when our attention is focused upon a single 'object'."[50] Weber also recognized that social science cannot give "a causal explanation of even an individual fact in any final sense, nor exhaustively describe the smallest slice of reality".[51] He also knew that the social scientist cannot approach his studies "without presuppositions" and that such presuppositions are imposed by the investigator on reality rather than drawn from it. The value-orientation of the social scientist is, for Weber, double-edged: it ensures that there cannot be any absolutely objective scientific analysis of culture and yet simultaneously makes science possible. It was clear for him that social science cannot be value-free in the sense that the assumptions, values and conceptualizations of the world made by social scientists, as Runciman notes, "cannot claim any objective validity themselves".[52] From this, therefore, we can see that Max Weber identifies, in his own manner, a number of salient factors which have an effect on the power of human reason to explain anything at all in a final sense.

There are, therefore, a number of important Akbarian insights isomorphically echoed in the epistemological motifs of Weberian metaphysics: (a) the limitation of human reason to uncover anything but an infinitesimal fraction of reality, (b) the constantly changing flux of the world-process and human experience, and (c) the presuppositional colouring of the investigator. But without the unitive ontology of Ibn 'Arabi's *wahdat al-wujud* these insights yield a very different conclusion indeed. These differences become acutely apparent in the following extract from "Weber as a theorist of modernity" by Bryan S. Turner:

> Weber's own view of his work (namely, to understand the characteristic uniqueness of our times) can probably be best understood as a quest after the nature of modernity. Weber's interests in rational law, administration, military technology, religious ethics and so forth can be seen in a broader context as a set of investigations into the peculiarities of modernity and in particular its fateful or even demonic properties. ... Like Marx, Weber believed that in capitalistic modernity "All that is solid melts into air" ... Modernization disrupts the traditional order and the ideology by which traditional authorities made the world intelligible and legitimate. Modernity questions everything against a unitary principle of rationality ... but Weber recognized that this questioning of reality by reason was ultimately self-defeating and self-destructive. Rationality began to question its own horizons, recognizing its self-limitation. How can reason be rationally justified? Are there many forms of reason? Is reason (in the shape of instrumental rationality) in fact life-denying? ... these questions had their origin in Neitzsche's probing of language, knowledge and power ... As we have seen these question increasingly haunted Weber's sociology.[53]

Putative answers to these questions have led, in the recent history of academic sociology, to a radical questioning of the "assumptions and certainties about the rational project of modernity".[54] Such deliberations about the nature of human reason and its limits have led, as we shall see, to further conceptual entanglements under the rubric of

postmodernism. However, they have not yet led to what Ibn 'Arabi
called "the domain beyond reason" or to the conception of the Unity
of Existence. But a deeper understanding of the perspectival nature of
much human knowledge has developed which interestingly opens up
the whole question of different kinds of epistemic affordances. This
notion of the type of epistemic access and what it can give access to
is a very important idea. In one way the whole of the present study
is heading towards an understanding of this idea. We can summarize the idea thus: that what there is, and what one finds out about
what there is, crucially depends on the particular type of epistemic
approach used by the investigator. Experimental methods are one
possible set of affordances, phenomenological investigations another.
However, there are many possible affordances: humanistic, political, religious, for example. As a prelude to further discussion of this
important issue it is useful, then, to examine how the implications of
Nietzsche's insight into the perspectival nature of all human knowledge has been taken up and utilized in the modernism/postmodernism
controversy regarding the nature of modernity and its epistemological
paradigms.

Modernity, postmodernity and relativism

As mentioned earlier in this chapter, central to much of the critical
literature on the postmodernist challenge to the assumptions of
modernist theory is a discussion and evaluation of what, in his contemporary defence of it, Jürgen Habermas named "the Enlightenment
project." In contrast to what he regards as the "metaphysical" or
religious terms of pre-modernity, the eighteenth century European
Enlightenment heralded the *ideals* of non-metaphysical, scientific and
technological forms of rationality. For Habermas the term "metaphysical" is a pejorative term and he dismisses it with a hostility
reminiscent of logical positivism. Scientific and technological
forms of thinking are, of course, regarded, by him as fundamentally
non-metaphysical in nature. He also identifies two other forms of
non-metaphysical thinking: namely, art and morality. In this way
the concept of what constitutes legitimate forms of rational discourse
is extended to include morality and aesthetics. This move counters

the original Enlightenment tendency to restrict the rational to the scientific, the technological and the logico-mathematical. For Habermas, non-metaphysical forms of rationality constitute the defining characteristics of modernity and indicate its intrinsically scientific world-view. This epistemological orientation differentiates modernity from pre-modernity and, if we are to follow Habermas, it holds the key to human progress. What he offers is a purified view of knowledge denuded of what he considers to be unverifiable speculative metaphysics, religious dogma, intolerance, magic and mystification. This ideal of knowledge was bequeathed to us by the Enlightenment epoch. The Enlightenment was essentially future-oriented, rational and emancipatory, and for Habermas it is an ongoing unfinished project. Sometimes the Enlightenment ideals have been described as a set "of beliefs and expectations about the role of knowledge in the improvement of the human condition".[55] Put like this the Enlightenment project may seem eminently reasonable in its epistemological recommendations. But such a broad generalization of the beliefs and expectations of the *philosophes* tends to obscure the fact that they did, at least in the *Encyclopédie*, promote a very particular view of what constituted legitimate human knowledge. Their foundational ideas of validity, rationality and truth were based on the paradigm of science (they were deeply impressed by the new Newtonian physics): reason and observation were the sole means for the scientific interrogation of nature and for the attainment of impartial and objective truths. The postmodern onslaught is essentially a radical critique of this Enlightenment view of rationality and truth and the privileged status it has achieved in modernity.

Lyotard subtitles his canonical text *The Postmodern Condition*: "A report on knowledge". This seminal work has come to possess the status of an inaugural statement of postmodernist theory. It is fundamentally an *epistemological critique* and it is Lyotard's assessment of the nature of knowledge that will inform the present discussion.

A useful way of approaching postmodernist epistemology is to consider it in relation to Habermas's defence of the Enlightenment project. But it is salutary to remember that in his defence of the Enlightenment Habermas admits that "the brutal history" of the twentieth century makes it impossible to countenance any naive view of the difficulties facing such a project. For Habermas the Enlightenment project is incomplete: we have not yet seen its full, true or potential benefits. Its ideals must not be underestimated and are as crucial as ever to the emancipation of the human mind and the promotion of rational practice: we abandon such ideals at our peril. Those postmodernists who attempt to deconstruct or devalue such forms of rationality can do so only because they themselves have already benefited from them. He reminds us of "the *positive* role of the original Enlightenment epoch".[56] Through the application of rational discourse, he argues, "the self-determination of all was to be joined with the self-realization of each." Habermas encapsulates what he means by this in his notion of "communicative action". His use of this term is well summarized by Best and Kellner as constituting a form of "undistorted communication" (Habermas's own locution) "based on a willingness to engage in rational discourse on topics of controversy, to allow free and equal access, to all participants, to attempt to understand the issues and arguments, to yield to the force of the better argument, and to accept rational a consensus".[57] He holds the view that through the processes of open-ended rational discourse some degree of agreement can be reached about how to decide "what is true and good".[58] However, we must remember that Habermas rules out of the modernist rational agenda "the mythological, cosmological, religious and ontological modes of thought" of pre-modernity.[59] His view of reason is one which is purified of its two major distorting metaphysical elements: "dogma" and "ultimate grounds". Given this purified view of human reason, each and every act of discursive communication is potentially an act of emancipation from distorting assumptions and practices which will then allow rationally resolvable "disputes concerning the truth of statements or the correctness of norms".[60]

Habermas's intellectual optimism (or, one might say, his faith in this purified form of reason) accepts that there are universal shared criteria of rationality which cut across the great divides of linguistic, cultural and value-orientation in the contemporary world. These shared criteria make possible mutual translation and understanding between different linguistic and cultural traditions and provide the context in which arguments "about what is good and true" can be productively engaged in. Habermas's view envisages the whole process of cultural evolution as an ongoing removal of forms of distortion through rational, social processes of open discussion and communicative interaction. He unremittingly defends the relative autonomy of reason and its essentially arbitrating function, which function, for Habermas, is located in the consensus and agreement that can be reached through it.

There is much to be recommended in such a view. Let us take, for example, the formal principle of *respect for persons*. This principle is one which would be likely to command general rational consensus and agreement in the manner envisaged by Habermas. In fact, for Ibn ʿArabi (and in the context of this present study), this principle would be an excellent example of where human reason rules over those human prejudices and passions incompatible with the intrinsic sacredness of human life: a situation in which it is both proper and necessary for reason to rule over personal irrational caprice. As Ibn ʿArabi puts it "For reason delimits its possessor, not allowing him to enter into that which is improper."[61]

More generally, however, the arguments deployed in the defence of such a universal and formal principle do not often, if ever, stand alone: they are holistically embedded in particular and often disparate humanistic, religious or cultural traditions, each possessing its own metaphysical picture of human nature. It is these incommensurable metaphysical architectures of the self which can engender permanent rational disagreement involving essentially contested concepts of the self, and are, in themselves, not necessarily such formal ethical principles.

In this respect let us consider the spiritual tradition of Ibn ʿArabi and its affirmation that the human being is "the highest and most venerable creature God ever created". What sustains Ibn ʿArabi's unequivocal remarks on the sacredness of human life is the metaphysical picture which locates human kind as the *raison d'être* of God's creative act: "God so exalted man that he placed under his control all that is in the heavens and the earth from its highest to its lowest".[62] In Ibn ʿArabi's view the dignity of man cannot be overrated and the preservation of the human species has a fundamental ontological priority over "religious bigotry, with its consequent destruction of ... human souls, even if it is for the sake of God and the maintenance of law".[63] Whilst Adamic kind scientifically, quantitatively, and geocentrically might be considered to be a mere speck in the universe, in terms of Ibn 'Arabi's account of what the human prototype qualitatively and spiritually synthesizes and summarizes of the Divine order then, by comparison, it is the universe which can be considered infinitely small. From this perspective it is not the cosmos which embraces human kind but the heart of the *insan-i-kamil* which embraces the cosmos.

This metaphysical inversion of our usual scientifically inspired picture of the place of the human species in the universe is not the outcome of inferential deliberation or rational arbitration. It is a visionary cosmology that "gathers up large portions" of human experience and metaphysically transforms them.[64] Reason may seek to articulate such a new vision but it does not originate it. It may variously be described as a new metaphysics, or a new metaphor, or a new perspective as long as it is recognized that it not only reconceptualizes our understanding of what constitutes undistorted communication but equally reconfigures the means by which such communication can be achieved. Ibn 'Arabi certainly does not see logical inference and rational arbitration as the key here. In quite a different context, neither does Lyotard. Any claim which advocates the autonomous, consensus directed, universal arbitration of human reason as the royal road to the solution of human problems is in the service of what Lyotard calls the "meta-narratives" of modernity. It is against these meta-narratives that the postmodernist Lyotard directs our incredulity. Meta-narratives are those overarching narratives of religion, politics, and ethics which bestow value and meaning on our lives and futures.

As a prelude to the further analysis of Lyotard's term meta-narrative, let us first consider the grounds on which Lyotard bases his attack on Habermas's "consensus-through-discussion" thesis. It is an evaluation which acknowledges the diversity, essential contestability and incommensurability of many of the "language games" which constitute contemporary social life. Lyotard asks, "Is legitimacy to be found in consensus obtained through discussion, as Jürgen Habermas thinks? Such consensus does violence to the heterogeneity of language games. And invention is always born of dissension. Post-modern knowledge is not simply a tool of the authorities; it refines our sensitivity to differences and reinforces our ability to tolerate the incommensurable."[65] Lyotard's postmodernism embraces an openness to a diversity and variety of ways of life and knowing which cannot be subsumed or judged under a single overarching spectatorial view of human reason. For Lyotard there is no such epistemologically privileged position. This is reminiscent of both Nietzsche's perspectival view of knowledge and Weber's metaphysics of the meaningless infinity of the world process onto which human beings project an almost infinite number and variety of cultural values. Lyotard's postmodernist acknowledgement of the "heterogeneity of language games" has led him to be accused of "uncritical polytheism".[66] But Lyotard's account is only uncritical in one direction: he certainly has no hesitation in criticizing those language games which he describes as the meta-narratives of modernity. Equally, to engage in such a posture of "incredulity towards meta-narratives" presupposes that there are overarching universal criteria of rational assessment. Much of the criticism levelled against Lyotard has revolved round his allegedly unremitting (and ultimately self-contradictory) tendency to relativism. But perhaps this is too easy and facile a criticism which fails to extract what is the real issue, even if Lyotard himself oscillates in his analysis of the problem.

According to our reading of the nature of essential contestability and, in the light of Ibn 'Arabi's comments on the proper playing field of human reason, human choice between incommensurable metaphysical pictures of the world has as much to do with the predispositional aptitude of the chooser as it is to do with any rational strategies. These two points are fundamental for they mean that, in fact, human reason alone cannot, in principle, be the decisive arbitrator. To some extent, Lyotard's postmodernist affirmation of different ways of life and ways of knowing, and his denial that any *one* form of rationality can claim arbitrating superiority, echoes some of these themes. But as Giddens comments,

> Rather than these developments taking us "beyond modernity",
> they provide a fuller understanding of the reflexivity inherent in

modernity itself. Modernity is not only unsettling because of the circularity of reason, but because the nature of that circularity is puzzling ... Modernity turns out to be enigmatic at its core, and there seems to be no way in which this enigma can be "overcome". We are left with questions where once there appeared to be answers, and I shall argue subsequently that it is not only philosophers who realize this. A general awareness of the phenomenon filters into anxieties which press on everyone.[67]

We are now in a better position to consider Lyotard's attack on the so-called meta-narratives of modernity. These typically include such things as the Enlightenment ideas concerning human progress through the advancement of science and technology, the ideology of human welfare and wealth creation, the marxist theory of the emancipation of the working subject, and so on. Such meta-narratives, for Lyotard, are ideological constructions rather than universal truths: they are the defining myths of modernity on a par with Greek mythology or Hindu cosmology. They are to be treated with profound incredulity, whether such stories "are to do with the historical march of Reason, Civilization, Wealth or the Proletariat",[68] or, one might add, religion. Lyotard carefully excludes science from his category of the meta-narrative but this does not leave science unscathed. When science and technology are aligned with the mythical discourses of human progress, and the promises of commodity culture, they become ideologically impregnated. They lose their epistemological purity.

But science itself is a form of discourse, although it does not constitute a meta-narrative in Lyotard's sense, except perhaps when science becomes a form of scientism. But it is analytically useful to pursue the idea of science as a form of discourse. As we know, science is in the business of producing causal narratives (or stories) which are constantly subject to rational scrutiny and revision. If we are to follow Rom Harré's account of the logical status of the causal stories and causal laws of modern science (for example, the Big Bang, black holes, anti-matter, the genetic code, and so on) we interestingly learn that "we have to rid ourselves of a fundamental error that people make about science – and with which scientists themselves are consumed – which is that science is the pursuit of truth, and that scientists have some sort of special monopoly and special method by which they are going to arrive at this".[69] All that scientists have, according to Harré, "are some local facts and a few experiments". But what is equally informative is the dispositional picture of the natural and social world which this analysis presents:

> The world is a very rich source of dispositions – physicists are forever discovering new ones – but we have to have the right equipment to bring them out, to make them reveal themselves. The same idea has application in psychology. There are many things of which a person is capable but we do not know what they are until they are put in the right circumstances. There is a myth that people have fixed personalities, but it is now widely accepted that they do not. Rather, it is thought that people are all kinds of possibilities and that their capabilities, intelligence etc. depend on the demands put upon them … The idea, then, is that the world will show what we ask of it. If you are a physicist then it is with apparatus and experiments that you question the world.[70]

For Harré, therefore, science does not possess, contrary to popular rumour, the universal objective "truth-telling" status ascribed to it by many scientists themselves, and he continues with the statement that "we are no longer able to form a picture of what lies behind" our epistemic affordances.

But the main point resides in the underlying ontology described by Harré, which is of direct interest *vis-à-vis* Ibn 'Arabi's understanding of reality. If reality itself is dispositionally multi-faceted and capable of revealing very different aspects of itself depending on *the way it is approached*, then the epistemic access to reality which scientific methodologies afford constitute *one* form of access. For most of us there are many other forms of epistemic access which often reveal quite different, possibly incommensurable, aspects of reality. Such a pluralistic view, by its very logic, tends not to give a monopoly to any one method of revealing the dispositional richness of phenomena. It still remains open, of course, that some approaches may reveal *more* of the dispositional riches of phenomena than others. The proper conclusion seems to be that there are many forms of epistemic access to reality and that the approach of the physicist is but one. For Ibn 'Arabi, self-knowledge is another.

In the context of Akbarian metaphysics, self-knowledge, however, is not just one way among many, but the central key in our possession which can give epistemic access to the Unity of Being. And this key is itself a Divine gift. Ibn 'Arabi unambiguously reaffirms, "The Messenger of God said that there is no path to knowledge of God but knowledge of self, for he said, 'He who knows himself knows his Lord.' ... Hence he made you a signifier. That is, he made your knowledge of yourself signify your knowledge of Him."[71]

When seen from the perspective of Ibn 'Arabi's metaphysics of unity, Lyotard's postmodernist recognition of the sheer variety of ways of knowing fits well – perhaps rather unexpectedly – into a dispositional view of reality of the kind Ibn 'Arabi proposes, but it still remains unbridgeably distant from the Akbarian logic of self-knowledge. More positively, postmodernism has characteristically raised – in the name of reason – profound doubts about the foundations of reason itself, doubts aimed particularly at the promotion of the Enlightenment view of knowledge as a universal timeless truth. Lyotard was engaged to counter the codification of knowledge as a privileged mind-set guarded jealously by academics, scientists and philosophers. For him, knowledge is, sociologically speaking, embedded in a labyrinth of discourses, each with its own logic and criteria of assessment: in industrial society knowledge has become *commodified* – that is, geared to particular consumers and interest groups – and can claim little pretension to universality or privileged status. But as the authors of *Modernity and its Futures* remark, by way of redressing the postmodernist imbalance, modernity itself is "as much about intellectual puzzlement and existential doubt as it is about intellectual conviction in the powers of reason".[72]

It seems that the Kantian view of human reason as possessing an illegitimate propensity to view the whole as a whole informs both sides of the Habermas/Lyotard intellectual confrontation. For Habermas, traditional metaphysics has to be replaced with a non-metaphysical, pragmatic, enlightened and broad-based view of the processes of rationality and communicative action; whereas, for Lyotard, Habermas's championing of a revised view of the role and nature of human reason is on a par with the intellectual productions of traditional metaphysics. One way or another, therefore, *totalizing* metaphysics has come under attack. It is rejected either as potentially totalitarian, or it is rejected as the partial and local parading as the universal and objective.

Postmodernism has been summarized as an

> antinomian movement that assumes a vast unmaking of the Western mind ... deconstruction, decentering, disappearance, dissemination, demystification, discontinuity, *difference*, dispersion, etc. ... Such terms ... express an epistemological obsession with fragments or fractures, and a corresponding ideological commitment to minorities in politics, sex, and language. To think well, to feel well, to act well, to read well, according to the *episteme* of unmaking, is to refuse the tyranny of wholes.[73]

It is now appropriate to take stock of the modernist/postmodernist problematic *vis-à-vis* Ibn ʿArabi's cosmology of the perpetual Self-disclosure of Being. The fundamental epistemological orientation, for Ibn ʿArabi, is an epistemology of "Who is known?" – that is, "Who is known?" amidst, in, by and through the Heraclitian flux known as the era. For Ibn ʿArabi, the existence of the era is "the Breath of the Merciful". Neither the modernist theorizing of Habermas nor the postmodernist critique of knowledge of Lyotard envisages the possibility of such a radically alternative epistemological emphasis.

Postmodernism recognizes, as Tarnas remarks, that "Reality is not a solid, self-contained given but a fluid, unfolding process, an 'open universe', continually affected and moulded by one's actions and beliefs. ... One cannot regard reality as a removed spectator against a fixed object; rather, one is always and necessarily engaged in reality, thereby at once transforming it whilst being transformed."[74] But this postmodernist insight into the radical self-involving openness and continuous movement of reality issues in a form of epistemological relativity which veils the possibility of a more encompassing, universal point of view. In this respect postmodernist ontology would seem to provide an unusual example of what Ibn ʿArabi describes as the world being its own veil. Postmodernism only appears to be able to re-certify relativism.

In conclusion: both modernist and postmodernist theories of knowledge are human intellectual constructions which, if we are to follow the warnings of Ibn 'Arabi, cannot arrive at decisive certainty concerning knowledge of the Real. Modernism extols the efficacy of human reason and postmodernism affirms its inevitable relativity. Both are simply *theories* of knowledge which, from the point of view of Akbarian metaphysics, lack the theophanic epistemological credentials of *wahdat al-wujud*. When Giddens asserts that "modernity is enigmatic at its core, and there seems to be no way the enigma can be 'overcome'", he is perhaps not only attesting to the inability of the circularity of reason to overcome this enigma but also implicitly recognizing the boundaries of reason's own proper playing field. According to Ibn 'Arabi it is a kind of progress for reason to recognize its own epistemological boundaries, for it attests to the incapacity of human beings to reach knowledge of the Real via unaided reason. The enigma of modernity can therefore be seen as an indication that we take seriously the possibility of alternative epistemic means of grasping and recognizing the significance of the era. We can perhaps be reminded of what George Berkeley in *The Principles of Human Knowledge* records, "We should believe that God has dealt more bountifully with the sons of men than to give to them a strong desire for that knowledge which he had placed quite out of their reach."[75]

Before leaving this discussion on Ibn 'Arabi and the Era, there is a final observation which it is useful to make. For Ibn 'Arabi, the modern era with its particular determining qualities of science, technology, calculative rationality, globalization, its polytheism of values and its matrix of meta-narratives testifies, like all eras, to the ontological fact "Each day He is upon some task". The unique configuration of predominating qualities of the modern era which constitute what the historian Eric Hobsbawm described as "the greatest transformation in history since remote times" is none other than part of the infinity and inherent contents of the Self-disclosure of Being in Its love to be known. To envisage the era in this manner, or to contextualize it from the universal point of view of Ibn 'Arabi, is not to alter phenomena – for they are what they are – but to begin to see "the theatre of manifestation" from its own point of origin and essence rather than it being coloured by the predisposition of a particular theorizer. That such a universal vision is existentially possible and attainable is at the heart of Ibn 'Arabi's metaphysics.

To delve into this more fully we need to look now at how the concept of the Self is portrayed by Ibn 'Arabi and refracted in the lens of modern thought.

Notes

1 R. Tarnas, *The Passion of the Western Mind* (London, 1996), p. 411.
2 T. Izutsu, *Sufism and Taoism* (Berkeley, 1984), p. 215.
3 Izutsu, *Sufism and Taoism*, p. 492.
4 Izutsu, *Sufism and Taoism*, p. 206.
5 W. C. Chittick, *The Sufi Path of Knowledge* (Albany, NY, 1989), p. 97.
6 Chittick, *Sufi Path*, p. 101.
7 Chittick, *Sufi Path*, p. 13.
8 Chittick, *Sufi Path*, p. 395, n. 7.
9 Chittick, *Sufi Path*, p. 95.
10 Muhyiddin Ibn 'Arabi, *Ismail Hakki Bursevi's Translation of Kernel of the Kernel by Muhyiddin Ibn 'Arabi* [trans. from Ottoman Turkish by B. Rauf] (Sherborne, Gloucestershire, [1981]), p. 27.
11 Chittick, *Sufi Path*, p. 395, n. 7.
12 Izutsu *Sufism and Taoism*, p. 205.
13 Chittick, *Sufi Path*, p. 297.
14 A good example of the phenomena of inversion is the bowl of a sufficiently reflective spoon. If you look into the bowl of the spoon your image will be vertically inverted; if you turn the spoon over and look at what was the underside of the bowl your image will be laterally inverted.
15 Chittick, *Sufi Path*, p. 99.
16 Chittick, *Sufi Path*, p. 107.
17 Chittick, *Sufi Path*, p. 107.
18 Chittick, *Sufi Path*, p. 44.
19 K. Kumar, *Prophecy and Progress* (Harmondsworth, Middlesex, 1983), p. 47.
20 Kumar, *Prophecy and Progress*, p. 48.
21 Kumar, *Prophecy and Progress*, p. 48.
22 A. Giddens, *The Consequences of Modernity* (Cambridge, 1990), pp. 38–9.
23 Giddens, *Consequences*, p. 39.
24 Giddens, *Consequences*, p. 39.
25 B. Magee, *Popper* (London, 1990), p. 28.
26 Giddens, *Consequences*, p. 40.
27 Giddens, *Consequences*, p. 38.
28 Ibn 'Arabi. *The Wisdom of the Prophets*. Partial translation of the *Fusus al-Hikam*, from Arabic to French by T. Burckhardt, and from French to English by A. Culme-Seymour (Swyre Farm, Gloucestershire, 1975), p. 17.
29 Giddens, *Consequences*, p. 40.
30 Giddens, *Consequences*, pp. 40–78.
31 S. Hill, *The Tragedy of Technology* (London, 1988), p. 211.
32 M. Weber, *The Protestant Ethic and the Spirit of Capitalism*, trans. T. Parsons (London, 1967).
33 Kumar, *Prophecy and Progress*, p. 52.
34 J. E. T. Eldridge, ed., *Max Weber* (London, 1972), p. 13.
35 Eldridge, *Max Weber*, p. 10.

36 M. Weber, "Science as a vocation", in *From Max Weber*, ed. H. H. Gerth and C. Wright Mills (London, 1970), p. 148.
37 W. G. Runciman, *Weber Selections* (Cambridge, 1978), p. 4.
38 L. Mumford, *Technics and Civilisation* (London, 1934), p. 3.
39 Mumford, *Technics and Civilisation*, p. 58
40 Mumford, *Technics and Civilisation*, p. 6.
41 Kumar, *Prophecy and Progress*, p. 75.
42 Kumar, *Prophecy and Progress*, p. 75.
43 Kumar, *Prophecy and Progress*, p. 75.
44 D. MacKenzie and J. Wajcman, eds., *The Social Shaping of Technology* (Milton Keynes, 1988), pp. 9–10.
45 MacKenzie and Wajcman, *Social Shaping*, p. 10.
46 MacKenzie and Wajcman, *Social Shaping*, p. 5.
47 R. Cowan, cited in MacKenzie and Wajcman, *Social Shaping*, p. 23.
48 M. Heidegger, *The Question of Technology and Other Essays*, trans. W. Lovitt (New York, 1977), p. 14.
49 D. Cooper, "Technology: liberation or enslavement?", in *Philosophy and Technology*, ed. R. Fellows (Cambridge, 1995), pp. 7–18.
50 Eldridge, *Max Weber*, p. 11.
51 Eldridge, *Max Weber*, p. 11.
52 Runciman, *Weber Selections*, p. 4.
53 B. S. Turner, Preface, in *From Max Weber*, ed. H. H. Gerth and C. Wright Mills (London, 1970), p. xxvii.
54 Turner, in *From Max Weber*, ed. Gerth and Wright Mills, p. xxviii.
55 S. Hall, *et al.*, *Modernity and its Futures* (Cambridge, 1992), p. 328.
56 Hall *et al.*, *Modernity*, p. 334.
57 S. Best and D. Kellner, *Postmodern Theory: Critical Investigations* (London, 1994), p. 237.
58 Habermas cited in Hall, *Modernity*, p. 340.
59 S. Lukes, "Of gods and demons: Habermas and practical reason", in *Habermas: Critical Debates*, ed. J. B. Thompson and D. Held (London, 1982), p. 134.
60 Thompson and Held, *Critical Debates*, p. 9.
61 Chittick, *Sufi Path*, p. 161.
62 A. E. Affifi, *The Mystical Philosophy of Muhyid Din Ibnul Arabi* (Lahore, 1979), p. 83.
63 Affifi, *Mystical Philosophy*, p. 83.
64 T. Kuhn, *The Structure of Scientific Revolutions* (Chicago, 1996), p. 123.
65 J.-F. Lyotard, *The Postmodern Condition* (Minneapolis, 1984), p. 75.
66 S. Benhabib, cited in Best and Kellner, *Postmodern Theory*, p. 246.
67 Giddens, *Consequences*, p. 49.
68 Hall *et al.*, *Modernity*, p. 333.
69 R. Harré, "Ontology and science", *Beshara Magazine* (Issue 3, 1987), p. 8.
70 Harré, *Beshara Magazine*, p. 11.
71 W. C. Chittick, *The Self-Disclosure of God* (Albany, NY, 1998), p. 8.

72 Hall *et al.*, *Modernity*, p. 344.
73 I. Hassan, cited in Tarnas, *Passion*, p. 401.
74 Tarnas, *Passion*, p. 396.
75 G. Berkeley, *The Principles of Human Knowledge* (Britannica Great Books Series, Vol. 35 of 54, Chicago, 1987), p. 405.

4 Ibn 'Arabi and the self[1]

The metaphysics of self-knowledge

The metaphor of the heart which Ibn 'Arabi deploys with such a formidable lucidity opens up a vast epistemological landscape which depicts the very great nature bestowed by God on the human self. For Ibn 'Arabi the heart is that which knows God; it is the centre and focus of Divine activity. In this sense it is the fundamental organ of perception and awareness which constitutes the essence, or core, of each human self. The heart as the foundational locus of perception is capable of receiving directly the divine inspirations and of knowing and recognizing the theophanic nature of all self-experience. One might be inclined to say that the heart is the foundational centre of mystical perception. This is to some extent a logically proper designation. But such a characterization leaves open the question of deciding between mystical and non-mystical forms of perception and can easily result in a misleading dualism between different categories of perception: a situation which, above all, needs to be avoided when discussing Ibn 'Arabi's treatment of the metaphor of the heart. Ibn 'Arabi's metaphysics acknowledges that all perception is theophanic, whether it is realized as such or not by the recipient. But it is the heart (and, one might add, only the heart) that is capable of acknowledging, recognizing, and knowing and perceiving the reality of the Unity of Being: in both its transcendent and immanent dimensions. Accordingly it is the heart to which God looks and to which He addresses Himself.

Ibn 'Arabi's metaphysics of the heart strictly implies that there can be no dualism between knower and known, object and subject, or between original and image. The philosophy of *wahdat al-wujud* recognizes only the seamlessness, singleness and identity of the One Being and the non-existence of all else. From this it follows without any logical impropriety that the metaphor of the heart depicts, for Ibn 'Arabi, the epistemic kernel of the human self through which "the clarification of the mirror of the world" can take place whereby God can manifest by it "His mystery to Himself".[2]

Such a metaphysical picture of the foundations of the human self – of its original nature, beauty, potential grandeur, and intrinsic Divine purpose – entails a radical conceptual reconfiguration of much modern theorizing about the self. This is nowhere more evident than in the realm of contemporary scientific psychology which has, to some extent, laid claim to the study of the self, even in those domains of modern psychology which avowedly deny the unitary nature of the self. However, before we head off in this direction let us be as accurate as we can about the extraordinary conception of the self which constitutes the fulcrum of Akbarian metaphysics. We can fairly say that for Ibn 'Arabi the human self is to be properly viewed as essentially and unequivocally a point of vision (or a locus of awareness) which acts as a mirror in the unitive Divine act of Self-Expression. Ibn 'Arabi tells us that the human self in its primordial universal condition is a point of vision which possesses "no essential characteristic other than totality and absoluteness".[3] Its very nature is to mirror the totality and absoluteness of the Unity of Being. What such a topology of the self conveys is a metaphysical landscape in which the heart of the *insan-i-kamil* veridically reflects totally and absolutely the transcendent and immanent aspects of the one and unique Being. Put another way, the heart of the Perfect Man images, in total, the entire Divine order. As Titus Burckhardt remarks in a note to his translation of the *Fusus al-Hikam*, the claim to totality by the creature is "by virtue at once of his Divine origin ... and of his natural root".[4] Let us attempt to unravel further what this means.

The status and meaning of the human self (i.e. Adamic kind) is expressed by Ibn 'Arabi in the following remarkable affirmation:

For the vision that a being has of himself in himself is not the same as that which another reality procures ... for him as a mirror: in this he manifests himself to his self in the form which results from the "place" of the vision; this would not exist without the "plane of reflection" and the ray which is reflected therein.[5]

The human self is intrinsically a place of vision and a plane of reflection and a place whereby God manifests Himself to Himself. Ibn 'Arabi tells us that it is in the heart of Perfect Man that this Divine manifestation is total and absolute: the heart of Perfect Man reflects the entire Divine order without blemish or distortion. This constitutes the essential vision which fulfils the Divine love to be known in the most universal and complete manner. It is known as the "most-saintly effusion" and "consists in the self-revelation of God manifesting Himself from all Eternity to Himself".[6] Logically consecutive to this essential vision is the exterior manifestation or the further imaging and unfolding of the essential revelation in the "theatre of manifestation" known as the universes, including all that occurs within the matrix of space and time and thereby all that occurs within the co-ordinates of history and culture.

We can perhaps say that for Ibn 'Arabi the "infinity of the world process" is in reality the intrinsic unfoldment in space and time of the original unitive act of Self-envisioning of the one and only Being.

From this it is clear that for Ibn 'Arabi the core nature or heart of the human self is as a witnessing isthmus which expresses and synthesizes both the Divine and the Human aspects of the single unique reality. One might equally say that the heart of Perfect Man unites and expresses perfectly the Source and its Self-expression as apparent other. In this manner the *insan-i-kamil* utterly instantiates "the clarification of the mirror of the world". It is for this reason that the Perfect Man is referred to by Ibn 'Arabi as the cause of creation and the object in which the purpose of creation is fully realized. In so far as God manifests Himself *as* the world the jewel of that world *is* the *insan-i-kamil*. He is the jewel in the sense in which the whole purpose and meaning of creation is brought together in a most perfect, beautiful and preferred manner; preferred manner, because the jewel-like luminosity of the heart of the *insan-i-kamil* accords with and varies with God's love to be known in its infinite and universal constant transmutation. In other words, it is according to God, and not itself. This is the only principle which constitutes its ever-changing universal luminosity. Because of this it is possible to say that the *insan-i-kamil* is the macrocosm and the universe is the microcosm, providing such a locution is understood not to imply the egotistic elevation of the creature. In short, "the clarification of the mirror of the world" *is* the heart of Perfect Man. It is in such a heart that God procures for Himself a vision of Himself as apparent other and beholds, as if in another, His own beauty. This is a situation of such ontological elevation that, as Affifi accurately remarks, it is the place wherein God is known to Himself through Himself. Ibn 'Arabi continually reaffirms that it is the heart (and only the heart) that possesses knowledge of this mystery and receives its contents.

In summary, the whole movement of God's love to be known, from the original essential revelation to the exteriorizing manifestation, constitutes the metaphysics of self-knowledge according to Ibn 'Arabi. It articulates a universal theophany and cosmology of the self in which the origin of the self is no other than the Self-expression of Divine beauty, Divine compassion, Divine generosity and Divine grandeur. Such a conception of the Divine root and identity of human selfhood is intrinsically antithetical to any concept of selfhood which robs the phenomena of the self of its unitive and universal theophanic nature. For Ibn 'Arabi a person's biological, psychological and cultural matrix (and the historical circumstances and events which define and constitute their particular era) provide too narrow a compass from which to form an ontologically adequate conception of the nature of the human self. This is clearly not to deny the biological, psychological and cultural–historical determinants of human identity. What is required, if we are to follow the logic of Ibn 'Arabi's metaphysics of the self, is to envisage such determinants (if they can ultimately be regarded as such) as partial expressions of something more vast and fundamental. Any analytical failure to see them from the universal point of view recommended by Ibn 'Arabi necessarily results in a fatal loss of phenomena and a misconstruction of human possibility. From the perspective of *wahdat al-wujud* the assumptions of human selfhood largely prevalent in contemporary theorizing in psychology are likely to amount to no more than human mental constructions: constructions which are ultimately coloured by the predispositions of the theorizers themselves. Such partial insights can easily become reified and parade themselves as universal objective truths. When this happens, such partial pictures of ourselves tend to become identity-defining and inevitably influence what is conceived of as human possibility. Such partial pictures of ourselves can send us hurtling along a particular existential life trajectory, largely unaware of our more essential and universal human possibility. In a slightly different context the fundamental ontology of this situation is alluded to in Ibn 'Arabi's important reference to Junayd's affirmation that "the colour of the water is the colour of its receptacle".[7] We colour the world in certain ways. These colouring adjectives, as we might call them, can conceal from us our original nature: they can act as veils. Nevertheless, such colourings are not without veracity for even as they veil they simultaneously indicate their origin. The essential point to note here is that, whatever else, they most definitely stand in dependent relation to what they colour.

Given the universality of Ibn 'Arabi's treatment of the metaphor of the heart, it comes as no surprise to find that it has a clear semantic affinity with the deployment of the metaphor of the heart in much ordinary folk psychology. Everyday psychology recognizes the metaphor of the heart as depicting (and referring to) an individual's inner state, attitudes and life-orientation. Heart-felt issues often relate to the question of a person's integrity, authenticity and intentions. In fact, the question of human authenticity was the staple diet of much contemporary twentieth-century existentialism. In an Anglo-Saxon philosophical vein, P. F. Strawson[8] has pointed out that the good or bad intentions of others towards us form the axiomatic basis of our reactive attitudes towards them in all the infinitely complex forms that such attitudes can take – from resentment to forgiveness to love. Such complexes of reactive attitudes form the bedrock of ordinary interpersonal relations. Crucially these reactive attitudes express fundamental human values and constitute ends rather than means. Let us take as an illustration one such reactive attitude: generosity. Intentional acts of spontaneous generosity, though perhaps infrequent, can and do occur. To ask of the originator of such an act why they performed it or what purpose it was serving, would be likely to betray a radical misunderstanding of the intention and nature of the act itself. Such acts, when genuine, are not performed for self-gain or as part of a clever strategy. Neither do they constitute elements in a social or economic policy aimed at achieving certain ends. They are performed for generosity's sake alone, stripped of any other consideration. If this is the case with human acts of generosity, what then of the Divine act of generosity in creating the human self in His own image? The heart-felt appreciation of this original Divine act can only be wholly embraced when and if the recipients are stripped of any other consideration but Divine love itself. This stripping away or letting go of all else *is* indeed Ibn 'Arabi's ontological recommendation for the *salik* (seeker). But what results is not (to use an image from modern cosmology) a black hole but rather the removal of ignorance in favour of a knowledge of what essentially is and always has been.

But to return to the theme of human acts of generosity. Such acts are an index of a deeply held human value. In this sense the metaphor of the heart deployed in everyday psychology semantically identifies the essential role that such values, intentions and reactive attitudes play in our assessment of others and of ourselves. In short, the metaphor of the heart in everyday psychology alludes to the existential orientation of the self: its decisions, direction, acts and intentions.

In this general sense Ibn 'Arabi's delineation of the concept of the heart has its analogue in ordinary everyday psychological experience. It is part of the stock of common-sense psychology that there are many things which can possess the heart – love of power, wealth, family, country, art, literature, science, goodwill, resentment, and so on. It is not possible, or even desirable, as Strawson points out, to be precise or scientific about the range of phenomena which can constitute our intentions and attitudes: for the field is infinitely complex. All we need note is that the metaphor of the heart is a semantic index of that which we hold most dear. In this sense a person's heart can be said to correspond with their fundamental predisposition. This is perhaps why the phrase "a change of heart" is regarded, to some extent, as a change in the quality and orientation of the person to whom it is ascribed. In the spiritual topography of Ibn 'Arabi the locution "a change of heart" indicates a qualitative change which tends to issue from and realigns them with their own original predisposition, known as their *'ayn al-thabita*.

It must be kept in mind, however, that for Ibn 'Arabi the heart depicts an ontological spiritual landscape which reconfigures and re-dimensionalizes (or perhaps, un-dimensionalizes) many of the findings of everyday folk psychology. In short, Ibn 'Arabi transposes the experiential findings of everyday psychology regarding the meta-phor of heart to their essential spiritual foundation in the context of *wahdat al-wujud*. The heart, in the final analysis for Ibn 'Arabi, is a Divine gift. Its fundamental ontological orientation is love of God: indeed, it is God who puts love of God into the heart. All other forms of love are pale reflections and potential indices of God's love to be known. For Ibn 'Arabi and those who follow him, the lament of the person who fills their heart with other than God is somewhat akin to the lament of the tin man in the *Wizard of Oz* who cries "if I only had a heart". Following the Akbarian metaphysics of self-know-ledge, we might say that the tin man's plea *is* a cry of the heart: a cry for the revivification of the heart, or the awakening of the heart to its true ontological role, nature, and magnitude. If we are inclined to say that each human self possesses a heart we must undoubtedly recognize, according to Ibn 'Arabi, that the human realization of the heart's inherent orientation requires the *awakening* of the heart. Ibn 'Arabi utilizes the traditional term "Know thyself" to denote the inner orientation necessary for such a revivification. This is expressed in the saying "He who knows himself knows his Lord". This process is some-times alluded to as "the polishing of the mirror of the heart": that is, the removal of all those things which prevent the heart from perfectly mirroring the unity of being.

Even a precursory glance at the many passages in the *Fusus al-Hikam* and the *Futuhat al-Makkiyah* which deal explicitly with the question of knowledge of the heart confirms that they characteristi-cally exemplify a compelling lucidity and directness which demands of the reader a shift in perspective. We are repeatedly reminded that it is the heart that gives direct access to "the knowledge inherent in God" (*'ilm laduni*). Such unequivocal emphasis on the centrality of the heart as the fundamental locus of perception naturally raises the further question: How then does the heart's knowledge relate to the other human faculties of knowing? How does it relate to the knowledge conveyed by the senses? By reason? By memory? By imagination?

Epistemologically Ibn 'Arabi's answer is quite clear: the heart's knowledge of God (which it is continually receiving even when we are unaware of it) can inform *all* other human faculties, including the human mind and the intellect. In this sense, the heart's knowledge can transpose itself into cognitive and intellectually communicative forms: it can represent itself in sensation, images, memories, dreams and even in syllogistic arguments and number theory. The heart's contents can assume cognitive articulation and mental representation. And not only this but potentially all sensory, imaginative, intellectual, and social experience are imbued with multivariate spiritual meaning. This is a situation also alluded to, for example, in William Blake's memorable lines, "To see a World in a grain of Sand and Heaven in a Wild Flower". It is this formidable power of the heart to perceive the essential realities that Ibn 'Arabi encodes in what is perhaps the most famous line of his collection of mystical poetry, the *Tarjuman al-Ashwaq*: "My heart has become capable of every form".[9]

But to return to the question: How then does the heart's knowledge relate to the other human faculties of knowing? According to Souad Hakim's[10] account of Ibn 'Arabi on this matter, the inspired-intellect (or the inspired-mind) is one which has acknowledged the existence of the heart and turned its attention undividedly to it, thereby receiving knowledge directly from it. When this alignment between the heart and the mind happens, the human receptor is said to possess understanding. One might say that a person who possesses such an understanding instantiates something of the Divine Wisdom. This also implies that the ordinary intellect may quite easily fail to understand. The mind which is not attuned to the heart can quite easily fail to cognitively grasp the fuller and deeper meanings of much human experience. By contrast, where such understanding exists, it is to be regarded as a great gift, in accordance with the saying "God bestows wisdom on whom He pleases and when He does so great good is established."

Viewed for a moment in analytical isolation, the intellect or the mind is, according to Souad Hakim, simply a receptive "centre of judgement". By this is meant that the intellect is capable of receiving the contents from all the normal sources of perception: that is, the senses, reason, memory, imagination and any other forms of representation. These four organs of perception constitute the epistemic mechanisms by which certain putative forms of knowledge are conveyed to the intellect. Each one of these mechanisms conveys that form of knowledge peculiar to it: the senses convey one form of knowledge, reason another, memory another, imagination another, and so on. The role of the intellect as a centre of judgement is to give its assent or dissent to what is received from these various epistemic sources. For instance, the senses, memory, or imagination may deceive. As René Descartes is famous for pointing out, we may be dreaming. What the intellect as a centre of judgement can do is to judge that it is a dream and evaluate the epistemological credentials of its claims accordingly.

But there is another and more profound sense of this matter alluded to in Akbarian metaphysics. In the chapter in the *Fusus al-Hikam* concerning the Word of Joseph, we learn that the whole of the Prophet Muhammad's life is to be regarded as a "dream within a dream", and we also learn, in the same chapter, that "people are asleep and when they die they awake".[11] A key to understanding the meaning of these somewhat enigmatic allusions is to recognize that, for Ibn 'Arabi, all cosmic and human experience is God appearing as apparent other: that is, to recognize the non-existence of anything but God. This requires the acknowledgement of the Unity of Being in the face of the multiplicity of ever-changing, apparently separate, phenomena. The witnessing by the *salik* of the cinematographical quality and theophanic nature of all experience of the self is the recognition that one's life is, if we can be permitted a certain poetic licence, a series of cinematographical frames in the greater Divine cosmic film-show. More soberly, it is the recognition of the truth of the saying "The world is illusion but it is the Truth in Truth." This realization is critical if the true situation is to dawn upon the receptor. Without this realization, Ibn 'Arabi reiterates, "men will remain asleep".

Ultimately, for Ibn 'Arabi, it is the judgement of the heart and not the intellect alone which facilitates insight into the true state of affairs. The intellect as a centre of judgement may have some glimmerings of this matter but only in an intellectual kind of way – as we saw much earlier in the discussion of the question put to Ibn ʿArabi by Ibn Rushd. To recognize life as "a dream within a dream" is to recognize who it is and what it is that is constantly concealing and revealing itself. In essence, to recognize life as a dream within a dream is to witness completely, without there being any notion of a separate witnesser, the Unity of Being.

The nearest we have to such a view in modern Western philosophy is probably contained in Berkeley's *Essay Towards a New Theory of Vision*.[12] In this unusual work Berkeley attempts to show that the kaleidoscopic transformation of the universe from moment to moment constitutes a language through which the Divine communicates and is witnessed. But nowhere in Berkeley's deliberations is there anything comparable to the philosophically astute remark of Ibn ʿArabi that the strangest and most paradoxical error in the human sphere which "has appeared on earth … is … that man imitates his reason. God created this faculty to serve intellect, but instead of that, intellect serves reason".[13] The great epistemological error that "has appeared on earth" is that human reason, not the intellect, becomes the judge. When this is the case it seems that the intellect cannot exercise its power of judgement over the findings of reason and is thereby disallowed from countenancing the "truths beyond reason". The metaphysical picture of physical reality as possessing an atomistic ontology of separate independent entities, is one which it would have been difficult to gainsay until the advent of quantum physics. When the prevailing forms of scientific reason alone become their own judge and jury it is difficult, though perhaps not impossible, to alter a particular scientific paradigm. It is not impossible to do so because twentieth-century developments in relativistic and quantum physics and, more recently, in chaos theory, have arguably cast considerable difficulties in the way of any naive atomistic ontology, and reasserted the irreducible interconnectedness of physical reality and the inseparability of the observer and the observed. But these developments themselves have been based as much on new thought experiments and re-conceptualizations of physical reality as on reason and observation. Reason has served and articulated new imaginative insights rather than the reverse. Of course, such insights are subject to rational scrutiny but they do not originate in it.

Ibn 'Arabi's view is that if human reason becomes the sole arbiter of truth (as, for instance, Kant and others would like it to be) then the function of the intellect as a centre of judgement becomes impaired and to all intents and purposes largely inoperative, at least consciously. For Ibn 'Arabi the intellect which serves reason represents a one-winged intellect unable to travel beyond the truths of reason. By contrast, the fully-fledged intellect is capable of flying (and designed to fly) to the proximity of the heart and thereby register the findings brought to it by the promptings of the heart. When this happens the intellect is transformed into the heart-inspired intellect and the main epistemological focus becomes the understanding and wisdom of the heart. All the other mechanisms of perception (i.e., the senses, memory, reason, intuition and imagination) are now in the service of the heart. In this situation human reason does not transgress its proper boundary: it serves the intellect which, in turn, receives its knowledge from the heart itself. In brief, all the human faculties become subservient to the heart. When the heart and the mind are inseparably aligned in this manner they tend to become logically synonymous: the perceptions of the Intellect, Mind and Heart constitute a single indivisible reality sometimes referred to by Ibn 'Arabi as Light. And Light is, for Ibn 'Arabi, synonymous with knowledge of God and knowledge of the Unity of Being. Even human reason with its inherent limitations ultimately constitutes a kind of light. But this is to say no more than, for Ibn 'Arabi, that reason is one of the subordinate powers of the intellect and not the other way round. Interestingly, we can now see in clearer view the sense of the remarks noted at the beginning of this study, when Ibn 'Arabi informs us that

God never commanded His Prophet to seek increase of anything except knowledge, since all good (*khayr*) lies therein. It is the greatest charismatic gift. Idleness with knowledge is better than ignorance with good works ... By knowledge I mean only knowledge of God, of the next world, and of that which is appropriate for this world, in relationship to that for which this world was created and established. Then man's affairs will be "upon insight" wherever he is, and he will be ignorant of nothing in himself and his activities.[14]

This is a point reconfirmed in its own way by George Berkeley's apt remark in *The Principles of Human Knowledge*:

> We should believe that God has dealt more bountifully with the sons of men than to give them a strong desire for that knowledge which he had placed quite out of their reach. This were not agreeable to the wonted indulgent methods of Providence, which, whatever appetites it may have implanted in the creatures, doth usually furnish them with such means as, if rightfully made use of, will not fail to satisfy them.[15]

The heart, then, represents, for Ibn 'Arabi, the most comprehensive and deepest level at which the drama of each human self is existentially played out. The heart is the core of the self: indeed essentially it constitutes the self. Of the many analogous terms like breast, intellect, soul and breath, it is the term heart which centrally signifies that God has, out of His own intrinsic beauty and thereby compassion, made, in essence, man in His own image. In its most profound depths the human self is no other, for Ibn 'Arabi, than the Self-expression of the One Being. The heart of the *insan-i-kamil* is the most complete instantiation of this Self-expression and *ipso facto* englobes all other modalities of the One Unique Existence. Essentially all other modalities of the One Being are the necessary details of the ever-new, ever-continuous, global, universal unfoldment of God's love to be known. The details and detailing of the entire divine order (the ever-changing furniture of the world) are englobed by and consequential to such a heart.

Perhaps enough has been indicated to convey, if necessarily in an embryonic manner, the sheer vastness of Ibn 'Arabi's concept of the heart and the magnitude of his conception of the human self and its possibilities. The heart is seen to represent the very Self of Compassion known as the *nafs al-rahman*. From the point of view of *wahdat al-wujud*, the Self of Compassion is logically co-terminus with all that there is. There is for Ibn 'Arabi nothing that exists over which God's compassion does not prevail, for the very condition of there being anything at all is that it is essentially moulded and made out of compassion: compassion is its inner reality. To borrow an image from modern chaos theory, the fundamental "hidden attractor" of all that there is and to which hidden order the universe itself conforms, is the compassion of the Bounteous One. But to some, like Ibn 'Arabi, this reality is not hidden but abundantly apparent and overwhelmingly and constantly present. As Ibn 'Arabi insists in his opening statement of *Sufis of Andalusia*, if you "take the Bounteous One alone as your companion, He will speak to you without the need for any intermediary".[16]

The reality of the self in the metaphysics of Ibn 'Arabi is the reality of God's wanting "to see His own Essence in one global object which having been blessed with existence summarized the Divine order so that there He could manifest His mystery to Himself".[17]

It is apparent from the foregoing discussion that Ibn 'Arabi's ontology of the self necessarily recasts the topographical features of much contemporary theorizing about the self. Theories of the self in modern scientific psychology provide an interesting and informative illustration of the issues raised for modern theories of the self by Ibn 'Arabi's metaphysics.

Modern psychology and the self

The treatment of the self in modern scientific psychology

The impact of modern psychology on the self-images and mental outlook of the twentieth century can hardly be underestimated. To confirm this we need only cite a few of the more well-known examples: the cultural assimilation of Freudian and Jungian anthropology; the immense psychological emphasis on the individual and individual differences; the ubiquitous deployment of psychometric testing in education, in the military and in industry; the widespread appeal of the emancipatory programmes of humanistic psychology and counselling; the affinities of cognitive science with the processing logics of artificial intelligence; and, finally perhaps, the emergence of computational theories of the human mind itself. In short, modern psychology has made its indelible contribution to the *Zeitgeist* of the twentieth century.

In an important sense (and in a diversity of areas) it has helped to prepare the ground for a monumental re-examination of who and what we are in the light of the scientific epistemological assumptions of

the Enlightenment project.[18] Although psychology has not produced
a single unified overarching paradigm (or anything even comparable to the law of gravitation in physics), it has tilled the ground
and directed our attention to new insights into the psychological
conditions of knowledge-acquisition, and insights into the psychological consequences and demands of modern life, as well as instituted
and professionalized clinical and therapeutic emancipatory practice.
Modern psychology has secured its place in the process of reflexivity
which characterized the epistemology of the twentieth century. Its
paradoxical nature has been to provide the hope of an adequate
twenty-first century metaphysics of the self and the mind whilst
being predominantly experimentalist and statistical in its methodology. The early pioneers of modern scientific psychology conceived
of its distinctive object as human consciousness and mental life. We
see this emphasis, for example, in Gustav Theodor Fechner's psycho-
physics, Wundt's attempt to analyse consciousness into its elementary
building blocks, and William James's functionalist affirmation of the
unity of consciousness. But in the latter half of the twentieth century
academic psychology came to define itself almost exclusively by its
methodology rather than by its subject matter. Whether consciously
or not, much later twentieth-century psychology followed William
James's recommendation in *Principles of Psychology* that the mind
"*works under conditions*; and the *quest of the conditions* becomes the
psychologist's most interesting task".[19] Such an emphasis absolves the
psychologist from producing any overall metaphysics of the self and
is compatible with the assumption that it is not the job of the science
of psychology to produce any such overall schema. This may seem all
well and good, but, as soon as psychology is conceived as embracing
aspects of the self other than brain-science, the plausibility of such a
delimitation of its scope (to brain-science or perhaps computational
mechanisms of the mind) seems unduly restrictive and metaphysically incomplete. To many, such metaphysical and methodological
restriction greatly reduces the potential value of psychology. From
the very beginning of modern psychology up to the present there has
been pressure within the discipline itself for a broader, more universal
perspective than that provided by an experimentalist, brain-science
paradigm. Perhaps, just as Aristotelian logic was once seen as

IBN 'ARABI AND THE SELF ~ 137

comprising the *whole* of logic but in the twentieth century was known to constitute but a fraction of logical theory, the movement to reconstitute psychology in the context of a much larger theoretical and methodological universe will prove equally fruitful and more complete. It is this movement towards grounding psychology in a more theoretically adequate and appropriate epistemology which is one of the most interesting developments in later twentieth-century philosophy of psychology.

Put simply, the sheer diversity of psychology's subject matter has unequivocally attested to the multi-dimensionality of the human self. It is a multi-dimensionality that demands a perspective larger than any experimentally defined psychology alone can provide. Ever present in psychology is an intrinsic pressure to develop a more metaphysically adequate basis for dealing with the multi-dimensional, value-laden nature and complexity of the self. The demand for psychology not to fix itself in a one-dimensional experimental form of rationality lies at the root of many of the major debates, issues and themes which have plagued modern psychology in one way or another since its inception as a predominantly experimental enterprise in the nineteenth century. The essential problem confronting psychology in the twenty-first century is the question of its epistemological adequacy to deal with the larger questions facing any adequate theory of the self. The self is beginning once again to be addressed as a fundamental explanatory category and not simply as a by-product of brain physiology or the outcome of computational processes. It is arguable that the concept of the self is not an added-on, emergent product but a fundamental presupposition of there being the science of psychology at all.

The relative invisibility of the self under the searchlight of experimentalism
As an overall record of the achievement and impact of psychology there is no better or more accurate statement than Roger Smith's in his *History of the Human Sciences*:

> The development of academic disciplines and professional
> institutions in the human sciences does not immediately seize
> the imagination as a turning-point in human self-discovery. It
> is necessary, however, to give it great weight. In the twentieth

century the presence of these disciplines and professions was the
visible sign of belief in and the special status of specialist knowledge and techniques about human nature. The internalization of
belief in psychological knowledge, so that it acquired a taken-for-
granted quality, altered everyone's subjective world and recreated
experience and expectations about what it is to be a person. The
result was an emphasis on "the personal" in psychological terms,
with ramifications in every aspect of life. It became possible to
refer to the existence of "psychological society" in the twentieth
century ... there is a significant sense in which everyone in the
twentieth century learned to be a psychologist; ... able and willing
to describe life in psychological terms. The twentieth century was
a psychological age, and in this it differed from earlier ages.[20]

Whilst this may be interesting and true as a statement regarding the
general cultural influence of psychology on the popular imagination,
the concept of the self within the professional domains of scientific
psychology remained relatively under-theorized and marginalized.

As we have glimpsed in the history of Western nineteenth- and
twentieth-century psychology, experimental scientific psychology has
been largely successful in defining itself as psychology *par excellence*.
There have been other pretenders to the throne, such as humanistic
psychology or psychoanalysis, but none have established themselves
as paradigmatic. And this is in spite of the household or near-house-
hold names of some of their respective advocates, like Freud, Jung,
Rogers and Maslow. Only experimental psychology has succeeded in
legitimizing itself (at least within its own ranks) as being incontrovert-
ibly scientific in its methods and outlook. None except experimental
psychology has succeeded in codifying so thoroughly its claim to
scientific supremacy and securing its place in the epistemic assumptions of a modernist industrial Western technological world-view.
This is well illustrated in one of psychology's most recent and central
analytical concerns – cognitive science. Paul Thagard, in his introduction to cognitive science in *Mind*, comments:

> Although cognitive psychologists today often engage in
> theorizing and computational modelling, their primary method

is experimentation with human subjects. People ... are brought into the laboratory so that different kinds of thinking can be studied under controlled conditions ... psychologists have experimentally examined the kinds of mistakes that people make in deductive reasoning, the ways that people form and apply concepts, the speed of people thinking with mental images, and the performance of people solving problems using analogies. Our conclusions about how the mind works must be based on more than "common sense" ... since these can give a misleading picture of mental operations, many of which are not consciously accessible ... To address the crucial questions about the nature of mind, the psychological experiments need to be interpretable within a theoretical framework that postulates mental representations and procedures. One of the best ways of developing theoretical frameworks is by forming and testing computational models intended to be analogous to mental operations.[21]

This attempt to understand the mechanisms of the mind based on the construction of computational models, coupled with a representational theory of mind, has faced various serious challenges. Cognitive science, however, has brought to psychology people from widely differing disciplines such as artificial intelligence, mathematics, linguistics, philosophy and neuroscience, often quite independently from experimental psychology. This itself indicates the conceptual inevitability of going beyond the bounds of strictly experimental psychology when postulating theories which attempt to encapsulate, successfully or otherwise, the nature of the human mind and human consciousness.

Because of the perceived difficulty of incorporating a comprehensive metaphysics of human values into the framework of psychology as an objective natural science, the self has never been granted the status of an irreducible central explanatory category. Accordingly, crucial aspects of the treatment of the self (that is, its inherent metaphysical, ideological and cultural dimensions) have been noticeably absent and relatively invisible in a strictly experimental paradigm logically wedded to the objective and the factual. The products of experimental psychology have issued in a plethora of theories and

observations concerning the brain, behaviour, perception, informa-
tion-processing, artificial intelligence, consciousness, mind, language,
personality, communication and the like but have noticeably paid little
explanatory analytical attention, if any, to an overall metaphysics of
the self. In modern scientific psychology the self has been treated in
a piecemeal fashion and has not generally been taken as the unifying
investigatory centre of analysis. It is true, of course, that in some areas
of psychology the category of the self is optimal and explicit – for
instance, in the person-oriented architectures of various models of
counselling and therapy. But this is the exception rather than the rule.
In the hegemonic areas of modern psychology (like psycho-biology
and cognitive science) there is much talk of neural networks, memory,
perception and consciousness but little, if any, sustained conceptual
analysis of the self in which they are embedded or rooted, either
as process or structure. At best, explanatory priority is given to the
category of the brain or the category of consciousness, or to computational models of cognition and its simulation; at worst, there is an
implicit reductionism of the self to one or other or some of these
categories. What this results in is a potential loss of an adequate metaphysics of the self; that is, a metaphysics which is adequate to deal with
the self as an essential, irreducible ontological category presupposed
by, and in, all human experience.

This absence of an explicit universal metaphysics of the self is
conceptually and logically the most important contrast between traditional thought forms such as Ibn 'Arabi's and the presuppositions of
modern scientific psychology, particularly experimental psychology.

Its absence is all the more puzzling if for no other reason than it is
a commonly held assumption of much ordinary folk-psychology that
psychology does, and ought to, have the self as its central object of
study. In line with this common sense assumption, traditional theories
of knowledge, like that of Ibn 'Arabi, have always emphasized as axiomatic (under various descriptions) the Socratic dictum "Know thyself".
No such axiom or its analogue figures in the official agenda of modern
experimental psychology or computational theories of mind. Some of
the consequences of such an absence can be discerned in the recurring
criticisms of psychology typified, for example, in such pronouncements
as the 1994 statement by the president of the American Psychological

Association who suggested that psychologists "stand very close to being [involved in] a discipline concerned with superficial problems" and that in the future a return to "a psychology of meaning in the broadest sense ... will become increasingly important".[22]

Whether one agrees with this statement or not, the question of the need for modern psychology to address itself to "meaning in its broadest sense" has remained one which has haunted the limitations and orientation of experimental psychology since its alleged inception with Wilhelm Wundt's self-promotion of psychology as a natural science in the latter part of the nineteenth century. But this did not blind Wundt from recognizing the limitations and inappropriateness of the experimental method when it came to investigating the products of higher mental processes – such as myth, religion, morality, art, culture and law – the investigation of which, he argued, belonged to cultural psychology. Cultural psychology (*Volkerpsychologie*) demanded a historical rather than an experimental methodology. Wundt acknowledged that the methods used for investigating physiology are not appropriate for investigating history and culture. This conceptual insight is one which is radically reconfirmed in the conceptual and methodological strategies of late twentieth-century discursive psychology in its insistence that "all social psychological phenomena are properties of discourse".[23] Such a view has important implications for our understanding of the concept of the self.

Self and experience beyond the experimentalist paradigm

In relation to the sheer diversity of subject matter of twentieth-century scientific psychology, Sloan's point that "many of psychology's subfields implicitly or explicitly incorporate one personality theory or another" is enough to indicate that some theory of the self, implied or otherwise, is inevitably presupposed by the psychological enterprise. But it is equally clear that the personality theories to which Sloan refers do not constitute a universal metaphysics of the self of the kind deemed necessary by Ibn 'Arabi. Many modern psychological theories of personality are aligned to the demands of modern industrial and post-industrial technological culture and the entrepreneurial assumptions about individuality which are most characteristic of it.

By contrast, the logic of a universal metaphysics of the self of the kind presented by Ibn ʿArabi demands the articulation of a much larger metaphysical picture of the whole as a whole. Personality theories in modern psychology fall well short of this in their attempt to provide, as Sloan puts it, "the big picture on human nature". Their major limitation seems to be that their big picture turns out to be a very particular cultural snapshot. And even when it is granted that many of psychology's subfields either implicitly or explicitly do incorporate a theory of the self, this is not, in practice, coincidental with making the self a central explanatory category. Neither is it a widespread practice in psychology to subject such theories, when and if they are incorporated, to comparative evaluation. As a rule, as Sloan shrewdly observes, psychology students are not taught how to assess theories of personality "as theories":

> Instead, in keeping with general practice in mainstream
> psychology, future psychologists are taught that the validity
> of theoretical concepts is to be ascertained by operationalizing
> them for experimental or correlational studies. In conjunction
> with this practice, they are trained to describe personality
> mechanistically with an impoverished vocabulary, reducing the
> complexity of personal experience to a few quantifiable dimensions
> or dichotomous categories ... Put simply, mainstream approaches
> have systematically reduced our capacity to understand
> personality.[24]

This reduction in our capacity to understand personality and the impoverished vocabulary which accompanies it become apparent when such accounts are compared with the infinitely rich vocabulary deployed in ordinary folk-psychology or, indeed, for the purposes of the present study, when they are compared with the vocabulary of the self which is evident in the writings of Ibn ʿArabi.

As well as the tendency in scientifically defined psychology to "supplement or replace subjective human judgements by supposedly objective personality descriptors", it is not surprising to find that, in the debates concerning the study of personality, the question of how to approach the study of personality becomes an essentially contested issue, the answer to which depends on the paradigmatic preferences of the theorizer: behavioural, phenomenological, cognitive, psycho-analytical, or whatever.

As a consequence of this, Sloan's observation that we may profitably regard personality theorists as "generalists who stand back to get the big picture on human nature (and) ... who hope to synthesize or integrate the knowledge produced by the various subdisciplines of psychology" multiplies the problem of the essential contestability of theories of the self and renders any such final integration partial at best, and any particular theory likely to be subject to the very disagreements it seeks to resolve.

As we have already highlighted, Akbarian metaphysics depicts such potentially intractable disagreements concerning the ultimate nature of the human self as finally located in the predispositional ontology of the theorizers themselves. This state of affairs concords with Ibn 'Arabi's general principle of the *immanencing of knowledge according to the place of reception*, a state of affairs equally seen as the Self-disclosure of the Real refracting itself through the predisposition of the person and, thereby, conforming to the value and belief orientation of the theorizer.

The picture presented by the principle of the immanencing of knowledge in the ontology of Ibn 'Arabi is one of reality being of such a nature that it configures itself to the place of human reception and, in this sense, mirrors back the individual's predisposition to view the world in certain ways. Basically, therefore, each human subject constitutes a uniquely configured predispositional point of vision within the Unity of Being. This predispositional diversity is itself the grounds for the diversity of belief about the nature of reality. But it is not possible to render this Akbarian insight accurately without adding that such diversity is a non-coercive "intentional diversity".[25] Fundamentally, it is the human receptor who constructs and holds certain beliefs about the nature of reality according to personal predisposition. In its metaphysical depths, Ibn 'Arabi informs us, the Oneness of Being precedes and remains unassailable by this process of predispositional refraction.

From such a vantage point our understanding of the essentially contested issues that permeate modern psychology undergoes, at the very least, a radical conceptual transformation: it entails a profound change in our ideas about ourselves, about the world, about what we think we know and about the nature of knowledge itself.

Perhaps the nearest modern psychology comes to recognizing such a view of knowledge is recorded in Kirk J. Schneider's "Towards a science of the heart", when he remarks, "when the lifeworld becomes a theme of knowledge, it always includes the co-constitution of the investigator and participant. The investigator is a participant–knower and understands that he or she is part of the phenomenon that is being studied."[26] Something more of the implications of such a view are expressed by Tarnas when he observes:

> The fund of data available to the human mind is of such intrinsic complexity and diversity that it provides plausible support for many different conceptions of the ultimate nature of reality. The human being must therefore choose among a multiplicity of potentially viable options, and whatever is chosen will in turn affect both the nature of reality and the choosing subject. In this view although there exist many defining structures in the world which resist or compel human thought and activity in various ways, on a fundamental level the world tends to ratify, and open up according to, the character of the vision directed towards it. The world that the human being attempts to know and remake is in some sense elicited by the frame of reference with which it is approached.[27]

For Ibn 'Arabi each person constitutes a unique frame of reference or approach to reality – that is, a unique point of vision in the kaleidoscopic transmutation of reality at every moment. The non-stop predispositional refraction of reality can also be understood as the one unique existence revealing multifaceted aspects of itself in the form of the nature, condition and uniqueness of its human receptors. From this perspective biology, culture and history are the enabling conditions: they are part of the conditions which allow the immanencing of the predispositional consequences in all their ongoing infinity. If we generalize this quintessential Akbarian point of view, we may also add that the unprecedented nature of the modern era is the here and now consequence of the internal contents of *wahdat al-wujud*.

Ibn 'Arabi's account of the predispositional refraction of reality leaves us with a surprising glimpse of why it is that people of equal intelligence and education and comparable background can hold with enduring tenacity profoundly opposed views concerning human nature and human destiny.

Even where there exists broad agreement within modern psychology concerning, for example, the unemancipatory nature of any theory of human personality which impedes "self-reflection, agency, autonomy, mutuality, and other capacities that characterize meaningful living", the more fundamental issue of what constitutes the "fully human" cannot be avoided for long. C. S. Peirce[28] is reputed to have remarked that the only thing worse than someone with bad metaphysics is someone who thinks they have no metaphysics at all. It is clear that different metaphysical assumptions about what constitutes the fully human lie at the heart of much modern psychology, explicitly or implicitly.

Ibn 'Arabi's account of the importance of the predispositional grounds of the diversity of belief presupposes that we locate the complex dimensionality of the human self in the whole as a whole. There have been some partial attempts in recent psychology to locate the self in a much wider perspective which acknowledges the centrality of subjective experience and its location in physical, biological, cognitive, cultural, historical and moral contexts. A recent formulation of such a view is documented in "Towards a psychology of experience".[29] The following is part of the inaugural statement: "The goal is still to describe, interpret, explain and facilitate our experience of ourselves and the world around us. Experimental, phenomenological and transformative approaches will all have their part to play." The desire for the subjective and the experiential to be regarded as a core topic in psychology has its roots in the historical foundations of the discipline and it is an index of the invisibility of the self in much modern psychology that such a plea for its resuscitation needs to be made at the turn of the new millennium.

By contrast, for Ibn 'Arabi, an adequate psychology of experience could not be arrived at by an inclusive concatenation of perspectives and methodologies of the kind suggested by this observation. The comprehensiveness and unity of the self alluded to by Ibn 'Arabi *already is*, and it is only from the point of unity that all else, including psychology and our self-experience, can be most completely viewed. Our assessment of the noticeable shift in psychology towards a more comprehensive view of the self, whilst commendable, still involves a loss of phenomena and impoverishment of the stature of the self when compared with the phenomenology of the self which imbues the very woof and warp of the *Fusus al-Hikam* and the *Futuhat al-Makkiyyah* of Ibn ʿArabi.

The turn towards a discursive–critical perspective[30]

Sloan's position, which was briefly examined earlier, transcends the locus of attention from the brain and the individual to the social, political, cultural, historical and the global. We discern here an unambiguous movement towards a more universal perspective. In line with this the inherent logic of a critical–discursive psychology rejects any theory of the person which underestimates or naively ignores the culturally positioned nature of all human theorizing. Critical–discursive psychology reaffirms that all theories of the human self are socially constructed, historically located products. The difficulty facing such a global constructivist perspective on the human self is that of avoiding the complete relativizing of the self within the theoretical co-ordinates of biology, culture and history. This is a rather different order of problem than the one which issues from the tendency to regard the self as primarily an emergent function of the brain or alternatively from the problems facing a full-blown biological Darwinizing of the self. The point here is that the conception of the self as discursively embedded in culture and history entails a redimensionalizing of the methodology and parameters of a psychology of the self beyond the boundaries of brain-science or biology. The turn towards discursive psychology (rather than experimental neuropsychology) requires the self to be viewed from a larger conceptual canvas: one might say it represents a more total view of the self.

Discursive and critical psychology have the advantage of treating people as primarily inhabiting symbolic and conversational universes, in contradistinction to treating people simply as causal happenings or experimental subjects. From this perspective what is specifically human about us (rather than just animal) is the extent of our linguistic competence and capacity, and the accompanying forms of discursive thought. We inhabit linguistic universes and it is through such discourses that the notion of the self emerges. Within the very recent history of the twentieth century, Western discursive psychology represents the nearest approach to a metaphysics of the self which recognizes the historical as well as the biological, the social as well as the individual, the environmental as well as the brain, the moral as well as the causal: in short, a psychology which recognizes the central importance of discursive, creative and emancipatory human practice and adheres to a broad view of the multidimensionality of the human self. Nevertheless, such views of the possibilities open to the human self remain comparatively restricted when compared with the universal metaphysics of *wahdat al-wujud*. Let us see further why this is so.

Discursive psychology conceives of the human agent and human agency as being inextricably entangled in hegemonic cultural and linguistic forms: it is a position which logically disallows any theoretically naive view of the self as a pre-given "uncomplicated subjectivity".[31] Quite the reverse, from the point of view of discursive psychology, the self is necessarily to be regarded as a "complex subjectivity" because it is discursively produced by the ever-changing vicissitudes of history and culture. Accordingly, what is taken to be human nature at any historical or cultural juncture is, in reality, the outcome of a series of discursive practices, practices which possess no epistemological finality or privilege. Whilst many of the advocates of discursive psychology, particularly Ian Parker,[32] wish to avoid dissolving the notion of self *in* discourse, they are also radically sceptical of the modernist–humanist view "of a unified self that lies underneath discourse". This sceptical stance is partly because of the tendency of culturally specific and historically located discourses on the nature of the self to parade themselves as ahistorical universal truths. For analysts like Parker such claims themselves constitute ideologically located positions on human nature. When such essentialist ideologies of the self prevail they enclose the self within an iron-cage of dogma and ideology: a dogma which is necessarily a product of specific cultural and historical discursive formations.

To some extent such a view would, in part, be acceptable to Akbarian metaphysics. It is true for Ibn 'Arabi that human beings *are* immersed in the relative – in biology, in history, in culture and language, for example. But Ibn 'Arabi also insists that "(The world) is to itself its own veil".[33] In this he is partly suggesting that the matrix of secondary causes (like history, culture and biology) on which our very existence as human selves depend can veil us from the deeper theophanic nature of self-experience. From an Akbarian perspective the theoretical assumption that discourse, history and culture constitute the ultimate ever-changing grounds of the self would be regarded as part of the manner in which their status as secondary causes is veiled from the perception of the theorizer and remains opaque to their conjectural assumptions.

Whilst, therefore, the epistemological parameters of discursive and critical psychology locate the self within a much broader conceptual matrix than evolutionary, experimental or computational paradigms, they do not yet grasp, if we are to follow Akbarian metaphysics, the actual nature and full ontological status of the phenomena with which they deal. The picture of the self presented by discursive psychology has acted as a valuable corrective to reductionist conceptions of the self; but, it is still far from a metaphysics of the whole as a whole. For Ibn 'Arabi, the secondary causes of biology, culture and history cannot be regarded as the ultimate foundations of the self or its logical progenitors.

Further comments on the treatment of subjectivity and self in psychology and computational models of mind

By way of summary we may conclude that discursive psychology does not regard the self as an irreducible psychological category; rather, it envisages the self as essentially a discursive construction. In this sense the self has no ultimate solidity other than as a social product. Such a view has the merit of treating our concepts about ourselves as the outcome of an ongoing, open-ended process rather than treating the self as thing-like and fixed. The self is not a thing but a process.[34] The discursive and cultural processes which generate particular conceptions of the self and self-identity are taken as the primary data. The individual's sense of self is given in social discourse and is contingent on collective cultural life. Whilst the self, in this view, becomes conceptually conspicuous, it also remains potentially unstable and deconstructable. There is no such thing as a fixed human nature: what is taken as human nature, or the self, is itself ultimately the product of particular historical, cultural and linguistic formations. However, this does not entail a deterministic picture of the self for it is recognized that the individual is *both* shaped by and capable of shaping social and historical circumstance.

Discursive psychology furnishes us with a highly theorized and sophisticated account of the self compared with the conceptually under-theorized topography of the self in much experimental and computationally inspired psychology. But neither discursive, experimental or computational paradigms treat the self as an irreducible, central and explanatory category.

This refusal to treat the self as a central explanatory category has been significantly influenced by the Jamesian preference to take as the axiomatic object of explanation mental life rather than the self. The modern analogue to the Jamesian focus on mental life is, of course, cognitive science. This marginalizing of the self is itself a very interesting fact.

The conceptual and practical implications of this marginalizing tendency are convincingly illustrated by Wendy Hollway when she notes:

Despite the fact that experimental psychology has been most interested in the mind (perception, cognition, learning, attention and memory), it has defined these in physiological terms and set up experiments which deal exclusively with performance (or behaviour). Yet on the other side of the experiment the psychologist is engaged in just the sorts of activities that would be associated with mind when it is not reduced to physiology (accounts of events or experience, questioning, giving answers ... – in a phrase, making sense). Such manifestations of mind in the experimental "subject" are bypassed and in effect suppressed ... While the scientist-psychologist retains reason or mind in the full sense, the mind which is the object of psychology is reduced in the process of psychology's allegiance to natural science.[35]

The author here is clearly concerned to restore the experimental subject to full rationality and avoid the asymmetry between investigator and investigated. But we can note with interest that the emphasis is on the mind, not on the self which possesses such a mind, a self, one might add, to which may be ascribed the dignity of being a human subject even when deprived of, or unable to exercise, full rationality or cognitive competence.

For Ibn ʿArabi, neither the brain nor mind, in this contemporary psychological sense, represents the most comprehensive and deepest level at which the drama of each human self is existentially played out. From the universal point of view of the Unity of Being, the body (including the brain) is an inseparable existential part of the self's own phenomenal field, agency and awareness. But the body in the form we know it is *not* co-extensive with the self. It is logically inseparable in the sense that it is a particular form or image assumed by the Real and in this respect it is none other than the Real or, as one might legitimately put it, the Self. But it is only a particularized mode acting as a *locus* for the self's phenomenal field and agency. From the metaphysics of the Unity of Being the death of the body is the dissolution of a particular form, not the dissolution of its ultimate reality. The self and the body are logically identical (that is, the body is a particular form or appearance assumed by the Reality as one of Its unique Self-manifestations) but they are not logically co-extensive. Because of this, and in contradistinction to the premise of much modern psychology, the dissolution of the brain cannot essentially compromise the integrity, unity and oneness of the reality of the human heart as the *locus* of the self. The brain and body are a kind of dismantleable and reorganizable hardware. The software, if you want, is the heart: the brain and the body are particular kinds of hardware.[36]

In general there are many modalities for Ibn ʿArabi through which the self *can function* or *be realized* or *be given expression*. In this respect, the physical body (including the brain) is *one* such modality of the infinite Self-expression of the One and Unique Being. The Akbarian principle indicates that in order for anything to be given phenomenal expression a receptive modality (*or* form *or* body *or* image of some kind) is necessary. But, for Ibn ʿArabi, this does not confine us to physical bodies in the form we know them.

Interestingly, and surprisingly, this point is one which is acknowledged, at least conceptually, in modern computational models of the mind. In his discussion of machine functionalism, Jaegwon Kim emphasizes that the single most important idea which gave rise to computational theories of mind was that of *"the multiple realizability of mental properties".*[37] This means, for a computational theory of mind, *mental properties* (mind-stuff or qualia) can be realized or function through varied and very different hardware – just as the same software program can be run on very different types of computers. Mental states such as knowing, desiring, believing, perceiving and imagining can be, as Kim puts it, multiply realizable in "a large variety of physical/biological structures". Kim goes on to say "Perhaps not many of us now believe in angels, purely spiritual and immortal beings supposedly with full mental life ... If the idea of an angel with beliefs, desires and emotions is a consistent idea, that would show that there is nothing in the idea of mentality itself that precludes purely non-physical, wholly immaterial realizations of psychological states." Kim does not, of course, comment on whether the idea of disembodied mentality is coherent but he does insist that from his own point of view "Minds, if they exist, must be embodied."

What Kim calls embodiment, Ibn 'Arabi calls form or image or frame. For Ibn 'Arabi such embodiments or images differ considerably in their coarseness or fineness, in their density or subtlety, in their spiritual luminosity and receptivity. But essentially all embodiments (including animals and inanimate matter) share the capacity to act as loci for spiritual realities, which realities themselves need a place of reception to display their properties. This Akbarian way of describing the situation invites us to reconceptualize our ordinary view of objects, bodies and things as being images: analogous to pictures on a television screen or perhaps to holographic images. Essentially what we are presented with is a *non-thingified* ontology in which phenomenal objects, including people, have a reality only in relation to what they are images of. The self, in this respect, is a *relational term* which gains its significance from its embeddedness in the totality of the relational forms of the Real. As Izutsu remarks "The ontological status of phenomenal things is rather that of relations, that is, various and variegated relational forms of the Absolute itself ... in this sense only, they are all real."[38]

The notion of the multiple realizability of love and knowledge in a myriad of different forms (and kinds of forms) is, as we have already seen, a very familiar Akbarian theme. In this sense the machine functionalist conception of the *multiple realizability of mental properties* has its analogue in Akbarian metaphysics.

For Ibn 'Arabi, every single human intellectual production and thought (and every theory of mind) is an instant in the infinite multiple realizability of God's love to be known. And this clearly includes all the conditions necessary for there to be human beings to have thoughts in the first place. This situation is alluded to in the famous line "My heart has become capable of every form": a heart capable, we may say, of cultural, cosmic, physical, mental, moral, linguistic and spiritual forms *ad infinitum*. Reality, thus conceived, is of a formidable, ever-changing and immense nature, sometimes referred to by Ibn 'Arabi as "God's Vast Earth".[39] Whilst God's Vast Earth necessarily includes as one of its possibilities human intellectual and creative production, it cannot itself (because of its multidimensional vastness and kaleidoscopic infinity) be comprehended under any single mental representation or metaphor or theory of mind or body. Human intellectual productions can at best capture only an infinitesimal fraction of the nature of phenomenal reality. Phenomenal reality as understood by Ibn 'Arabi is itself intrinsically symbolic and possesses (as Izutsu points out) no reality in itself. The status of phenomenal reality is relational and dependent. It is therefore ontologically incorrect, if we are to follow Ibn 'Arabi in this matter, to envisage phenomenal reality as a collection of separate things or a concatenation of individual objects. Rather, the phenomenal world is the result of the One Unique Reality's disposition to appear as this or that, just as an image of a person's face in a mirror appears to be other than its originator. The human self is consequently neither a thing nor an object. It is accurate to say that the self, as we normally know and experience it, exists as a determinate point of vision. It also subsists, Ibn 'Arabi informs us, in the Divine Consciousness as in a Divine mirror. It is only the perfected self, known as the *insan-i-kamil* (also sometimes described by Ibn 'Arabi as "the heart which is devoid of wrong beliefs"),[40] which instantiates the essential Oneness of Being in its totality and absoluteness.

Bearing this in mind, let us consider once again cognitive science's attempt to unravel the mechanisms of the human mind. The chief and perhaps the most fundamental project of modern cognitive science has been the attempt to understand the architecture of the human mind as being computational in nature. Such a venture is beset with all kinds of theoretical problems and there have been many critics. One of the seminal texts in this programme has been Jerry A. Fodor's *The Modularity of Mind*.[41] In a recent assessment of the progress of the computational theory of mind Fodor regards such a project as one to which "most sensible psychologists and philosophers of mind, (*including Plato*[42]) have always been more or less wittingly devoted": that is, "the construction of a representational theory of mind; the reduction of minds to symbols". And he adds, "I sort of like the work. The pay is no good, and the progress is *very* slow. But you do get to meet interesting people on the way."[43] This conception of the mind as a symbol manipulator, as a dealer in symbols necessarily emphasizes the symbolic nature of all human knowledge and in this respect, at least, opens non-empiricist doors in so far as it rests on a view of the nature of knowledge which does not confine epistemological investigation to sense-experience or observable behaviour. Cognitive science presents us with a more subtle and variegated epistemology than was customary in the heyday of behaviourist psychology. Computational theories of mind accept the efficacy and reality of mental causation and mental worlds in a way that was forbidden by the behaviourist manifesto. But the acceptance of the world of mental phenomena itself poses the further question of the relationship between the mind and the world outside the mind. This is why some advocates of computational theories of the mind argue that such theories of mind must beware "of putting too much in the head" and also should "beware of *narrow* visions of the form and content of putative representational systems" which fail to deal adequately with action-oriented, environmentally related aspects of the human mind.[44] It is here that we can discern the beginnings of a broader conception of the human mind as being "a brain/body/world system". This hints at a kind of intrinsic, unavoidable ecological interdependence and interconnectedness between the outer world and inner aspects of the human mind. This recognition opens up promising vistas of reconceptualizing the mind–matter dualism much as, for example, space–time was conceptually reconfigured by Einsteinian physics. But, contrary to Fodor's understanding of Platonic ontology, Plato arguably regarded the *whole* of phenomenal reality (both internal mind-stuff and external observable reality) as analogous to shadows on the Cave wall. For Plato (but not Fodor, and not for computational theories of mind in general) we possess an essential knowledge of the pre-natal origin of these images which is epistemologically accessible through self-knowledge or recollection.[45] This is a far cry from any Fodorian modularity of the mind thesis. The axiom of self-knowledge does not, one might say cannot, figure in a computational theory of the mind such as Fodor's. How could a computer have self-knowledge in the Platonic sense? The important thing to grasp from the point of view of Ibn 'Arabi studies is that, while inanimate matter may be said to possess knowledge of a certain kind, it cannot possess the comprehensive knowledge of reality bestowed potentially on the human self by God as made in His image. So, whereas the theorists who construct computational theories of the mind may (at least potentially) possess epistemic access to the comprehensive knowledge of reality, the computational processes they theorize about cannot. It seems, then, that computational theories of the mind remain firmly rooted in a modern scientific world-view: a scientific view of reality which, as Roger Sperry in "Holding course amid shifting paradigms" insists, whilst allowing for today's new trends towards wholeness, subjectivity and qualities, "does not presage a further degree of general loosening or change in the conceptual foundations of science".[46]

This reiterates the impossibility of the prevailing epistemological co-ordinates of science of ever producing more than a *set of theories* about the ultimate nature of reality. This is a view interestingly endorsed by Karl Popper's[47] insistence on the conjectural and provisional nature of all scientific theorizing. For Popper there are never any true scientific theories, or at least we can never know them to be true. It follows, from a Popperian point of view, that the value of modern cognitive explanations of mind remain no more than provisional and conjectural theories: they do not, and cannot, constitute knowledge.

In almost Popperian fashion, but for very different reasons, Ibn 'Arabi's metaphysics would regard the theories and findings of science as being conjectural and provisional but also add that they can only reveal a small fraction of the nature of reality.

It is when we consider the vastness and centrality of Ibn 'Arabi's conception of the self that the findings of contemporary experimental psychology and cognitive science seem fragmented and diverse, and unable (or unwilling) to conceive of the human subject as the synthesis and locus for biological, psychological, linguistic, historical, cultural, spiritual and cosmological realities without these dimensions of the self implying any fissure in the Unity of Being.

In God's Vast Earth, computational theories of mind encode (at its most general abstract and theoretical level) the technological and scientific mindset of the new millennium. In the context of the metaphysics of *wahdat al-wujud* such theories of mind may reveal, to some extent, the complicated mechanisms of the brain's information processing systems, but they equally put a veil over the very mind whose working they seek to causally unfold. Such theories offer an example of the way in which the mindset of an era can become its own veil. Cognitive scientists may regard the human self (or mind) as an intelligent, information processing, evolving, adaptive system but the limitations of this model become even more clear when we see what questions they leave off their computational agenda. Two of the most telling questions are "What ends ought we to pursue?" and "How ought we to live?" These contemplative Platonic invitations to self-knowledge do not figure, even remotely, in any proposed computational architecture of the human mind. For such theories of mind the self-enhancing power of contemplative and meditative ways of being and knowing remain profoundly unaccounted for and inessential. Computational theories of mind seem singularly devoid of any adequate metaphysics of the self.

Leaving aside these fundamental problems with computational theories of the mind, it is noticeable that within the history of psychology the concentration of such theories on mechanisms, theoretical models and simulations has brought to bear a larger set of disciplinary perspectives (mathematical, philosophical and linguistic) on the problem of mind than were previously deployed. In this sense, the rise of cognitive science has contributed to the inclusion of wider disciplinary perspectives. But it would be remiss not to see this wider inter-disciplinary flowering as having its roots in the very beginnings of modern psychology and to see how some of the nineteenth-century progenitors of modern psychology dealt with the central epistemological problems which the study of mental life raised.

Wider perspectives on the mind and self in the early history of psychology: the case of Wundt and James

We have seen that the historically diverse range of interests which gave rise to modern psychology mitigated against the self becoming a central, unifying explanatory concept. It was also that very same diversity which prompted the need for viewing the self from a widening variety of psychological viewpoints. Even a precursory look at the history of psychology makes Roger Smith's observation, that "psychology is a cluster of activities with a family resemblance but no common identity, and the field undoubtedly has multiple origins", into a self-evident truism.[48] Historically its multiple origins are as diverse as brain physiology, sensation, higher mental processes, perception, consciousness, philosophical empiricism, Darwinian biology, American functionalism, and pragmatism, animal studies, and more recently as we have seen, theories of artificial intelligence, computer programming, and technology. From the very beginnings there was the attempt to supersede philosophical armchair speculations about the nature of mind (like Cartesian dualism, for example) by using strictly empirical experimental psychological methods. The unambiguous aim was to open the human mind itself to experimental investigation. In fact Wilhelm Wundt in his promotion of psychology as an experimental science felt that psychology could put to one side, once and for all perhaps, the metaphysical questions concerning "God, Freedom and Immortality" so beloved by Kant. Looking back from the vantage point of this century, such a programme seems philosophically naive and on a par with the logical positivist's dream that, as Carnap insisted, "there is no question whose answer is in principle unattainable by science".[49]

In hindsight we may be philosophically inclined to smile at Wundt's conviction, in the 1873 edition of *Principles of Physiological Psychology*, that the findings of scientific psychology may be capable of mediating "a total comprehension of human existence".[50] By contrast (in his more metaphysical moments), the American psychologist William James considered psychology to be considerably more restricted in its capabilities.

In his *Principles of Psychology*, William James memorably codifies the view that the psychologist is necessarily a *cerebralist*. He argued that "a certain amount of brain-physiology must be presupposed or included in psychology" because mental life "works under conditions" and "the quest conditions of the conditions becomes the psychologist's most interesting task".[51] Damage or alteration to the physiology of the brain can seriously affect the human faculties of perception, sensation, memory, and so on. Our mental life depends on the conditions of our brains. However, in spite of his cerebralist axiom, such a preoccupation with brain-science did not sustain William James's interest in psychology for very long, primarily because he was constantly drawn to larger metaphysical questions concerning the human condition. James oscillated between scientific and more mystical–philosophical interests. Eventually, in spite of his fame as a founder figure of psychology in America, he abandoned psychology altogether.

James situated the object of psychology as the investigation into the brain mechanisms which govern memory, reason, volition, imagination, language acquisition, and the like. These themselves become the diverse objects of psychological investigation. Under such an investigative rubric the self does not figure as a primary object of psychological investigation. Rather, the object of investigation becomes mental phenomena: in short, the object is the mind. The self becomes an emergent and secondary product of the mind or brain. By recommending this emphasis on the correlation between brain and mind, James defined what was to constitute the new science of psychology. James clearly recognized that this emphasis on the brain conditions under which mental life operates relieved psychology of having to pronounce on the more metaphysical questions concerning the human self and its destiny. This simply was not psychology's task:

the modern psychologist didn't need to choose between a *psychology with a soul* or *without a soul*.[52] This, in effect, meant that for psychology such questions could largely be ignored and the presumptions of a scientific world-view promoted. Secondly, because psychology was now deemed scientific it meant that psychology need not engage in metaphysical reflections on its own assumptions. Its method was empirical and experimental and that was that. William James's argument summed up the case for psychology being a natural science whose theorizing and methods aimed to produce models of the causal mechanisms which condition mental life. Much twentieth-century psychology followed the Jamesian recommendation to concentrate its analytical attentions on aspects, mechanism and method. Even James's famous conclusion (which is in direct contradiction to Wilhelm Wundt's view) that "consciousness, then, does not appear to itself chopped up in bits"[53] is the result, says James, of the proper application of the empirical method when the mind examines itself from within. The epistemic access to mental life was, for James, some form of empirical internal perception which was taken to be analogous to the role of observation in the physical sciences.

Both James and Wundt took seriously the internal, mental worlds of the individual and both considered human consciousness and its contents to be the proper object of psychological investigation. Equally, they both sought to authenticate the scientific credentials of psychology as science. Much later William James, in *A World of Pure Experience*, advocated an even more radical form of empiricism. It was a view in which objective realities exist as a function of our mental life, or mind, or consciousness. So the purely cerebralist assumptions of the earlier James began to recognize the need to broaden the scope of psychology to a psychology of mental experience which breaks down any naive duality between subject and object, observer and observed.

In the work of Wilhelm Wundt we also find a psychologist grappling with some of the wider conceptual issues facing a psychology of consciousness. Wundt's *Principles of Physiological Psychology*, like James's famous work, reflects a self-conscious desire to promote psychology as a natural science whose experimental methodology was, for Wundt, replicable "experimental self-observation".[54] Wundt uses this term to distinguish it from what he considered to be the scientifically unsatisfactory practice known as introspection, with which it was sometimes seen as identical. The aim of this methodology was to discover and examine the atomic elements of human consciousness. In effect Wundt was committed to two psychologies: the first investigated experimentally the alleged building bricks of human consciousness (like sensation and feeling), but the second (which concerned itself with the higher mental processes like language, memory and thinking) needed to employ a historical methodology. The products of the higher mental processes like language, myth, religion, morality, art, culture, law and history were culturally mediated and required a science of culture rather than a science of nature for their analysis and investigation. Wundt's ten-volume work, *Cultural Psychology* (*Volkerpsychologie*), provided the theoretical basis for the later development of social psychology. For Wundt, a psychology of consciousness and a psychology of culture necessarily deployed logically distinct methodologies.

The deeper conceptual issue raised by Wundt's work was the question of whether psychology was a science of nature or a science of the mind or spirit, that is, *Naturwissenschaft* or *Geisteswissenschaft*. Behind this distinction lies the view of the human self as being simultaneously located in two distinct orders: the self as part of the physical and biological order of causally determined happenings, and the self as part of the cultural, historical order of human freedom, values, meanings, language and symbols. Wundt recognized that the methods used for investigating the former are inappropriate for investigating the latter. The products of higher mental processes (belief-systems, cultural values, religion and so on) could only be examined by using the historical method of investigation, not experimental self-observation. Even Wundt's view of the atomistic nature of consciousness as being built from elementary parts allowed for a process of "apperception" (as he called it) by which conscious experience is no mere addition of the parts. The situation is analogous to a combination of chemical elements resulting in a new compound which is more than just a collection of its basic elements. His atomistic view of the building blocks of human consciousness therefore allowed for dynamic qualitative synthesis. The human mind was not to be regarded as a passive, mechanical receptor of its atomic constituents but rather, via its higher mental processes, an active organizer and synthesizer into meaningful wholes. For this reason he named his view of the mind "voluntarism". What, then, did Wundt make of the notion of the self? The self, he suggests, is simply the result of "the unity of volition plus the universal control of our mental life which it renders possible".[55] The self was none other than the power and control we have over our mental lives, and is akin to the human will. In this case, would this mean that some people would have less self than others? Or even less self at one moment than at another moment? There are many analytical questions one would like to raise here but the important point is the linking of the concept of the self with the concepts of human volition, agency, control and autonomy. This conceptual move indicates that even in the work of the inaugurators of modern scientific psychology a wider metaphysics of the self was unavoidable. For Wundt the self is ultimately an unexplained power: the power we have over our mental lives. Strangely, this unexplained power can be virtually left out of the picture when investigating such things as feelings. Consider Wundt's tri-dimensional theory of feeling. All human feeling, concludes Wundt, can be plotted on a physiological matrix of pleasant/unpleasant, high/low arousal, concentrated/relaxed attention. Such a mathematically generalized picture of feelings leaves completely untouched the infinite shades of meaning and value which conceptually impregnate our myriad feelings of love, patience, diligence, hope, belief, confidence, resentment, wonder, beauty, power, loss, compassion. He attempts to explain human feeling without any recourse to a wider concept of the human self. When it is recognized that it is in discourse, not physiology, that the meanings of human feeling are given cognitive value, the wafer-thin physiology of feeling proposed by Wundt seems unconvincing. A physiology of feeling (like an arithmetic of happiness) is an analytically spartan exercise which intrinsically fails to capture the subtle richness, variety and modalities of felt human experience. Wundt's attempt to arithmeticize and physiologicize feeling seems to dissociate feelings from having any higher cognitive function.

Over all, much of the treatment of the self in the history of psychology oscillates between either an evolutionary biologizing view of the self as part of the causal, physical and biological order, or the view that the self is a historical, cultural and social construction whose nature is unfixed. Wundt's two psychologies embrace both positions: he recognizes that we are both biological and cultural beings. But even Wundt's view of consciousness did not go unchallenged. By contrast, James emphatically opposed the Wundtian view that consciousness could be analysed into elements. The nature of consciousness, James famously insisted, is a continuous unified stream whose evolutionary function is to enable us to successfully adapt to the environment. The development of higher mental processes (such as desires, cognitions, reasonings, decisions and the like) were evolutionarily advantageous and this is the reason for their emergence in sentient beings. James defined mental phenomena as actions done for an end which show a choice of means: only these, he says, "can be called indubitable expressions of mind".[56] In a rather memorable example James emphasizes the intrinsic intentionality of conscious mental phenomena and the intrinsic non-intentionality of purely physical causes of events. He recounts:

> Romeo wants Juliet as the filings want the magnet; and if no obstacles intervene he moves towards her by as straight a line as they. But Romeo and Juliet, if a wall be built between them, do not remain idiotically pressing their faces against its opposite sides like the magnet and the filings with the card. Romeo soon finds a circuitous way, by scaling the wall or otherwise, of touching Juliet's lips directly. With the filings the path is fixed; whether it reaches the end depends on accidents. With the lover it is the end which is fixed, the path may be modified indefinitely.[57]

What then was James's theory of the self? There is a whole chapter of the *Principles*[58] devoted to it. There is the empirical self, or me, which consists of the body and the social self. He says, "A man's social self is the recognition he gets from his mates." This entails that we can have many social selves, some of which, James recognizes, may conflict with others. The empirical me can be full of internal contradictions. However, the I, by contrast with me, is that which recognizes the old man as being the same person as the young boy – but grown older. James concludes his discussion of the self by suggesting that the I need not be regarded as an unchanging metaphysical entity like the soul, or a principle like the pure Ego, viewed out of time. The consciousness of self can simply be accounted for by the stream of thought hypothesis: the I is a thought which simply appropriates all other thoughts to itself and which "can remember those which went before, and know the things they knew". He recognizes that this view of the self cannot assign a reason "why successive thoughts should inherit each others' possessions". In a more mystical turn of mind James allows "that why such finite streams of thought are called into existence in such functional dependence on brains" must lie in "the total sense or meaning of the world".[59] He acknowledges that we must trust that there is such meaning but that such a question lies outside the province of psychology as a natural science. It was partly James's fairly constant awareness of the limitations of the psychological enterprise that led him into more metaphysical pastures. Of Wundt, William James remarked: "he isn't a genius, he is a professor – a being whose duty is to know everything, and have his own opinion about everything". The whole tenor of James's writings, both in psychology and elsewhere (for example, in *The Varieties of Religious Experience*), whilst always lucid and interesting, exemplifies a tentative openness to alternative perspectives. He seems to have recognized that no single method of investigation or single discipline can legitimately claim to deal with the human subject as the locus or matrix of multivariate biological, psychological, cultural, historical, rational and linguistic factors.

James and Wundt, then, in their different ways, were grappling with, and acknowledging some of the wider conceptual issues facing the scientific investigation of the human mind. But their metaphysics was generally confined to the scientific investigation of the conscious aspect of mind. The human mind was defined essentially as exhibiting consciousness, including volition and intentionality. The notion of any kind of profound *unconscious* motivation hidden from conscious intro-spection could not readily feature on their agenda. The psychoanalysis of Freud and Jung is unmistakably opposed to such a one-dimensional view of the human mind.

The Jungian assault on the unsatisfactoriness of adopting a one-dimensional view of the mind, once again, reflects the perceived need within psychology for a more comprehensive philosophy of mind. Jung's position on the nature of mind and self is encapsulated in his remark that "A high regard for the unconscious psyche is by no means such a delusion as our Western rationalism likes to suppose."[60] Whatever the value of analytical psychology may turn out to be, it undeniably contributed to a paradigm shift in our understanding of the hidden, non-rational depths of the human mind and the self. This shift of emphasis (from the conscious to the unconscious dimensions of the self) offered a topography of the self which recognized its subterranean and almost geological immensity. The self, for the inaugurators of psychoanalytic psychology, had a much vaster and deeper landscape than hitherto imagined, at least as imagined by some of the founder figures of modern scientific psychology.

In summary, the treatment of the self in modern psychology has been complexly embedded in the prevailing paradigms (from early experimentalism to psychoanalysis, to Gestalt psychology, to behaviourism, to humanistic psychology, to modern cognitive science and computational theories of mind, to discursive and critical psychology), all of which have faced the need to provide an adequate theory of the self which acknowledges the multidimensionality of the human self as being located in both the physical and biological orders, and in cultural, historical and value-laden universes. None of these psychological enterprises can ultimately avoid the essentially contested nature of the preferred theories of mind and self which inform them. Overall, the prevailing metaphysical picture of the self presented by late twentieth-century psychology might be one of the human self conceived of as an intelligent adaptive organism. Whatever its merits (and it probably seems particularly meritorious if you are a cognitive scientist), it leaves so much off the metaphysical agenda that the picture it presents, by comparison with the metaphysics of Ibn ʿArabi, is a metaphysically impoverished, microcosmic landscape of the self.

When we remember that Ibn ʿArabi's metaphysics of the self insists that potentially it is the human self which integrates and synthesizes all aspects of reality and that it is this ontological fact which constitutes the *raison d'être* of human existence and distinguishes human kind from all other species, then we realize that we are confronted with a metaphysical picture of an entirely different grandeur, order, and magnitude. For modern psychology the human self is decidedly microcosmic. The human species is generally conceived of as only part of the evolutionary and cosmological order, perhaps considered only a small speck in an infinitely vast universe. For Ibn ʿArabi such views are a total inversion of the actual situation: the human self is essentially macrocosmic. The essential reality of the human self is not evolutionary or cosmological: these universes themselves are small compared with the inheritance which God has bestowed upon the human self. We read:

> Thus, this being (Adamic) was called Man and God's Represent-
> ative. As for his quality as a man it designates his synthesised
> nature (containing virtually all other natures created) and his
> aptitude to embrace the essential Truths. Man is to God that
> which the pupil is to the eye (the pupil in Arabic is called
> "man within the eye"), the pupil being that by which seeing
> is effected; for through him (that is to say, the Universal Man)
> God contemplates His creation and dispenses His mercy. Thus
> is man at once ephemeral and eternal, a being created perpetual
> and immortal, a Verb discriminating (by his distinctive knowledge)
> and unifying (by his divine essence). By his existence the world
> was completed.[61]

Such is the case that the *insan-i-kamil* can be said to instantiate the "manifested consciousness of God". The scale of this radical transfiguration of the self in favour of the Divine Identity is nowhere more clearly stated than when God says of such a person "I am his hearing and his sight".[62] From such a macrocosmic and total vision the self-involving dynamics of the Unity of Being becomes ubiquitous and transparent. And for such a person the reality of such sayings as "He is the first, He is the last, He is the outward, He is the inward" remains unassailable. This totally transfigured vision of reality is described by Ibn ʿArabi as the Station of Light which seems to be a situation in which the normal coordinates of space and time are suspended and become merely hypothetical:

> I ... saw a light which seemed to illumine what was before me,
> despite the fact that I had lost all sense of front or back, being as

if I had no back at all. Indeed during this vision I had no sense of direction whatever, my sense of vision being, so to speak, spherical in its scope. I recognized my spatial position only as a hypothesis, not as a reality.[63]

The general idea of a self-involving modal reality has, perhaps unexpectedly, an analogue in our own theoretical culture. We can glimpse the plausibility of this idea by examining some of the developments in post-empiricist philosophy of science. The analogy is only partial, but it is a fruitful one.

Psychology, post-empiricist views of science and the self

Certain developments in the philosophy of science (in the latter part of the twentieth century) have been characterized as a transition from understanding science as a mirror to reality (which depicts unchangeable ahistorical truths about the way the world is) to a view of science as simply a tool for the manipulation of reality. It is a transition from viewing science as being in the business of representing the truth about the way things are to a largely pragmatic view that the findings and methodologies of science are simply one form of theory and practice which manipulates reality in particular kinds of ways. Science is one kind of epistemic affordance, as it is sometimes put.

To understand why this conception of science is so important and radical is to understand that it is attacking both the truth-telling account of science and the alleged epistemologically privileged nature of science. It is argued that the old empiricist view of science (called by Rorty the "spectator theory of truth")[64] needs to be replaced by the view that the scientist is not an aloof ahistorical spectator but *an active manipulator of reality*. In this sense, the observer and the observed are inextricably entangled and what we take as "the real" is more accurately to be regarded as a function of our interaction with the phenomena we study and the way we study it. This posits a view of reality which replaces the assumption that science pictures reality as it is in itself with a view of reality as revealing aspects of itself according to the manner in which it is approached and investigated. To this must be added the more general statement that all we ever have at our disposal are a matrix of approaches to reality: scientific, artistic, moral, political, and religious, and so on. Within the context of the philosophy of science it is this ontological emphasis on the *self-disclosing dynamic nature of reality* which distinguishes post-empiricist from empiricist views of science. As Werner Heisenberg (the founder of the uncertainty principle in quantum physics) puts it, "What we observe is not nature itself but nature exposed to our method of questioning."[65] This idea of a self-disclosing dynamic reality is not a million miles away from the Akbarian understanding of the metaphysics of Being. Let us consider this issue a little further.

The substance of the attack on the empiricist theory of truth is succinctly summed up in the following:

> Interestingly, in the philosophy of science attention has shifted recently from a view of knowledge as (linguistic) representations, to knowledge as *skills and practices*, that is, it has shifted from representation to manipulation. Scientific knowledge is a matter of actively disclosing the world rather than merely picturing it. This suggests a more pragmatic, interactive view of reality, as dependent on practical exploration, than is implied in the classical realist tenet of a mind-independent reality: "science (is) a pragmatic exploratory coping with the world" ... the real is what we manipulate.[66]

According to this view there is no reason why reality could not disclose apparently paradoxical aspects of itself, for instance, the wave–particle duality mentioned in an earlier chapter. This general idea of reality being of such a dynamic nature that it configures itself to the way we grapple with it, makes our beliefs about, and approach to, reality somewhat pivotal. It is interesting that this point should throw some light on Ibn 'Arabi's insistence on the conformity of reality to the servant's opinion of it. This Akbarian insight needs to be understood with care for it is not the case that reality always conforms to our beliefs and practices, for it often simply does not. The point is a much more interesting and far-reaching one. It is the view that our predispositional beliefs and practices radically affect what reality can show (or not) of its deepest recesses and universality. What we are dealing with, as far as Ibn 'Arabi's metaphysics is concerned, is ourselves as potentially no other than an image of the whole: that is, we are dealing with a picture of the self as capable, in potential and in principle, of completely and totally imaging and witnessing reality in all its modalities and non-modalities. If Ibn 'Arabi's metaphysics of the self is to be taken seriously then we are faced with a situation in which the image and the original form an inseparable, indissoluble and seamless unity. For Akbarian metaphysics there is no God-independent reality. There is only a Self-involving Unity rigorously identical with Itself. It is a dynamic ontology mirroring Itself in a myriad of its own Self-nesses, either partially or wholly.

This means that the human self, in its primordial universal condition, is a point of vision which possesses "no essential characteristic other than totality and absoluteness". Its very nature is to mirror the totality and absoluteness of the Unity of Being. This *is* the human potential. If this potential is to be realized by the individual it requires an approach to reality which involves the whole of oneself, so that the polishing of the mirror of the heart can take place and the heart can become devoid of "wrong beliefs" about the nature of the Real. For this purpose the tools of modern science are simply not the right tools but we ourselves are. Science can, of course, legitimately continue to roam in its own specific playing field and uncover certain aspects of what Einstein called "the Ancient One". But the true nature of the Real, if we are to follow Ibn 'Arabi on this matter, cannot be arrived at by such means. This conclusion does not impugn the open-endedness or creativity of science, but it does set epistemological limits concerning the kind and type of knowledge science can, in principle, provide. But even within these limits it is, as Einstein carefully points out, inaccurate to consider the scientist as being in the business of systematic epistemology:

> the external conditions which are set for [the scientist] by the
> facts of experience do not permit him to let himself be too
> much restricted, in the construction of his conceptual world,
> by the adherence to an epistemological system. He, therefore,
> must appear to the systematic epistemologist as a type of
> unscrupulous opportunist.[67]

Similarly, in the context of the metaphysics of unity, the seeker after truth may appear to the rationalist or empiricist to be a kind of unscrupulous opportunist whose conception of reality is not limited or restricted by what appear to others to be the facts of experience – for the very landscape and architecture of the *salik*'s self-experience is recast in the very process of grappling with it. The Divine Principle is simple: respond to Me and I will respond to you. This axiomatic principle is hinted at in the Arabic name *mujib* – the One who necessarily responds. This opens up the human possibility, according to Ibn 'Arabi, of dealing directly with reality "as it is in Itself", without intermediary and not masked by the phenomena of secondary causes. By contrast, modern science necessarily deals with the secondary phenomena of cosmological, physical, biological, psychological, historical, social, and cultural causation and it deals with them by means which are, according to Ibn 'Arabi, relatively indirect and limited – incapable of discovering the theophanic secret of the atom. Much post-empiricist philosophy of science tends also to emphasize the conjectural and provisional nature of scientific knowledge and its inevitable entanglement in interpretative schema.

But to see the science of psychology as perspective-bound may be considered by some of its practitioners as its prime heuristic virtue, which resists grand theory in favour of painstaking empirical research. However, the apparent modesty of such a claim is incongruent with the immodesty of the claims (made by some very influential schools of psychology) which accord epistemological privilege to their own paradigm as the paradigm: as the only way of acquiring legitimate knowledge or as the only way of practising psychology. In the history of psychology such a claim to paradigmatic superiority is nowhere better illustrated that in behaviourist psychology. I simply quote illustratively the behaviourist manifesto by J. B. Watson:

> Psychology as the behaviourist views it is a purely objective experimental branch of natural science. Its theoretical goal is the prediction and control of behavior. Introspection forms no essential part of its methods, nor is the scientific value of its data dependent upon the readiness with which they lend themselves to interpretation in terms of consciousness.[68]

This must itself be a paradigm case of predispositional beliefs limiting what "reality" can show of itself.

Psychology and essential contestability

We have seen that it is the multivariate dimensionality of the self which makes it intractable to overall explanation from any single disciplinary perspective, including psychology. It is this same architectural complexity of the self which can generate permanent and irresolvable disagreement about the nature of the self from within, and across, particular perspectives. That is why it is possible to read the history of psychology as the history of an essentially contested concept. The competing schools of psychology have tended to result in a fragmented view of the self or a reductionism of the self to brain or mind to machine. If we add to this the tendency of experimental psychology to view itself as a mirror to nature – a mirror which stands objectively aloof in its findings from the cultural assumptions and historical conditions of the modern era which have produced it – then the epistemological assumptions of such a psychology are likely to remain unquestioned and unquestionable. It is when we look at psychology as a human social construction (and a potentially human emancipatory practice) that we see it as serving human interests and inevitably coloured by prevailing conceptions of the self, whether stated or unstated, investigated or left unexamined.

The ways in which each era and its theoretical culture is influenced by a prevailing sense of the self is importantly developed by Logan in his paper "Historical change in the prevailing sense of self". He proposes "that a major component of the broad cultural context for theorizing is the *prevailing sense of self* [my italics] of members of that culture and that era, and the prevailing sense of self ... be viewed as central in historical and cultural change".[69]

Equally, the inclusion of widening interdisciplinary perspectives in psychology (such as linguistics, artificial intelligence, philosophy and computational theory) reflect and recursively influence theoretical changes in our understanding of the self. Such reconceptualizations of the self have themselves been forged by the monumental and unprecedented changes of modernity. The cognitive melting-pot of modernity has somewhat traumatized the theoretical understanding of the self: its traditional parameters have been questioned, its solidity dissolved and its status deemed problematic. Old ways of theorizing about the self have become less compelling and new ways unproven, uncertain and relativistic. The changing contours of modernity have fundamentally shaken the experiential foundations of the meaning of selfhood, whilst at the level of individual self-identity there has remained a need for people to hang on to some centrally defining topology of the self. When under strain traditional views of the self have sometimes been reasserted with new dogmatic vigour. However, such reinvigorated fundamentalisms, both secular and religious, may also be seen ironically as testifying to the increasing need for a fundamental reconfiguration of the parameters of the self: a more global view of the self perhaps. At any rate, it is worth pondering on the possibility that it is not simply coincidence that Ibn Arabi's universal metaphysics of the self is becoming widely available in Western culture at the start of the twenty-first century.

The self as sui generis

It is pertinent now to gather together from the sum of these discussions of Ibn 'Arabi's metaphysics a view of the self which is isomorphic with its main outline. In doing so it is useful to regard Ibn 'Arabi's concept of the Self as *sui generis*, that is, as an irreducible metaphysical category. Individual selves, as they are ordinarily understood, turn out to be, for Ibn 'Arabi, more accurately described as "Himself-nesses". They can be strictly regarded as expressions of the Divine Identity. We remember the line "I wrapped myself in flesh and bones and appeared as Yunus" or, one might equally assert (in order to indicate Ibn 'Arabi's view of the conceptual magnitude and infinity of these determinate modes), appeared as the cosmos, appeared as the era, and appeared as the human species. We are also warned not to embark upon our own intellectual reflection about "God's Self" for only "His own Self" can "denote Him".[70] It is God who gives knowledge to us of Himself in the persons of prophets, saints, in revealed texts and in the hearts of his servants, according to His will. These are some of the means by which we learn of "the Self of the Real".[71] What we can say, in line with the metaphysics of unity of Ibn 'Arabi, is that the two fundamental dimensions of the Self of the Real – transcendence and immanence – denote what we might call macrocosmic and microcosmic aspects of the human self. In the macrocosmic sense the Self is dimensionless, and in the microcosmic sense the Self is configured in determinate modes or images. The microcosmic dimension embraces the infinity of the world process, including ourselves as determinate forms of the Real. Such a unitive metaphysics recognizes human individuality and uniqueness and the sacredness of the individual but does not, logically cannot, imply any form of individualism that regards human life as no more than a collection of individual separate selves. There is no metaphysics of individualism in Ibn 'Arabi.[72] In Ibn Arabi's metaphysical teachings the individual human microcosmic self is, in essence, made in the image of the whole and thereby images the ontological irreducibility of the whole and contains the potential to reflect the whole as a whole: in this respect it is itself *sui generis*. This means that, from the point of view of Ibn 'Arabi, the human self cannot be reduced to the brain, nor to biology, nor to culture. It also means that the human self is a locus for freedom, deliberation, choice and feelings. Consciousness, awareness and mental life are, according to this view, properties of the self. Equally it follows that it is the self which suffers patience and resentment; it is the self which expresses generosity and love and gratitude; it is the self which produces the conceptual worlds of art, mathematics, literature, music, medicine, law, religion and science, and so on. It is the self which recognizes the body as *its* body – not simply as an object – but as an inseparable existential part of its own phenomenal field, agency and awareness. It is the self which is capable of witnessing internally and externally the infinity of the world process. Some of these features of the self are interestingly encapsulated in Ninian Smart's working formula of the human self as a historical, decision-making, imaginative animal.[73] Smart's acknowledgement of the cultural aspects of the self (as a historical being), of the psychological aspects of the self (as a reasoning, decision-making, imaginative being), and the biological aspects of the self (as a member of the animal species) indicates something of the complex dimensionality of the human self. It also seems an implausible assumption to suggest that the human self can be reduced to any one of its own dimensions.

All this is implied in the notion of treating the concept of the person as a *sui generis* category. But, for Ibn 'Arabi, there is more. Ibn 'Arabi proposes *further* dimensions of "the Self of the Real", of which the historical, psychological and biological constitute *only* some of the dimensions. Even more fundamentally, the Self of Akbarian metaphysics transcends *any* dimensionality whatsoever. And this entails that *all* the immanent dimensions of the Self, its determinate modes and appearances, bear testimony to the transcendent vastness and uniqueness of the One and Only Being. For Ibn 'Arabi consciousness of the Self, in its metaphysical depths, is nothing less than consciousness of the Unity of Being. The dimensions of biology, culture, history, cosmology, adaptation to the environment, perception, memory, thinking, imagination and so on are some of the means by which God manifests His mystery to Himself in "one global object". This one global object, if regarded as a dimension of the eternal, is neither exhaustive of it nor co-terminus with it. This one global object is forever in the making.

We are now in a position to relate these general themes and issues regarding the metaphysics of the self to two important areas of modern psychology: therapy and feminism. These areas present us with an analytical opportunity to examine some of the central and underlying assumptions regarding the nature of the self in contemporary emancipatory discourse.

Psychology, therapy and the self

Subjective human experience has always remained essential to therapeutic theory and practice. And there have been other contemporary influences, like consciousness studies[74] and critical psychology, which involve broad and liberating parameters for understanding human possibility, development and subjectivity. These, together with the more mainstream therapeutic traditions of modern psychology, have kept alive a variety of epistemological strategies for investigating human identity and selfhood and engaging in the woof and warp of lived human experience. Such traditions offer psychology the methodological resources to repair "the exclusion of subjectivity" noted earlier. The modern therapeutic landscape deploys a variety of perspectives and practices, including the phenomenological, the existential, the social constructionist, the psychoanalytic, the clinical and the cognitive. Such methodological pluralism acknowledges the multivariate factors which facilitate subjective human experience. All these forms of emancipatory psychology incorporate some assumptions about the nature of the self and its proper functioning. Often the starting point is the person's subjective interpretation of experience and events: that is, the stories they tell us about themselves. Some of these traditions offer the individual prescriptive replacement narratives, others are more ideologically fluid and flexibly postmodern. Even in scientifically based cognitive therapy, in which it is theoretically postulated that the cognitive assumptions of the client sometimes produce psychological dysfunction, the starting point is the client's first-person account.

Overall, emancipatory psychology is one of the most fundamental seams in the complex archaeology of the human self at the beginning of twenty-first-century psychology. The very presence of psychotherapy indicates that we need not be unduly alarmed by the conclusions of cognitive science "that there is no self, no mind or observer sitting at the center of the brain to receive mental images or initiate movements".[75] Did anyone ever believe that there was a self sitting at the centre of the brain anyway?

The founders of the various schools and approaches to psychotherapy are legion. These include such well-known names as Sigmund Freud, Carl Jung, Abraham Maslow, Carl Rogers, George Kelly, Eric Erikson and Aaron Beck, and such central analytical concepts associated with these figures as the Oedipus complex, individuation, hierarchy of needs, unconditional positive regard, personal constructs, normative crises, cognitive distortion and so forth. Some approaches are typically conducted on a one-to-one basis whilst others are family-, group-, gender- or even community-based practices. There is no need to engage in unravelling any further the theoretical labyrinth and methodological diversity of modern psychological therapeutic practice. What is more appropriate is to relate the overall picture of emancipatory and transformative psychology in the early twenty-first century to issues concerning modernist and postmodernist theories of knowledge. We will then be in a better position to assess how they stand in relation to Ibn 'Arabi's metaphysics of the Self.

According to Gergen and Kaye, the modernist view is the view of the therapist as a scientifically trained professional who has at their disposal objective empirical scientific theories with which to diagnose and hopefully remedy psychological dysfunction. In this case, the scientific narratives of the therapist have epistemological privilege over the client's narrative to such an extent that the therapist's account is deployed to replace the essentially pre-scientific folk psychology of the client. And, hopefully, to replace a "failure story" with a "success story". Of course, the therapist may be, and often is, eclectic in his or her approach, having recourse to a variety of scientifically validated theoretical and methodological procedures. To the extent that such scientific accounts remain, to their advocates at least, relatively invio-lable, epistemologically privileged and somewhat fixed in the range of their "narrative formulations", they can often amount "to a constric-tion of life possibilities". That is, in so far as

> the therapist's narrative becomes the client's reality, and his or
> her actions are guided accordingly, life options for the client
> are severely truncated. Of all the possible modes of acting in
> the world, one is set on a course emphasizing, for example, ego
> autonomy, self-actualization, rational appraisal, or emotional
> expressiveness, depending on the brand of therapy inadvertently
> selected [by the client].[76]

Postmodernism offers two main objections to any such modernist assumptions. Firstly, it denies the epistemologically privileged posi-tion of scientific accounts – for postmodernism scientific narratives are just one kind of narrative among many. They do not necessarily have any intrinsic superiority over other forms of narrative – they simply constitute one way in which reality might be represented or manipu-lated. Secondly, it is argued, scientific formulations tend to be abstract and decontextualized from the historical and cultural settings of both the therapist and the client. Following Gergen and Kaye further in this matter, such scientific formulations "are, in this sense, clumsy and insensitive, failing to register the particularities of the client's living conditions. To emphasize self-fulfilment to a woman living in a house-hold with three small children and a mother-in-law with Alzheimer's is not likely to be beneficial."[77]

Central to the postmodernist conceptual landscape, therefore, is the denial that science has a monopoly over the truth. In general, this constitutes a denial that *any* representation of reality is epistemologically privileged or is directly able to know reality "as it is in itself". For postmodernism the nature of reality is mediated through linguistic and social constructions, which are necessarily themselves relative to historical and cultural ways of life.

If we couple this postmodernist view of the perspectival, historically positioned and mediated nature of all human knowledge with the post-empiricist tendency to regard science as a form of pragmatic manipulation of reality, then we can begin to see that much postmodernism is committed to the view that we can never get behind the back of language (as Gadamer insists).[78] This means that there is no unmediated access to "things as they are in themselves". And it follows that the objective "truth of self" assumption of modernist therapy is an epistemological non-starter. Gergen and Kaye conclude that the ambivalent result of postmodernism is, on the one hand, to encourage the client "to explore a variety of means of understanding the self", and, on the other, to discourage a commitment to any of these accounts as standing for the truth of self. Postmodernism, notwithstanding this unreassuring implication, has the merit of potentially freeing people from any dogmatic narratives about who and what they are. And this itself has the merit of allowing a variety of metaphysical views of the self to co-exist. How, then, does this stand in relation to Ibn 'Arabi's landscape of the self?

The crucial caveat which radically differentiates Ibn 'Arabi's view of the self from postmodern pluralistic accounts of the self is that liberation from limiting beliefs is necessary, for Ibn 'Arabi, *only* so that the universal reality of the Self can be grasped. For Ibn 'Arabi it is axiomatic that the Self cannot be dissolved in a pluralistic relativism or a labyrinth of secondary causes, but it can and does *express* itself in and through these means. Within the context of Akbarian metaphysics the Self of the Real can be attained when the imagined individual separateness of the self gives way to its ontological origin, as no other, in the Unity of Being. This is why in the *Sufis of Andalusia* Ibn 'Arabi insists that if we want to know our reality we must take God alone as our guide and He will teach us. This vital fundamental commitment is the only epistemological key which can truly liberate us from "immersion in limiting constructions of the world".[79]

Consequently, for Ibn 'Arabi there cannot be any microcosmic dissolving of the self in the vicissitudes of linguistic and cultural discourse. There can, in fact, be no dissolving of the Self at all but only the dissolving of misconceptions and ignorance regarding it. This point is scrupulously in line with the Metaphysics of Unity. It is in the contemplation of self-experience that the Unity of Being can be consciously reaffirmed and consciously re-cognized providing, as the relentless logic of Ibn 'Arabi's *wahdat al-wujud* ubiquitously affirms, that when this realization "comes upon thee thou understandest that thou knowest God by God, not by thyself".[80]

We may generalize and say that all relative and limiting constructions about the nature of reality are ultimately cognitive constructions of our own making, even including many of our conceptions of God. The paradigm-shift necessary for understanding Ibn 'Arabi's point of view on this matter is alluded to in his observation that "you think of yourself as a small thing, whereas in you there is hidden the biggest of the universes".[81] It is because of this tendency of human beings to be caught up in their own belief systems that we are reminded that "Whatever may happen the gnostic will not be caught up in one definite belief because he is wise unto himself."[82] This direct epistemological recommendation to undergo a paradigm-shift in our conception of ourselves carries with it no implication that the gnostic, himself or herself, is without belief or direction or knowledge. The implication is quite the reverse. In so far as the 'arif (that is, "the one who knows") is immersed, like a drop in the ocean, in "reality as it is in itself", such a person is totally and cognitively secure from being immersed in any limiting constructions of reality. Any limiting constructions of reality are viewed from the point of the Unity of Being and not from the point of view of the limiting constructions themselves. From this perspective all knowledge is viewed *sub specie æternitas*. The 'arif's knowledge of reality is irredeemably non-fractional. In the ontological schema of Ibn 'Arabi "human selves" are essentially relational forms of the Real to Itself. In effect, they are the Self-disclosures of the Real.

This idea of the reality of the human self as being fundamentally *relational* arises in much recent feminist re-theorizing about the self and for the sake of completeness it is informative to examine some of the insights of feminist psychology on this point.

Feminism and the self

In a collection of essays entitled *Feminists Rethink the Self* [83] there is a central analytical concern to situate conceptions of the self in their historical, cultural and gendered context, and to examine the notion of what the self, as relational, may mean in regard to "the care-giving responsibilities traditionally assigned primarily to women".

The collection of essays begins by acknowledging that the "implications of one's account of the self reverberate throughout one's world-view, opening up social, intellectual, and aesthetic possibilities". Any particular theory or idea about the self, whilst opening up a particular set of possible life trajectories, necessarily forecloses others. This seems to emphasize the point that perhaps "just as important as the kind of beings we are is the kind we *think* we are".[84] We can, for example, be locked into constrictive and unhelpful pictures of ourselves. This particular group of feminist philosophers suggests that one of the most important functions of any concept of the self is its potentially emancipatory role. It is recondite to add that emancipatory theories of the self often carry with them quite powerful moral or ethical prescriptions.

By comparison, one unusual feature of Ibn 'Arabi's account of the Self is that, whilst it does offer a universal invitation to self-knowledge, the omni-encompassing predispositional ontology of *wahdat al-wujud* necessarily includes *all* human possibility and diversity. From the perspective of such an ontology, the outpouring of the inherent multiplicity and predispositional contents of the Divine knowledge into the "theatre of manifestation" is not limited to producing a preferred type of person or kind of life. In effect, all human possibilities are given their chance in the ongoing "infinity of the world process", including what John Stuart Mill called "experiments with living". The Divine Wish, nevertheless, is for the individual to choose consciously to return to Him. But the paths are legion and the predispositions diverse; and although all necessarily return to Him, the manner and mode of return conforms itself to the predisposition of the servant. There is no Divine coercion in this matter. Further, the infinity of predispositional diversity engenders "diversity of belief" regarding the Real. Nevertheless, Ibn 'Arabi warns us to be on our guard against our own beliefs about the nature of reality and to be "free from pretentiousness on matters which we have realised or embraced by our individual knowledge".[85] But importantly, the predisposition of the individual is not necessarily the final arbiter or overriding determinant in this matter of knowing ourselves in order to know God: there is the possibility of escaping from the limits to which our predisposition submits us. This is because of Adamic kind's integrative nature and "aptitude to embrace the essential Truths".[86] So whilst, as Claude Addas[87] so rightly affirms, Ibn 'Arabi's is a universal message of hope, it is not given to any naive over-moralizing about the self. But let us see further how some of these issues are refracted through the lens of feminist theorizers on the self.

It is the claim of the authors of *Feminists Rethink the Self* that "paying attention to the experience of women" can profoundly "affect our understanding of the self". One of the ways in which this is indelibly demonstrated is by the autobiographical examination (by one of the contributors)[88] of the effects of a traumatic experience on her understanding of (and relationship with) what she refers to tripartitely as "the embodied self", "the narrative self", and "the autonomous self". She contrasts her approach with traditional philosophizing about the self which "at least since Locke, ha[s] puzzled over such questions as to whether persons can survive the loss or exchange of their minds, brains, consciousness, memories, characters, and/or bodies". These "imaginary scenarios", she argues, "however farfetched, are at least *conceivable*, whereas the experience of rape victims, Holocaust survivors, and war veterans are, for most of us, unthinkable." In her case, she recounts that the result of the trauma of being raped was the "undoing of the self" – the disintegration of the belief that one can be oneself in relation to others or even to oneself "since the self exists fundamentally in relation to others". She recounts:

> My hypervigilance, heightened startle response, insomnia, and other PTSD [post-traumatic stress disorder] symptoms were no more psychological, if that is taken to mean under my conscious control, than were my heart rate and blood pressure.[89]

Attempts to overcome harrowing trauma "by dissociation from one's body or separation from the self that one was either before or during the trauma", the author suggests, are never wholly successful.

The effects of trauma seem deeply imprinted on the body itself and the victim's relationship with it. The rebuilding of the self after trauma begins with *narrative* and "bearing witness" which re-establishes the survivor's identity: the empathic other is essential for the continuation of the self. There is a profound need to be believed and listened to. As well as the need to reconstruct the narrative self, the re-establishment of the autonomous self is also crucial for recovery, and we read:

> If a rape victim is unable to walk outside without the fear of being assaulted again, she quickly loses the desire to go for a walk. If one's self, or one's *true* self, is considered to be identical with one's will, then the survivor cannot be considered the same as her pre-trauma self, since what she is able to will post-trauma is so drastically altered. Some reactions that were once under the will's command become involuntary, and some desires that were once motivating can no longer be felt, let alone acted upon.[90]

This loss of their former relationships with themselves – with their body, with their will, with the kind of person they took themselves to be – is often described as "analogous to the loss of a beloved other".

The concluding suggestion is that the deepest truth about the self is its *connectedness and relational nature*. And so "by finding (some aspects of) one's lost self in another person, one can manage (to a greater or lesser degree) to reconnect with it and to reintegrate one's various selves".

Such conclusions about the nature of the human self, irrespective of the traumatic circumstances which gave rise to them, do strike a universal chord and they echo many familiar Akbarian themes. What is conceptually invisible from these conclusions, from the point of view of Ibn 'Arabi's metaphysics of unity, is, of course, any intimation that the aspects of the self which have been so carefully, convincingly and dramatically identified are isomorphic with a universal cosmology of the self larger than gender, history or culture. The idea that one of the deepest truths about the self is its relational nature is axiomatic to Ibn 'Arabi's conception of the *insan-i-kamil* as possessing no other function than that of a bridge or isthmus between the inner and outer aspects of the Unity of Being. It is the *insan-i-kamil*, as the manifested consciousness of God, who dispenses God's mercy and bears witness *par excellence*. In this context the dependence on others and the need for others is, in reality, the dependence on God and the need for God. To come to know this with God's knowledge (not one's own knowledge) is a potential which resides, according to Akbarian ontology, in the *raison d'être* of the Adamic form. The possibility of realigning with one's lost self by finding aspects of one's lost self in another person has a clear analogy with the Akbarian prescription "He who knows himself knows his Lord." The true beloved is the Divine Subject, that is, God: in God we find ourselves. From the perspective of the Unity of Being the seeker is also the sought. Feelings "analogous to the loss of a beloved other" (which our feminist author portrays with such devastating honesty) ontologically image universally, for Ibn ʿArabi, the profound need to return to the original integrative and unitive state of oneness and totality. And such feelings can (and do) occur to people without them having any clear knowledge of the universal significance or foundation of such feelings.

The deeper significance of such longings is touched on in much of Ibn ʿArabi's poetry, particularly in the *Tarjuman al-Ashwaq*, whose title translates as "The Interpreter of Desires". In this remarkable collection of poems Ibn ʿArabi traces the journeys and trials and the myriad states and vicissitudes of the lover in search of the Beloved. The *Tarjuman* is super-saturated with metaphorical meaning capable of reconceptualizing the significance of much lived and felt human longing for "the beloved". His poetry, like all his writings, possesses a multivalent, contagious and revivifying propensity in keeping with the meaning of his name *Muhyiddin*: the revivifier of religion. Or perhaps one should say the revivifier of the heart: that is, the revivifier of the religion of love.

Postscript

If for no other reason than to mitigate against some of the less acceptable human consequences of modernity, the seismic changes in Western and global twentieth-century human life have made the need for a new and renewed sense of human response and responsibility urgent and unavoidably obvious. There is evidence of a growing perception that what is required is a revitalized sense of unity, beyond the self-descriptions and divisions of the age. Much of the twentieth century has profoundly affected people's "subjective ... expectation about what it is to be a person".[91] Such a reorientation in the topography of the self has been inescapably entangled with all the other unprecedented cultural changes wrought by modernity. In the context of the Unity of Being these global, cultural changes in lived human experience can be no other than the consequential aspects of "the clarification of the mirror of the world". For this reason it would be a fundamental misconstruction to view the increasing interest in Western culture in Ibn 'Arabi's metaphysics of unity as an accidental (or even unwelcome) by-product of modernity. The increasing interest in the work of Ibn 'Arabi is not a throw-back to a pre-scientific, pre-technological, pre-industrial age. Such a conclusion could only rest on a denial of what the very doctrine of unity is insisting upon, that is, that modernity is itself an inseparable dimension of the Unity of Being. It is a perspective which conceives of modernity as indissolubly tied to that process of the "clarification of the world" whose meaning is ultimately we ourselves. The question which stands on the immediate horizon of this new millennium and which faces each one of us, collectively and separately, consciously or unconsciously, is "Who are we?" in the light of the Unity of Being. Ibn 'Arabi is categorical about the answer: the era is no other, we are no other, there is no other. It is the existential realization of this state of affairs which is, for Ibn 'Arabi and his followers, the fundamental human project and possibility. The *wahdat al-wujud* of Ibn 'Arabi requires that we go beyond the self-descriptions of modernity, beyond its individualisms, beyond its ideologies, beyond its divisions and its boundaries, and beyond its conceptual and theoretical categories. The metaphysics of the Unity of Being challenges citizens of the new millennium to reconceptualize their epistemological and theoretical co-ordinates and adopt as their *axiomatic* descriptor the *very idea* of the Unity of Existence. As Plato so accurately understood so long ago, we can be sure that such a universal perspective contains "no secret corner of illiberality".[92] For, as Plato himself insists, "nothing can be more antagonistic than meanness to a soul which is ever longing after the whole of things both divine and human".

The grounds and experiential landscape of this longing informs the entire corpus of Ibn 'Arabi. His writings are a monumental documentation of the topography of self-knowledge. It is an epistemology of Who is known rather than what is known. It is an epistemology capable of transforming our view of ourselves, our self-experience and our understanding of modernity. One might say that what echoes through every line, every paragraph and every chapter of Ibn 'Arabi's prodigious corpus of work is the classical Quranic address "Ah, what will convey unto thee …!"[93] What is unsurpassably conveyed is an immense spiritual archaeology of the origin of the human self and its destiny. Its beauty is matched only by its unassailable certainty concerning the Unity of Being.

Notes

1 As far as possible, in specifically Akbarian contexts, the expression "the Self" refers to its comprehensive metaphysical ontology as understood by Ibn 'Arabi. By contrast, the term "the self" refers to the empirical self as ordinarily understood.

2 Muhyiddin Ibn 'Arabi, *The Wisdom of the Prophets*. Partial translation of the *Fusus al-Hikam*, from Arabic to French by T. Burckhardt, and from French to English by A. Culme-Seymour (Swyre Farm, Gloucestershire, 1975), pp. 8–10.

3 Ibn 'Arabi, *Ismail Hakki Bursevi's Translation of and Commentary on Fusus al-Hikam*, trans. B. Rauf (4 vols, Oxford, 1986–91). Vol. 1, p. 94.

4 Ibn 'Arabi, *Wisdom*, p. 11, n. 26.

5 Ibn 'Arabi, *Wisdom*, pp. 8–9.

6 Ibn 'Arabi, *Wisdom*, p. 10, n. 15.

7 Ibn 'Arabi, *Wisdom*, p. 131.

8 P. F. Strawson, *Freedom and Resentment and Other Essays* (London, 1973), pp. 1–25.

9 Ibn 'Arabi, *The Tarjuman al-Ashwaq*, trans. R. A. Nicholson (London, 1911), XI, p. 67.

10 S. Hakim, "Knowledge of God in Ibn 'Arabi", in *Muhyddin Ibn 'Arabi: A Commemorative Volume*, ed. S. Hirtenstein, and M. Tiernan (Shaftesbury, Dorset, 1993), pp. 264–90.

11 Ibn 'Arabi, *Fusus*, Vol. 3, p. 534.

12 G. Berkeley, *Essay Towards a New Theory of Vision* (London, 1972).

13 Hakim, in *Muhyiddin Ibn 'Arabi*, ed. Hirtenstein and Tiernan, p. 269.

14 W. C. Chittick, *The Sufi Path of Knowledge* (Albany, NY, 1989), p. 148.

15 G. Berkeley, *The Principles of Human Knowledge* (Britannica Great Books Series, Vol. 35 of 54, Chicago, 1987), p. 405.

16 Ibn 'Arabi, *Sufis of Andalusia*. Partial translation of *Ruh al-quds* and *Durrat al-fakhirah* by R. W. J. Austin (Gloucestershire, 1988), p. 63.

17 Ibn 'Arabi, *Wisdom*, p. 8.

18 For an excellent treatment, see *The Enlightenment*, Studies 1 and 2 and Texts 1 and 2 (Milton Keynes, 1992).

19 W. James, *Principles of Psychology* (Britannica Great Books Series, Vol. 53 of 54, Chicago, 1987), p. 2.

20 R. Smith, *History of the Human Sciences* (London, 1997), pp. 575–7.

21 P. Thagard, *Mind* (Cambridge, Mass., 1996), p. 7.

22 K. J. Schneider, "Towards a science of the heart", *American Psychologist* (March 1998), p. 286.

23 R. Harré, "Appraising social psychology: rules, roles and rhetoric", *The Psychologist* (January 1993), p. 27.

24 T. Sloan, "Theories of personality: ideology and beyond", in *Critical Psychology*, ed. D. Fox and I. Prilleltensky (London, 1997), p. 89.

25 An incisive point made by B. Rauf in reply to an address given by C.-A. Gilis to the Muhyiddin Ibn 'Arabi Society, and documented in *"Report of the*

Annual General Meeting of the Muhyiddin Ibn 'Arabi Society", 26 October 1985, Note.

26 Schneider, "Towards a science of the heart", p.280.

27 R. Tarnas, *The Passion of the Western Mind* (London, 1996), p.406.

28 Charles Sanders Peirce (1839–1914), American pragmatist, influenced by William James. His identification of the metaphysical nature of positivism certainly implies this. See "Critique of Positivism", *Works of Charles Sanders Peirce*, www.door.net/arisbe/menu/library/bycspbycsp.htm, [cited 10 July 2001].

29 J. Henry, *et al.*, "Towards a psychology of experience", *The Psychologist* (March 1997), p.117.

30 See D. Fox and I. Prilleltensky, eds., *Critical Psychology* (London, 1997).

31 I. Parker, "Discourse analysis and psychoanalysis", *British Journal of Social Psychology* (36, 1997), pp.482–93.

32 Parker, "Discourse analysis and psychoanalysis", pp.479–95.

33 Ibn 'Arabi, *Wisdom*, p.17.

34 J. Pickering, "The self is a semiotic process", *Journal of Consciousness Studies* (6, No. 4, 1999), pp.31–47.

35 W. Hollway, *Subjectivity and Method in Psychology* (London, 1989), p.122.

36 R. A. F. Thurman, "Sophisticated software for the human brain", in *Mind-Science*, ed. D. Goleman and R. A. F. Thurman (Boston, 1991), pp.51–75.

37 J. Kim, *Philosophy of Mind* (Boulder, Colo., 1996), pp.73–4.

38 T. Izutsu, *Creation and the Timeless Order of Things* (Ashland, Oreg., 1994), p.27.

39 C. Addas, *Quest for the Red Sulphur*, trans. P. Kingsley (Cambridge, 1993), p.117.

40 Ibn 'Arabi, *Fusus*, Vol. 4, p.889.

41 J. A. Fodor, *The Modularity of Mind* (Cambridge, Mass., 1983).

42 My words in italics.

43 J. A. Fodor, in *A Companion to the Philosophy of Mind*, ed. S. Guttenplan (Oxford, 1996), pp.292–300.

44 A. Clark, "The dynamical challenge", *Cognitive Science* (Vol. 21, No. 4, 1997), p.475.

45 The technical Platonic word for this process of recollection is *anamnesis*.

46 R. W. Sperry, in *New Metaphysical Foundations of Modern Science*, ed. W. Harman and J. Clark (Sausalito, Calif., 1994), p.98.

47 K. R. Popper, *Conjectures and Refutations* (London, 1963).

48 Smith, *History of Human Sciences*, p.493.

49 S. Brown, *Verification and Meaning*, Units 11–13, "Thought and reality: central themes in Wittgenstein's philosophy", course book (Milton Keynes, 1976), p.21.

50 T. H. Leahey, *A History of Psychology* (4th edn., Upper Saddle River, NJ, 1997), p.196.

51 James, *Principles*, p.2.

52 James, *Principles*, p.1.

53 James, *Principles*, p.155.

54 Leahey, *History of Psychology*, p. 198.

55 Leahey, *History of Psychology*, p. 201.

56 James, *Principles*, p. 7.

57 James, *Principles*, p. 4.

58 James, *Principles*, Chapter X, pp. 188–220.

59 James, *Principles*, p. 259.

60 C. G. Jung, *Modern Man in Search of a Soul* (London, 1990), p. 214.

61 Ibn 'Arabi, *Wisdom*, p. 12.

62 Ibn 'Arabi, *Wisdom*, p. 18.

63 Ibn 'Arabi, *Sufis of Andalusia*, p. 30.

64 S. Bem and H. L. de Jong, *Theoretical Issues in Psychology* (London, 1997), p. 78.

65 S. Holroyd, *The Arkana Dictionary of New Perspectives* (London, 1989), p. 67.

66 Bem and de Jong, *Theoretical Issues*, p. 79.

67 P. Feyerabend, *Against Method* (London, 1975), p. 10.

68 J. B. Watson, "Psychology as the behaviorist views it", *Psychological Review* (Vol. 20, 1913), p. 158.

69 R. D. Logan, "Historical change in prevailing sense of self", in *Self and Identity*, ed. K. Yardley and T. Honess (London, 1978), p. 13.

70 Chittick, *Sufi Path*, pp. 63–5.

71 Chittick, *Sufi Path*, p. 366.

72 R. Harré, in *The Singular Self* (London, 1998), p. 7 notes interestingly and correctly that individuality does not imply individualism. Certainly, Ibn 'Arabi's metaphysics allows for each person's unique and irreplaceable individuality without any commitment to individualism.

73 N. Smart, "Creation, persons and the meaning of life", in *Six Approaches to the Person*, ed. R. Ruddock (London, 1972), p. 15.

74 See *Journal of Consciousness Studies* (Vol. 1, No. 1, 1994).

75 Smith, *History of Human Sciences*, p. 852.

76 K. Gergen and J. Kaye "Beyond narrative in the negotiation of therapeutic meaning", in *Therapy as Social Construction*, ed. S. McNamee and K. Gergen (London, 1994), p. 172.

77 Gergen and Kaye, "Beyond narrative", p. 172.

78 H.-G. Gadamer, *Truth and Method* (Part 3, London, 1989), pp. 381–474.

79 Gergen and Kaye, "Beyond narrative", p. 183.

80 *"Whoso Knoweth Himself ..."*, trans. T. H. Weir (London, 1976), p. 16. This work is no longer considered attributable to Ibn 'Arabi, but the quotation cited is clearly and accurately Akbarian in its meaning.

81 Ibn 'Arabi, *Ismail Hakki Bursevi's Translation of Kernel of the Kernel* [trans. from Ottoman Turkish by B. Rauf] (Sherborne, Gloucestershire [1981]), p. 14.

82 Ibn 'Arabi, *Kernel of the Kernel*, p. 8.

83 D. T. Meyers, ed., *Feminists Rethink the Self* (Boulder, Colo., 1997), p. 1.

84 R. Trigg, *Ideas of Human Nature* (Oxford, 1988), p. 169.

85 Ibn 'Arabi, *Wisdom*, p. 13.

86 Ibn 'Arabi, *Wisdom*, p. 12.
87 Addas, *Red Sulphur*, p. 293.
88 S. J. Brison, "Outliving oneself", in *Feminists Rethink the Self*, ed. Meyers, pp. 12–39.
89 Brison, "Outliving oneself", p. 17.
90 Brison, "Outliving oneself", p. 28.
91 Smith, *History of Human Sciences*, p. 575.
92 Plato, *The Republic*, Book VI, Section 486 (Britannica Great Books Series, Vol. 7 of 54, Chicago, 1987), p. 374.
93 A Divine mode of address, exemplified perhaps most famously in Surah 97 in the Quran, known as "Power".

Bibliography

Specific sources
Core texts consulted on the life and thought of Ibn 'Arabi

Abadi, A. "Ibn 'Arabi's theophany of perfection". *Journal of the Muhyiddin Ibn 'Arabi Society*, Vol. I, 1982, pp. 26–9.

Addas, C. *Quest for the Red Sulphur*, trans. P. Kingsley. Cambridge, 1993.

Addas, C. *Ibn 'Arabi: The Voyage of No Return*. Cambridge, 2000.

Affifi, A. E. *The Mystical Philosophy of Muhyid Din Ibnul Arabi*. Lahore, 1979.

Averroës (Ibn Rushd) *Tahafut al-Tahafut*, trans. S. Van Den Bergh. London, 1978.

Chittick, W. C. *The Sufi Path of Knowledge*. Albany, NY, 1989.

Chittick, W. C. *The Self-Disclosure of God*. Albany, NY, 1998.

Chodkiewicz, M. *An Ocean Without Shore*, trans. D. Streight. Albany, NY, 1993.

Chodkiewicz, M. *Seal of the Saints*, trans. L. Sherrard. Cambridge, 1993.

Coates, P. Review of T. Izutsu's *Sufism and Taoism: A Comparative Study of Key Philosophical Concepts*. *Journal of the Muhyiddin Ibn 'Arabi Society*, Vol. V, 1986, pp. 69–71.

Corbin, H. *Creative Imagination in the Sufism of Ibn 'Arabi*, trans. R. Manheim. Princeton, NJ, 1969.

Corbin, H. *The Concept of Comparative Philosophy*, trans. P. Russell. Cambridge, 1981.

Hirtenstein, S. *The Unlimited Mercifier*. Oxford, 1999.

Hirtenstein, S. and Tiernan, M. (eds.). *Muhyiddin Ibn 'Arabi: A Commemorative Volume*. Shaftesbury, Dorset, 1993.

Hourani, G. F. *Averroes: On the Harmony of Religion and Philosophy*. London, 1976.

Husaini, S. A. Q. *The Pantheistic Monism of Ibn al-Arabi*. Lahore, 1945.

Ibn 'Arabi, Muhyiddin. *The Wisdom of the Prophets*. Partial translation of the *Fusus al-Hikam*, from Arabic to French by T. Burckhardt, and from French to English by A. Culme-Seymour. Swyre Farm, Gloucestershire, 1975.

Ibn 'Arabi, Muhyiddin. *The Tarjuman al-Ashwaq*, trans. R. A. Nicholson. London, 1911.

Ibn 'Arabi, Muhyiddin. *The Bezels of Wisdom*. Translation of the *Fusus al-Hikam* by R. W. J. Austin. London, 1980.

Ibn 'Arabi, Muhyiddin. *Ismail Hakki Bursevi's Translation of Kernel of the Kernel* [trans. from Ottoman Turkish by B. Rauf]. Sherborne, Gloucestershire [1981].

Ibn 'Arabi, Muhyiddin. *Ismail Hakki Bursevi's Translation of and Commentary on Fusus al-Hikam*, trans. B. Rauf. 4 vols. Oxford, 1986–91.

Ibn 'Arabi, Muhyiddin. *Sufis of Andalusia*. Partial translation of the *Ruh al-Quds* and *Durrat al-Fakhirah* by R. W. J. Austin. Reprinted Gloucestershire, 1988.

Izutsu, T. *Sufism and Taoism*. Berkeley, Calif., 1983.

Izutsu, T. *Creation and the Timeless Order of Things*. Ashland, Oreg., 1994.

Jami, Nur-ud-din Abd ur Rahmani. *Lawa'ih*, trans. E. H. Whinfield. London, 1978.

Journal of the Muhyiddin Ibn 'Arabi Society. 1982 onwards.

Morris, J. W. "Listening for God: prayer and the heart in the *Futuhat*". *Journal of the Muhyiddin Ibn 'Arabi Society*, Vol. XIII, 1993, pp. 19–53.

Morris, J. W. "Seeking God's Face", Part 2. *Journal of the Muhyiddin Ibn 'Arabi Society*, Vol. XVII, 1995, pp. 1–39.

Niffari, Muhammad Ibn 'Abdi 'L-Jabbar. *The Mawaqif and Mukhatabat*, trans. A. J. Arberry. London, 1978.

Rauf, B. "Universality and Ibn 'Arabi". *Journal of the Muhyiddin Ibn 'Arabi Society*, Vol. IV, 1985, pp. 1–3.

Rauf, B. *"Report of the Annual General Meeting of the Muhyiddin Ibn 'Arabi Society"*, 26 October 1985, Note.

Rauf, B. *Addresses*. Gloucestershire, 1986.

The Twenty-Nine Pages: An Introduction to Ibn 'Arabi's Metaphysics of Unity. Edited extracts from *The Mystical Philosophy of Muhyid Din Ibnul Arabi* by A. E. Affifi. Chisholme House, Roberton, Roxburgh, 1998.

Weir, T. H. (trans.). *"Whoso Knoweth Himself…"*. Extracts from the *Risale-t-ul-wujudiyyah* (Treatise on Being). London, 1976.

General sources

Ackroyd, P. *Blake*. London, 1995.

Ayer, A. J. *Language, Truth and Logic*. London, 1987.

Ayer, A. J. and O'Grady, J. (eds.). *A Dictionary of Philosophical Quotations*. Oxford, 1995.

Bartholomew M., Hall, D. and Lentin, A. (eds.). *The Enlightenment Studies*, Studies 1 and 2. Milton Keynes, 1992.

Beck, L. W. (ed.). *Kant: Selections*. London, 1988.

Beck, L. W. "From Leibniz to Kant", in *Routledge History of Philosophy*, ed. R. C. Solomon and K. M. Higgins. Vol. VI. London, 1993, pp. 5–39.

Bem, S. and de Jong, H. L. *Theoretical Issues in Psychology*. London, 1997.

Benfey, O. T. "Chains and rings: Kekule's dreams", in *Faber Book of Science*, ed. J. Carey. London, 1996, pp. 137–8.

Berkeley, G. *The Principles of Human Knowledge*. Britannica Great Books Series, Vol. 35 of 54. Chicago, 1987.

Berkeley, G. *Essay towards a New Theory of Vision*. London, 1972.

Best, S. and Kellner, D. (eds.). *Postmodern Theory: Critical Investigations*. London, 1994.

S. J. Brison, "Outliving oneself", in *Feminists Rethink the Self*, ed. D. T. Meyers. Boulder, Colo., 1997, pp. 12–39.

Brown, S. *Verification and Meaning*. Units 11–13, "Thought and reality: central themes in Wittgenstein's philosophy". Course book. Milton Keynes, 1976.

Carr, E. H. *What is History?* London, 1961.

Chalmers, A. F. *What is This Thing Called Science?* Milton Keynes, 1999.

Clark, A. "The dynamical challenge". *Cognitive Science*, Vol. 21, No. 4, 1997, pp. 461–81.

Cooper, D. "Technology: liberation or enslavement?", in *Philosophy and Technology*, ed. R. Fellows. Cambridge, 1995, pp. 7–18.

Copenhaver, B. P. and Schmidt, C. B. *Renaissance Philosophy*. Oxford, 1992.

Darwin, C. *The Descent or Origin of Man*. Chicago, 1987.

Detlefsen, M. "Philosophy of mathematics in the twentieth century", in *Routledge History of Philosophy*, ed. S. G. Shanker. Vol. IX. London, 1996, pp. 50–123.

Eldridge, J. E. T. *Max Weber*. London, 1972.

Eliot, S. and Whitlock, K. (eds.). *The Enlightenment*, Texts 1 and 2. Milton Keynes, 1992.

Engels, F. and Marx, K. *Communist Manifesto*, intro. by A. J. P. Taylor. London, 1967.

Fellows, R. *Philosophy and Technology*. Cambridge, 1995.

Feuerbach, L. *The Essence of Christianity*, trans. G. Eliot. New York, 1957.

Feyerabend, P. *Against Method*. London, 1975.

Feyerabend, P. *Conquest of Abundance*. London, 1999.

Fodor, J. A. *The Modularity of Mind*. Cambridge, Mass., 1983.

Fodor, J. A. In *A Companion to the Philosophy of Mind*, ed. S. Guttenplan. Oxford, 1996, pp. 292–300.

Fox, D. and Prilleltensky, I. *Critical Psychology*. London, 1997.

Gadamer, H.-G. *Truth and Method*. London, 1989.

Gallie, W. B. "Essentially contested concepts". *Proceedings of the Aristotelian Society*, Vol. 56, 1955–56, pp. 167–98.

Gergen, K. and Kaye, J. "Beyond narrative in the negotiation of thera-peutic meaning", in *Therapy as Social Construction*, ed. S. McNamee and K. Gergen. London, 1994, pp. 166–85.

Gerth, H. H. and Wright Mills, C. *From Max Weber*. London, 1970.

Giddens, A. *The Consequences of Modernity*. Cambridge, 1990.

Goleman, D. and Thurman, A. F. (eds.) *MindScience*. Boston, 1991.

Hall, S. *et al. Modernity and its Futures*. Cambridge, 1992.

Harman, H. and Clark, J. *New Metaphysical Foundations of Modern Science*. Sausalito, Calif., 1994.

Harré, R. "Ontology and science". *Beshara Magazine*, Issue 3, 1987, pp. 8–15.

Harré, R. "Reappraising social psychology: rules, roles and rhetoric". *The Psychologist*, January 1993, pp. 24–8.

Harré, R. *The Singular Self*. London, 1998.

Heidegger, M. *The Question of Technology and Other Essays*. New York, 1977.

Henry, J. *et al*. "Towards a psychology of experience". *The Psychologist*, March 1997, pp. 117–20.

Hill, S. *The Tragedy of Technology*. London, 1988.

Hollinger, R. (ed.). *Contemporary Social Theory*. London, 1994.

Hollway, W. *Subjectivity and Method in Psychology*. London, 1989.

Holroyd, S. (ed.) *The Arkana Dictionary of New Perspectives*. London, 1989.

Horton, R. "African traditional thought and Western science", in *Rationality*, ed. B. R. Wilson. Oxford, 1970, pp. 131–71.

Irwin, T. *Classical Thought*. Oxford, 1989.

James, W. *Principles of Psychology*. Britannica Great Books Series, Vol. 53 of 54. Chicago, 1987.

Jenkins, K. *Re-thinking History*. London, 1991.

Jung, C. G. *Man and His Symbols*. London, 1990.

Jung, C. G. *Modern Man in Search of a Soul*. London, 1990.

Kanigel, R. *The Man Who Knew Infinity*. London, 1993.

Kant, I. *The Critique of Pure Reason*, trans. J. M. D. Meiklejohn. Britannica Great Books Series, Vol. 42 of 54. Chicago, 1987.

Kant, I. "What is enlightenment?", in *The Enlightenment*, Text 2, ed. S. Eliot and K. Whitlock. Milton Keynes, 1992, pp. 305–9.

Kierkegaard, S. A. *Journals*, trans. A. Dru. New York, 1959.

Kim, J. *Philosophy of Mind*. Oxford, 1996.

Kuhn, T. S. *The Structure of Scientific Revolutions*. Chicago, 1996.

Kumar, K. *Prophecy and Progress*. Harmondsworth, Middlesex, 1983.

Leahey, T. H. *A History of Psychology*. 4th edition. Upper Saddle River, NJ, 1997.

Logan, R. D. "Historical change in prevailing sense of self", in *Self and Identity*, ed. K. Yardley and T. Honess. London, 1978.

Lukes, S. "Some problems about rationality", in *Rationality*, ed. B. Wilson. Oxford, 1970, pp.194–213.

Lukes, S. "Of gods and demons: Habermas and practical reason", in *Habermas: Critical Debates*, ed. J. B. Thompson and D. Held. London, 1982, pp.134–48.

Lyotard, J.-F. *The Postmodern Condition*. Minneapolis, 1984.

MacIntyre, A. "Pantheism", in *The Concise Encyclopaedia of Western Philosophy and Philosophers*, ed. J. O. Urmson and J. Rée. London, 1991, p.227.

MacKenzie, D. and Wajcman, J. *The Social Shaping of Technology*. Milton Keynes, 1988.

Macquarrie, J. *Existentialism*. London, 1972.

Magee, B. *Popper*. London, 1990.

McNamee, S. and Gergen, K. J. *Therapy as Social Construction*. London, 1994.

Meyers, D. T. (ed.). *Feminists Rethink the Self*. Boulder, Colo., 1997.

Mitchell, B. *The Justification of Religious Belief*. London, 1973.

Mumford, L. *Technics and Civilisation*. London, 1934.

Nasr, S. H. *Knowledge and the Sacred*. Edinburgh, 1981.

Parekh, B. *The Concept of Fundamentalism*. Leeds, 1991.

Parker, I. "Discourse analysis and psychoanalysis". *British Journal of Social Psychology*, Vol. 36, 1997, pp.479–95.

Parkinson, G. H. R. (ed.). *An Encyclopedia of Philosophy*. London, 1989.

Peirce, C. S. "Critique of Positivism", in *Works of Charles Sanders Peirce*. www.door.net/arisbe/menu/library/bycsp/bycsp.htm [cited 10 July 2001].

Phillips, D. Z. and Mounce, H. O. "On morality's having a point", in *The Is/Ought Question*, ed. W. D. Hudson. London, 1969, pp.228–39.

Pickering, J. "The self is a semiotic process". *Journal of Consciousness Studies*, Vol. 6, No. 4, 1999, pp.31–47. (Published in the UK and USA.)

Plato. *The Collected Dialogues*, ed. E. Hamilton and H. Cairns. Princeton, NJ, 1961.

Plato, *The Republic*. Britannica Great Books Series, Vol. 7 of 54. Chicago, 1987.

Popper, K. R. *Conjectures and Refutations*. London, 1963.

Quine, W. V. O. *From a Logical Point of View*. New York, 1961.

Runciman, W. G. *Weber Selections*. Cambridge, 1978. Russell, B. *History of Western Philosophy*. London, 1961.

Russell, B. *My Philosophical Development*. London, 1985.

Ryle, G. *The Revolution in Philosophy*. London, 1956.

Schacht, R. *Nietzsche*. London, 1983.

Schneider, J. K. "Towards a science of the heart". *American Psychologist*, March 1998, pp.272–89.

Sloan, T. "Theories of personality: ideology and beyond", in *Critical Psychology*, ed. D. Fox and I. Prilleltensky. London, 1997, pp. 87–103.

Smart, N. "Creation, persons and the meaning of life", in *Six Approaches to the Person*, ed. R. Ruddock. London, 1972, pp. 13–36.

Smith, R. *History of the Human Sciences*. London, 1997.

Sperry, R. W., "Holding course amid shifting paradigms", in *New Metaphysical Foundations of Modern Science*, ed. W. Harman and J. Clark. Sausalito, Calif., 1994, pp. 97–121.

Spinoza, B. *Ethics*. Britannica Great Books Series, Vol. 31 of 54. Chicago, 1987.

Strawson, P. F. *Freedom and Resentment and Other Essays*. London, 1973.

Strawson, P. F. "Metaphysics", in *The Concise Encyclopaedia of Western Philosophy and Philosophers*, ed. J. O. Urmson, and J. Rée. London, 1991, pp. 202–8.

Strawson, P. F. "Scepticism and naturalism: some varieties", in *A Dictionary of Philosophical Quotations*, ed. A. J. Ayer and J. O'Grady. Oxford, 1995, pp. 435–7.

Tarnas, R. *The Passion of the Western Mind*. London, 1991.

Thagard, P. *Mind*. Cambridge, Mass., 1996.

Thompson, J. B. and Held, D. *Habermas: Critical Debates*. London, 1982.

Thurman, R. A. F. "Sophisticated software for the human brain", in *MindScience*, ed. D. Goleman and R. A. F. Thurman. Boston, 1991, pp. 51–75.

Tiles, J. E. "The truths of logic and mathematics", in *An Encyclopedia of Philosophy*, ed. G. H. R. Parkinson. London, 1989, pp. 99–120.

Trigg, R. *Ideas of Human Nature*. Oxford, 1988.

Turner, B. S. Preface, in *From Max Weber*, ed. H. H. Gerth and C. Wright Mills. London, 1970.

Unamo, M. de. *The Tragic Sense of Life*. New York, 1954.

Urmson, J. O. and Rée, J. (eds.). *The Concise Encyclopaedia of Western Philosophy and Philosophers*. London, 1991.

Wang, H. *Beyond Analytic Philosophy*. Cambridge, Mass., 1986.

Watson, J. B. "Psychology as the behaviourist views it". *Psychological Review*, London, 1913, pp. 158–77.

Weber, M. *The Protestant Ethic and the Spirit of Capitalism*, trans. T. Parsons, London, 1967.

Wilson, B. *Rationality*. Oxford, 1970.

Wittgenstein, L. *Tractatus Logico-Philosophicus*, trans. D. F. Pears and B. F. McGuinness. London, 1961.

Yardley, K. and Honess, T. *Self and Identity*. London, 1978.

Name index

Subject index

195